THE UNITED STATES
AND
LATIN AMERICA

THE UNITED STATES
AND
LATIN AMERICA

BY

JOHN HOLLADAY LATANÉ
PH.D., LL.D.

PROFESSOR OF AMERICAN HISTORY AND DEAN OF THE
COLLEGE FACULTY IN THE JOHNS HOPKINS UNIVERSITY

Author of "From Isolation to Leadership,"
"America as a World Power," etc.

GARDEN CITY   NEW YORK

DOUBLEDAY, PAGE & COMPANY

1920

TO THE MEMORY OF

MY FATHER

WHOSE DAILY COMMENTS ON PUBLIC QUES-
TIONS WERE MY FIRST LESSONS IN THE STUDY
OF POLITICS

AND TO

MY MOTHER

WHO IMPARTED TO ME A LOVE OF HISTORY
AND WHOSE APPROVAL IS STILL THE RICHEST
REWARD OF MY EFFORTS

PREFACE

THIS book is based on a smaller volume issued by the Johns Hopkins Press in 1900 under the title " The Diplomatic Relations of the United States and Spanish America," which contained the first series of Albert Shaw Lectures on Diplomatic History. That volume has been out of print for several years, but calls for it are still coming in, with increasing frequency of late. In response to this demand and in view of the widespread interest in our relations with our Southern neighbors I have revised and enlarged the original volume, omitting much that was of special interest at the time it was written, and adding a large amount of new matter relating to the events of the past twenty years.

Chapters I, II and V are reprinted with only minor changes; III, IV and VI have been rewritten and brought down to date; VII, VIII and IX are wholly new.

J. H. L.

BALTIMORE,
May 7, 1920.

CONTENTS

THE UNITED STATES
AND
LATIN AMERICA

THE UNITED STATES AND
LATIN AMERICA

CHAPTER I

The Revolt of the Spanish Colonies

The English colonies of North America renounced allegiance to their sovereign more through fear of future oppression than on account of burdens actually imposed. The colonies of Spain in the southern hemisphere, on the other hand, labored for generations under the burden of one of the most irrational and oppressive economic systems to which any portion of the human race has ever been subjected, and remained without serious attempt at revolution until the dethronement of their sovereign by Napoleon left them to drift gradually, *in spite of themselves,* as Chateaubriand expressed it, into the republican form of government. To carry the contrast a step further, when the conditions were ripe for independence, the English colonies offered a united resistance, while the action of the Spanish colonies was spasmodic and disconcerted. The North American revolution gave birth to a federal republic, that of the South to a number of separate and independent republics, whose relations with one another have at times been far from amicable. The causes for these striking dif-

3

ferences are to be explained not alone by race psychology, but by a comparison of the English and Spanish colonial systems and of the two revolutions as well. The history of the English colonies and of their revolt has been pretty well exploited, but information in regard to the Spanish-American revolution and its causes, although the sources are abundant, is not easily accessible to English-speaking people.

By virtue of the celebrated Bull of Pope Alexander VI, the Spanish-American colonies were looked upon as possessions of the crown, and not as colonies of Spain. Their affairs were regulated by the king, with the assistance of a board called the Council of the Indies. This council, which was on a footing of equality with the Council of Castile, was established by Ferdinand as early as 1511, and was modified by Charles V in 1524. It was to take cognizance of all ecclesiastical, civil, military, and commercial affairs relating to the colonies. From it proceeded the so-called Laws of the Indies, and all colonial offices in the gift of the crown were conferred by it. In the course of time, however, the personnel of this council became merged with that of Castile, and for all practical purposes the colonies became dependencies of the Spanish nation.

There were from the first establishment of Spanish rule in America, two viceroyalties on the continent. The viceroy of New Spain ruled over Mexico and Central America, whilst all South America subject to Spanish control was for about two centuries under the viceroy of Peru. In regions too remote to be under his immediate control, *audiencias,* or courts of justice, were established, the president of the *audiencia*

4

being known by the title of captain-general. Thus *audiencias* were established at Quito in 1542, at Charcas (in modern Bolivia) in 1559, in New Granada in 1564, in Chile in 1568, and later at Caracas and at Buenos Aires. In 1740, New Granada was raised to the rank of a viceroyalty, with its capital at Bogota; and in 1776 the same dignity was conferred on Buenos Aires. There were thus on the southern continent three viceroyalties widely separated: one on the Main, one on the Atlantic, and one on the Pacific.

The powers of the viceroy, or captain-general, as the case might be, were limited only by the *audiencia*, consisting of from three to five members, always of Spanish birth, whose functions were largely advisory, but who had the privilege of corresponding directly with the Council of the Indies, and who in case of emergency sometimes went so far as to depose the viceroy.

It should be borne in mind that in Spanish America the native Indian races were not driven beyond the frontier of civilization, as they were by the English settlers, but became, and remain to this day, an integral part of the population. There was thus in the Spanish colonies an unusual admixture of races. There were (1) European Spaniards; (2) Creoles, or children born in America of Spanish parents; (3) Indians, the indigenous race; (4) Negroes of African race; (5) Mestizos, children of whites and Indians; (6) Mulattoes, children of whites and negroes; and (7) Zambos, children of Indians and negroes.

The maladministration of Spain's colonies may be summarized under two heads: (1) acts of oppression against the native Indian race, and (2) regulations of a commercial and political character, which acted in restraint of the economic and social development of her own offspring in America.

Under the first head may be mentioned the *mita,* or forced labor in mines, farms, and factories, and the *repartimiento,* or *encomienda,* which was an allotment to Spaniards of territory including the native inhabitants as peons or vassals. In spite of humane restrictions placed by law upon them, these institutions degenerated into systems of fearful oppression, which led, in 1781, to the heroic but unsuccessful efforts of Tupac Amaru, the last of the Incas, to free the land of his fathers from the cruel rule of the Spaniard. So deep-seated was the dissatisfaction and so formidable the revolt, that it was not suppressed for more than two years. The unfortunate Inca and most of his family were cruelly put to death.

The economic and commercial restrictions imposed upon the colonies require fuller notice. The whole object of Spain's colonial policy was to extract gold and silver from America and to force Spanish manufactures and products upon that country. Commerce was confined to Spain and to Spanish vessels.

No South American could own a ship, nor could a cargo be consigned to him; no foreigner was allowed to reside in the country unless born in Spain; and no capital, not Spanish, was permitted in any shape to be employed in the colonies. Orders were given that no foreign vessel, on any pretence whatever, should touch at a South American port. Even ships in distress were not to be received with common hospitality, but were ordered to be seized as prizes, and the crews imprisoned.[1]

---

[1] Hall's "Journal on Chili, Peru, and Mexico," 2 Vols. Edinburgh, 1824, Vol. I, p. 249.

As late as 1816, when the United States protested against the blockade established by General Morillo, as contrary to international law, M. Onis, the Spanish minister, replied that the object of the blockade was to maintain the laws of the Indies, which during the Napoleonic wars had been somewhat relaxed, adding:

> You are aware that, agreeably to those laws, no foreign vessel was allowed to trade with the dominions of his majesty on that continent without a special license, and that vessels found near or evidently shaping a course towards them were liable to confiscation as interlopers.

When, later in the year, a United States commissioner was sent to Cartagena to reclaim American vessels so seized, the Spanish viceroy gave him to understand that he did not pretend to be acquainted with the law of nations.[2]

Not only were the colonists prohibited from engaging in manufactures which interfered with those of Spain, but restrictions were even placed on agriculture in the interests of the Spanish producer. Thus the cultivation of flax, hemp, and saffron was forbidden under severe penalty; the cultivation of tobacco was not allowed; and grapes and olives could be raised only for table use, so that oil and wine had to be imported from Spain. Upon one occasion (in 1803) orders were sent " to root up all the vines in certain provinces, because the Cadiz merchants complained of a diminution in the consumption of Spanish wines." [3]

The carrying out of this commercial system in all

---

[2] Am. St. Pap., For. Rel., Vol. IV, pp. 156-159.
[3] Hall's " Journal," Vol. I, p. 296. See also Rodney's report on South America, in Vol. IV, Am. St. Pap., For. Rel.

its details was entrusted to the *Casa de Contratacion,* or House of Trade, which was located at Seville until 1717, when it was transferred to Cadiz. The India House, as it was called, was established by warrant of Queen Joanna in 1503.[4] To this house were to be brought all merchandise for the colonies and all products from them of whatever character. The colonial trade was thus limited to one Spanish port. The affairs of the house were in charge of three commissioners or judges, who had jurisdiction, civil and criminal, over all cases arising out of the trade with America. Their authority was subordinated to no other court or council but that of the Indies.

Not only were no foreigners allowed to go to the Spanish colonies, but careful restrictions were placed on the movement of Spaniards to and from America. In 1511 King Ferdinand had by a special order permitted all subjects of Spain without distinction to go over to the Indies upon entering their names at the India House; but in the years 1518, 1522, 1530, and 1539 several orders were passed " that no person reconciled, or newly converted to our holy Catholic faith, from Judaism or Mahometanism, nor the children of such, nor the children or grandsons of any that had worn the St. Andrew's Cross of the Inquisition, or been burnt or condemned as heretics, or for any heretical crime, either by male or female line, might go over to the Indies, upon pain of forfeiting

---

[4] A full history of the India House and an account of its regulations is given by Veitia Linage in his " Norte de la Contratacion," Seville, 1672; translated into English by Captain John Stevens under the title, " Spanish Rule of Trade to the West Indies," London, 1702. Linage was for a number of years Treasurer and Comptroller of the India House. A good summary of the history and regulations of the House is given by Prof. Bernard Moses in his " Casa de Contratacion " in the Papers of the Am. Hist. Ass. for 1894, and in the third chapter of his " Establishment of Spanish Rule in America."

8

all their goods, of an hundred lashes, perpetual banishment from the Indies, and their bodies to be at the king's disposition." [5]

The commissioners might "grant passes to merchants to go over, or return if they came from thence, including married merchants, provided they have leave from their wives, and give 1,000 ducats security to return within three years." [6]

There were also strict rules about passing from one province in America to another. This could not be done without special leave from the king.[7] "The inhabitants of the Indies may not come to Spain without leave from the viceroys, presidents or governors of the places of their habitation, in which they are to express the causes of their coming, and whether it is to stay here or return." [8] "In the Indies, the magistrates are directed to apprehend any persons they find are gone over without leave, to imprison them till they can send them back into Spain, upon pain of losing their employments." [9] In 1594 and 1602 it was decreed that persons going over without leave should be sent to the galleys for four years. In 1622 King Philip IV decreed that a person simply going aboard a ship bound for the Indies without leave should be immediately sent to the galleys for eight years.[10] Other decrees equally severe were issued from time to time.

In order to keep the trade strictly under control and to properly protect it, intercourse with the colonies was held only once a year. Two squadrons, consisting of merchant ships and convoys under com-

[5] Linage, " Norte de la Contratacion," p. 107.
[6] Ibid., p. 110.
[7] Ibid., p. 113.
[8] Ibid., p. 114.
[9] Ibid., p. 109.
[10] Ibid., p. 109.

mand of an admiral and vice-admiral, made the trip each year. The fleet for New Spain (Mexico) sailed in the spring, and that for the mainland in the early fall. The first touched at some of the islands and then went to Vera Cruz; the latter touched first at Cartagena and passed on thence to Porto Bello, where the fair was held about the middle of March. This fair was the great event of the year, and lasted forty days from the time of the arrival of the fleet. From this point goods were distributed by way of Panama to Peru, Chile, and even across the continent to Buenos Aires. The gold bullion was sent in turn to this point by the viceroy of Peru. It came in fifteen days from Potosi to Arica, thence by sea in eight days to Callao, and in twenty days from Callao to Panama. The viceroy of Peru was to take care to have the plate at Panama by the middle of March. At Porto Bello it was taken aboard the galleons. About the middle of June the galleons met the fleet from New Spain at Havana, and from that point the two fleets with their convoys proceeded in greater safety to Spain. Thus for two centuries all intercourse between Spain and her colonies at one end of the line was limited at first to Seville, and then to Cadiz; and at the other to Vera Cruz and Porto Bello.[11] At a later period this arrangement was modified to some extent, and Buenos Aires was made a port of entry. The reason for not permitting trade with Buenos Aires during the earlier period was the fear that the British and Dutch would smuggle through that port.

While the relations of the colonies with Spain were kept under the strictest control, intercourse with for-

---

[11] Linage, " Norte de la Contratacion," pp. 191-193.

eign nations, although absolutely prohibited under the severest penalties, could not be entirely prevented. In speaking of Spain's restrictive policy, a British naval officer, who was on the South American station during the revolution, says:

Unfortunately, however, for that system, the South Americans, notwithstanding the network of chains by which they were enveloped, had still some sparks of humanity left, and, in spite of all their degradation, longed earnestly for the enjoyments suitable to their nature; and finding that the Spaniards neither could nor would furnish them with an adequate supply, they invited the assistance of other nations. To this call the other nations were not slow to listen; and, in process of time, there was established one of the most extraordinary systems of organized smuggling which the world ever saw. This was known under the name of the contraband or forced trade, and was carried on in armed vessels, well manned, and prepared to fight their way to the coast, and to resist, as they often did with effect, the *guarda costas*, or coast blockades of Spain. This singular system of warlike commerce was conducted by the Dutch, Portuguese, French, English, and latterly by the North Americans. In this way goods to an immense value were distributed over South America; and although the prices were necessarily high, and the supply precarious, that taste for the comforts and luxuries of European invention was first encouraged, which afterwards operated so powerfully in giving a steady and intelligible motive to the efforts of the Patriots in their struggle, with the mother-country. Along with the goods which the contraband trade forced into the colonies, no small portion of knowledge found entrance, in spite of the increased exertions of the Inquisition and church influence, aided by the redoubled vigilance of government, who enforced every penalty with the utmost rigor. Many foreigners, too, by means of bribes and other arts, succeeded in getting into the country, so that the progress of intelligence was gradually encouraged, to the utter despair of the Spaniards, who knew no other method of governing the colonies but that of mere brute force, unsupported by the least shadow of opinion, or of good will.[12]

The trade carried on by foreign interlopers grew to such alarming proportions that before the middle of the eighteenth century Spain found it necessary to relax the restrictions upon the private trade of her own subjects. This led, about 1748, to the discontinuance of the annual fleets or galleon trade.

The political administration of the country was absolutely in the hands of Spaniards, who as a rule were not allowed to marry, acquire property, or form any permanent ties in America. In the summary of charges against Spain appearing in the Argentine Manifesto of 1817, one of the specifications is, that of one hundred and sixty viceroys who had governed in America, four natives of the country alone were numbered; and of six hundred and two captains-general, all but fourteen had been Spaniards.

The monopoly of Spanish trade in South America was partially surrendered by the treaty of Utrecht, signed in 1713, at the close of the War of the Spanish Succession. By this treaty England agreed to recognize Philip V as king of Spain and the Indies, and in turn was granted the *assiento,* or contract for supplying the Spanish colonies with African slaves.[13] The importation of negroes into the Spanish possessions had been carried on under contract from the very first. The *assiento,* which had been previously granted to Spanish subjects, was, in 1696, granted to the Portuguese Company of Guinea, and in 1702 to the Royal

---

[12] Hall's "Journal," Vol. I, pp. 253-254.
[13] "The Assiento; or Contract for Allowing to the Subjects of Great Britain the Liberty of Importing Negroes into the Spanish America." Printed by John Baskett, London, 1713.

Guinea Company of France; but in 1713 England secured this lucrative monopoly and became the great slave-trading power of the world.

The *assiento* of 1713, which was very carefully drawn up in 42 articles, granted to an English company the sole right of supplying slaves to the Spanish West Indies and to South America for the period of thirty years from May 1, 1713. By it the Queen of England undertook to see that the company chartered by her should introduce into the Spanish West Indies, including South America, 144,000 negroes of both sexes and all ages within thirty years, at the rate of 4,800 a year. The company was to pay a duty of 33⅓ pieces of eight (dollars) for each negro imported. In addition to the 4,800 a year, other negroes might be imported at a duty of 16⅔ dollars each, thus encouraging larger importations. The negroes could be brought in either Spanish or English vessels, manned with English or Spanish sailors, provided only no cause of offense be given to the Catholic religion. The majority of the negroes were to be taken to Cuba and Porto Rico, and to the ports on the Main; but of the 4,800, the company had the right to take 1,200 to Buenos Aires, 800 to be sold there and 400 to be carried to the provinces up the Plata and to the kingdom of Chile. They were also allowed to carry negroes across the isthmus from Porto Bello to Panama, and there re-ship them to Peru. Either Englishmen or Spaniards could be employed in the business, provided that there were not more than four or six Englishmen in any port, and that these should be amenable to the laws in all respects as Spanish subjects. By no means the least remarkable provision of this treaty was that their British and Catholic majesties were each to receive one-fourth of the profits of this traffic.

Ships engaged in this trade were to be searched on arrival at port, and all merchandise found on board was to be confiscated and heavy penalties inflicted. On condition, however, that the company should not attempt any unlawful trade, his Catholic Majesty granted them the privilege, during thirty years, of sending annually a ship of 500 tons to the fair at Porto Bello. The Spanish king was to be concerned one-fourth in the profits.[14] It seems that the company stretched this privilege to the utmost. The ship always stopped at Jamaica, took on all the goods she could, and carried along with her five or six smaller vessels laden with goods. When she got near Porto Bello, all her provisions were put in the tenders and the goods these bore taken aboard. She then entered the harbor laden down to the water's edge. Thus this single ship was made to carry more than five or six of the largest galleons.[15]

Thirty years before the Spanish colonies began their war of independence, the British government had entertained the idea of revolutionizing and separating them from Spain. This idea seems to have arisen in 1779, during the administration of Lord North, when Spain joined France in the alliance with the American colonies against Great Britain.[16] It was suggested at

---

[14] "The Assiento; or Contract for Allowing to the Subjects of Great Britain the Liberty of Importing Negroes into the Spanish America." London, 1713.
[15] Ulloa, "Voyage to South America." English translation, London, 1806, Vol. I, p. 105.
[16] "Letters and Despatches of Castlereagh," Vol. VII, p. 266 ff. This volume is rich in information in regard to England's Spanish-American policy.

first, no doubt, as a measure of retaliation, but was frequently agitated in later years with the avowed object of opening up South America to British commerce. The same idea was the basis of Miranda's scheme for the liberation of his native land.

Francisco de Miranda [17] (1754-1816), a native of Caracas, Venezuela, was the first Spanish-American patriot. He was with the American army for a time during the Revolutionary War, but in what capacity is not quite settled. It is stated by some writers that he held a commission under LaFayette. The success of our war inspired him with the hope of freeing his own country from Spanish control. He confided his views to his friends in the United States, particularly to Alexander Hamilton, "upon whom he fixed his eyes as a coadjutor in the great purpose of his life." Shortly after Miranda had returned to his native land his schemes were discovered. He fled to the United States, and later to England, where he had repeated conferences with Pitt. Finding no help for his revolutionary schemes in England, he went to the continent and traveled through France, Germany, Turkey, and Russia. At the Russian court he was warmly received, but was soon dismissed at the demand of the Spanish minister. At news of the dispute between England and Spain about Nootka Sound in 1790, he hastened to England and communicated his scheme to the British ministry. Pitt lent a ready ear to his views as long as the dispute lasted, with the intention of making use of him in the event of a rupture with Spain. But when the dispute was peaceably settled,

---

[17] W. S. Robertson, " Francisco de Miranda and the Revolutionizing of Spanish America " (1909).

Miranda's hopes fell to the ground and he left England. His scheme was only temporarily abandoned, however. He considered himself to have been ill-used by Pitt on this occasion, as he subsequently stated to Rufus King, the American minister to England.

The French Revolution was now well under way, and the wars upon which the republic was entering offered an attractive field for a soldier of republican ideas. In April, 1792, Miranda went to Paris with introductions to Pétion and the leading Girondists, hoping that the revolutionary party might help him in his plans. He was given a commission as brigadier-general in the French army, and served in responsible posts under Dumouriez on the eastern frontier. He conducted the siege of Maestricht and commanded the left wing of the French army at the disastrous battle of Neerwinden, March, 1793, in which Belgium was reconquered by the Austrians. Dumouriez now declared against the Convention, but his troops having refused to follow him, he went over to the Austrians in company with the Duke of Chartres, Louis Philippe. Miranda fell under suspicion of treason and was forced to undergo a court-martial, but was acquitted. For some unexplained reason he was shortly after thrown into prison. He soon secured his release, but for several years disappears from public view. His services in behalf of the republic received in time due recognition. His name appears on the Arc de Triomphe in Paris in the list of the heroes of the Revolution.

In January, 1798, Miranda returned to England. As Spain was now the close ally of France, he hoped to secure the coöperation of Great Britain in his scheme. He also hoped to secure aid from the United States. The people of Kentucky and Tennessee were far from satisfied with the provisions of the Spanish treaty of 1795 in regard to the navigation of the Mississippi River. Then, too, just at this time, war between the United States and France seemed inevitable, on account of the resentment by France of the Jay treaty and her treatment of the American representatives. Washington had been called from his retirement at Mt. Vernon to assume the post of commander-in-chief of the army, while the active command was to be given to Hamilton. Hamilton had expressed great interest in Miranda's projects and was a man of known ambition. His appointment, therefore, as the virtual commander-in-chief of the American army made Miranda hopeful of his coöperation.

Mr. King, the American minister at London, entered heartily into the plans of General Miranda, and his correspondence on that subject, during the year 1798, with his government and with Hamilton is quite voluminous.[18] For a time it seemed as if Great Britain and the United States would coöperate for the purpose of revolutionizing Spanish America. The plan, as entertained by Miranda and Hamilton, was for England to supply the naval force and the United States the land forces. Miranda believed that six or eight vessels of the line and four or five thousand troops would be sufficient,[19] though Hamilton thought it would require ten thousand troops. England's participation in the scheme depended upon the relations be-

[18] "Life and Correspondence of Rufus King," New York, 1894, Vol. II, App. 5. For further information regarding his relations with Miranda, see extracts from his Memorandum Book, in Vol. III, App. 3.
[19] See Miranda's letter to President Adams, March 24, 1798. "Life and Corresp. of King," Vol. II, p. 654.

tween France and Spain. Mr. King wrote to his government, February 26, 1798:

Two points have within a fortnight been settled in the English cabinet respecting South America. If Spain is able to prevent the overthrow of her present government and to escape being brought under the entire control of France, England (between whom and Spain, notwithstanding the war, a certain understanding appears to exist) will at present engage in no scheme to deprive Spain of her possessions in South America. But if, as appears probable, the army destined against Portugal, and which will march through Spain, or any other means which may be employed by France, shall overthrow the Spanish government, and thereby place the resources of Spain and of her colonies at the disposal of France, England will immediately commence the execution of a plan long since digested and prepared for the complete independence of South America. If England engages in this plan, she will at Philadelphia propose to the United States to coöperate in its execution, Miranda will be detained here, under one pretense or another, until events shall decide the conduct of England.[20]

England's policy in regard to South America for the next twenty years substantially confirmed the interpretation of her motives here given by Mr. King.

During the summer of 1798 Mr. King had several conferences with the British ministry in regard to the Spanish-American question, but it was always understood that they were personal and wholly unauthorized. What occurred at these interviews was, of course, always communicated to the American government, but as they were unofficial and communicated merely in the nature of information, the State Department preferred to keep the matter on the same

[20] "Life and Corresp. of King," Vol. II, p. 650.

basis and did not refer to the matter in its dispatches to Mr. King. This caused him no little annoyance.[21] In the same way no notice was taken of General Miranda's letter to President Adams.

Hamilton, however, was very frank in the expression of his views both to General Miranda and to Mr. King. Under date of August 22, 1798, he wrote to the latter:

> I have received several letters from General Miranda. I have written answers to some of them, which I send you to deliver or not, according to your estimate of what is passing in the scenes where you are. Should you deem it expedient to suppress my letter, you may do it and say as much as you think fit on my part in the nature of a communication through you. With regard to the enterprise in question, I wish it much to be undertaken, but I should be glad that the principal agency was in the United States— they to furnish the whole land force necessary. The command in this case would very naturally fall upon me, and I hope I should disappoint no favorable anticipation.

The United States, however, succeeded in coming to an understanding with France, while England was unwilling to deal such a serious blow to Spain as long as there was a chance of arraying her against Napoleon. The communication of the views of the British government at Philadelphia, to which Mr. King referred as a preliminary, was never made. Miranda's hopes finally fell through at the reëstablishment of peace in Europe by the treaty of Amiens, which lasted until 1803. He lingered in Europe some time longer, until, wearied out by years of fruitless negotiation with the British government, he, for the time being,

---

[21] See King's letter to Hamilton, March 4, 1799. "Life and Corresp.," p. 662.

gave up all hope of success in that quarter and returned once more to the United States.

Arriving in New York from England in November, 1805, Miranda proceeded to lay his cause once more before Mr. King, who had so warmly befriended him in London, and to solicit his coöperation in fitting out an expedition for South America. While expressing his full sympathy with the cause, Mr. King stated emphatically that he could render him no assistance, nor could any individuals safely do so, without the countenance of the government. He, therefore, advised Miranda to go to Washington and lay his plans before the administration. This Miranda did. He was admitted to informal conferences both with President Jefferson and Secretary of State Madison. Upon his return to New York he represented to those interested in his schemes that he had secured from the government a secret sanction of his project, and that the administration, though unwilling to take the initiative, would support the undertaking so soon as the standard of revolution should once have been raised on the Spanish Main. Miranda's chief supporter was Colonel Smith, surveyor of the port of New York, whose influence as a public official in close touch with the administration was decisive in persuading many adventurous spirits to join the expedition with the belief that it was really secretly backed by the government of the United States.

Miranda left New York in the early part of February, 1806, in the *Leander,* with an imperfectly equipped force of about 200 men, most of whom were commissioned as officers and promised commands in the South American army, which was expected to spring from the soil at the magic touch of Miranda's step upon the shores of his native land. The ship proceeded to Jacquemel, San Domingo, where Miranda expected to get the necessary supplies and reinforcements. Here disappointments awaited him, disputes with the ship's captain ensued, and over a month was fruitlessly spent, while the Spanish authorities on the Main had time to put themselves on the alert. It was not until the last of April that the expedition, reinforced by two schooners, appeared off the coast of Venezuela near Porto Cabello. They were attacked by two Spanish vessels, which captured the schooners with about sixty men and large stores, while the *Leander* ignominiously took to flight.

Miranda then sailed for Barbados, where he solicited aid from the British admiral, Lord Cochrane, in command on the West Indian station. Lord Cochrane, without definite instructions from his government, but acquainted with its general policy in regard to South America, and knowing of the close relations in which Miranda had stood for years with the British ministry, decided to assist him in landing. With this understanding he signed with Miranda an agreement to the effect that in the event of the success of the expedition, Great Britain should always be held on a footing with the most favored nation, and that British ships should receive a deduction of ten per cent. upon duties paid by all other nations, except the United States.[22] On the twentieth of June, the expedition left Barbados under convoy of a part of Admiral Cochrane's squadron, and on August 2, 1806, effected a landing near Coro, Venezuela. They easily

---

[22] " Letters and Despatches of Castlereagh," Vol. VII.

took possession of the town, the unarmed inhabitants fleeing before them. Here Miranda remained about ten days, issuing proclamations and vainly waiting for the natives to join him. His position, meanwhile, was becoming unsafe, so he abandoned it and took possession of the little island of Aruba off the coast. Lord Cochrane, seeing that the expedition was a failure, and not wishing further to compromise his government, sent no reinforcements and finally ordered the withdrawal of the ships that had accompanied the expedition. Miranda was offered a convoy back to Trinidad, which he accepted, leaving Aruba, September 27, 1806. At Trinidad the members of the expedition dispersed.[23]

The Americans who had taken part in the expedition and survived were prosecuted in the United States courts for violation of the neutrality laws. They claimed that they had enlisted in the undertaking with the connivance of the government at Washington. Jefferson's enemies made great political capital of the affair. Members of the cabinet were summoned as witnesses, but refused to appear. Privately Jefferson and Madison both denied most emphatically having in any way committed the government to Miranda's undertaking, or having acted in any way in disregard of our obligations to Spain.[24]

Aside from accomplishing nothing, the expedition of 1806 was a great injury to Miranda's cause. He himself lost prestige as a military leader and brought his character into question as having misrepresented his connection both with the British and United States

---

[23] See Sherman, "General Account of Miranda's Expedition," N. Y., 1808.
[24] H. A. Washington, "Writings of Thomas Jefferson," Vol. V, p. 474; "Madison's Writings," Vol. II, pp. 220, 225.

governments. However, upon the occupation of Spain by Napoleon in 1808, Miranda again hastened to England and urged upon the ministry the claims of his country, in whose interests he had now been laboring incessantly as an exile for more than twenty years. We cannot but admire his tenacity of purpose in the face of the most disheartening failures.

Not only did the British government lend its encouragement, through Lord Cochrane, to the filibustering expedition from the United States with which Miranda hoped to revolutionize Venezuela, but about the same time it sent an expedition against the provinces of the Plate. This attack, like the assistance given to Miranda, was ill-timed and not properly followed up. The policy seems to have been outlined by Pitt, but was put into execution after his death by the short-lived ministry of Grenville and Fox. The government of the Duke of Portland, which succeeded after a few months, and in which Castlereagh and Canning were the most conspicuous figures, did not deem it expedient to follow up the undertaking.[25] In fact, the fate of the expedition was already sealed when Portland came into power.

The victory of Trafalgar had given the English control of the Atlantic. A force of some 6,000 men was dispatched to the South Atlantic without its destination being known. It proceeded to Rio Janeiro, Portugal then being in alliance with England. The viceroy of the Plate became alarmed and prepared to defend Montevideo, which he thought would be the first point of attack. The expedition, however, passed by and proceeded to the Cape of Good Hope, which

---

[25] "Letters and Despatches of Castlereagh," Vol. VII, p. 314 ff.

it wrested from the Dutch. In 1806 a dash was made from the Cape for the river Plate. Sir Home Popham commanded the fleet, and General Beresford the land force, which amounted to 1,635 men. On June 6 the squadron arrived at the mouth of the Plate. The ships had some difficulty in ascending the river, but on the 25th they came to anchor at a point fifteen miles below Buenos Aires. The city was captured with little or no resistance, the inhabitants having been led to believe that the British had come to liberate them. The contents of the public treasury were handed over to the invaders. The inhabitants were required to swear allegiance to George III, private property was respected, the free exercise of their religion was allowed, and all officials who took the oath were continued in office. When Beresford refused to proclaim the independence of the province, or to give any assurance for their future independence, the inhabitants, who had now learned how insignificant the invading force really was, began to prepare for resistance. A leader was readily found in the person of Jacques Liniers, a Frenchman, who had been for thirty years in the service of Spain. He and Juan Martin de Puyrredon began an organized movement for the expulsion of the English. On the 12th of August, Beresford, who had remained all this time without reinforcements, was compelled to surrender. Troops ordered to his support from the Cape did not arrive until later.

Sobremonte, the viceroy, had deserted Buenos Aires and established himself at Montevideo. The people of Buenos Aires, therefore, deposed him and chose Liniers in his place.

During the fall other English reinforcements arrived, and in January, 1807, Montevideo was taken by assault. As soon as the defeat of Beresford was known, General Whitelocke was sent to take command of the united English forces of the Plate, now some twelve thousand in number. He arrived in the spring. The reconquest of Buenos Aires now seemed an easy matter. It had been taken in the first instance by sixteen hundred men; there were now ten thousand available. On June 28 the British landed at the small port of Ensenada, forty-eight miles below Buenos Aires. The fighting continued on the outskirts of the city in a desultory maner and without any decisive action for several days. But finally, owing to the bad generalship and incompetency of Whitelocke, his troops got into such a muddle that half the force was captured or disabled. On July 6, Liniers decided to send a flag of truce with the proposal to surrender all the English prisoners, including those taken with Beresford, provided Whitelocke would evacuate the territory of Buenos Aires. One of Liniers' associates, Alzaga, insisted that the terms of surrender should include Montevideo. This demand seemed preposterous, but the clause was finally inserted, and to their surprise agreed to, so complete was the demoralization of the English. On July 7 the terms of capitulation were signed.[26] Thus through a lack of decision in the cabinet and a display of incapacity in the field, without parallel in British annals, the empire of the Plate was lost.[27]

With Napoleon's invasion of Spain in 1808, the

---

[26] See Watson, " Spanish and Portuguese South America." 2 Vols. London, 1884, Vol. II, p. 271 ff.
[27] See " Letters and Despatches of Castlereagh," Vol. VII, p. 316 ff.

Spanish-American question came to the front once more. Miranda returned to London and was detained there by the cabinet, as before by Pitt, with a view to using him if occasion should require. At the same time Castlereagh, now Foreign Secretary, had other solutions of the question in view. It was proposed, and the matter seriously discussed in the cabinet, to alienate the colonies from Spain, if possible, without revolution; and, instead of establishing republics according to Miranda's plans, to unite them all under a prince of the House of Bourbon. Louis Philippe, Duke of Orleans, was suggested as the most suitable person for the new crown. Some thirty years prior to this, immediately upon the recognition by Spain of the independence of the United States, Count de Aranda had advised Charles III to forestall the movement for independence, which must inevitably come in his own provinces, by establishing among them three great empires—one in Mexico, one in Peru, and one on the Main—each to be ruled by a prince of the royal family of Spain.[28]

Chateaubriand brought forward a similar plan several years later at the Congress of Verona. The present scheme was suggested by General Dumouriez in the interests of his friend, the Duke of Orleans. Several memorials on the subject, both by Dumouriez and the duke, were presented to the British government in 1807 and 1808.[29]

Napoleon's invasion of Spain constitutes at once the most contemptible and the most disastrous chapter in his career. In 1807, under the terms of an agree-

---

[28] Romero, "Mexico and the United States," Putnam, 1898, p. 287.
[29] "Letters and Despatches of Castlereagh," Vol. VII.

ment with Godoy, the unworthy favorite of the queen and the virtual ruler of Spain, a French army was introduced into the kingdom for the nominal purpose of punishing Portugal for her refusal to join the continental system. The Portuguese royal family, fully appreciating the danger in which they stood, fled to America and founded the empire of Brazil, which in 1815 was declared independent of Portugal. The Spanish rulers attempted to follow their example, but their intended flight became known and they were prevented by the populace from leaving the capital. In the meantime a disgraceful quarrel having arisen between the old king, Charles IV, and Prince Ferdinand, Napoleon, whose troops were now firmly established in Spain, stepped in as arbiter between father and son and summoned them both to meet him on the northern frontier. Having purposely lingered in France beyond the appointed time, he succeeded in enticing them over the border to Bayonne, where he compelled both to renounce forever the crown of Spain and the Indies, which he forthwith bestowed upon his brother Joseph. When the truth dawned upon them, the Spanish nation rose to a man. Napoleon had unwittingly aroused the latent principle of nationality; he had put into action a force which was new and one which the statesmen of Europe had hitherto left out of account, but which was to prove the most potent factor in the new epoch of political history introduced by the French Revolution.

Provisional juntas were rapidly organized in the various provinces of the kingdom of Spain and affairs administered in the name of Ferdinand VII. The Junta, or as it is better known, the Regency of Cadiz, rapidly gained a position of national importance and became the chief executive body of the Spanish nation. The American provinces, which had long been restive under Spanish rule, now claimed the same right of self-government that the provinces of the Peninsula had assumed, and began to depose the Spanish governors and to set up juntas of their own, still acting in the name of Ferdinand VII. The Americans claimed that they were not politically a part of Spain, but connected only through the sovereign, and that with the removal of the sovereign the connection ceased. The Regency of Cadiz, on the other hand, maintained that the colonies were integral parts of Spain, and claimed, therefore, the right to govern them in the absence of the sovereign.

The first throes of revolution were felt in 1809, almost simultaneously in Upper Peru, Quito, and Mexico. These movements were quickly suppressed with great cruelty. In the year 1810 the revolution opened upon a vast scale. All the Spanish colonies on the mainland, with the exception of Lower Peru, revolted at the same time and proclaimed their independence of Spain, although still professing allegiance to Ferdinand VII, the dethroned king.

The colonial authorities were deposed in most cases by force of public opinion and without violence. The revolution was municipal in character, that is to say, the *cabildos,* or town councils, the only popularly constituted political bodies in the colonies, assumed the initiative in the work of revolution and named the juntas. The junta of the capital city in each province was usually recognized as the chief executive body for that province, and assumed for the time being all the functions of government. National conventions were then called in many cases to decide upon the form of government. These in most cases entrusted the executive power to regencies or triumvirates, almost all of which rapidly gave way to military dictatorships.

The Regency of Cadiz had anticipated trouble from the colonies and had recognized their rights as freemen by inviting them to send deputies to the national Cortes, but at the same time had abridged those rights by allowing them only a very limited representation, absurdly out of proportion to their population and commercial importance. Upon the establishment of the provisional governments or juntas in the colonies, the Regency refused them the freedom of trade that had been promised, declined the proffered mediation of England, and proceeded to stigmatize the Americans as rebels and to declare them guilty of high treason, although they had been guilty only of the same conduct that the Spaniards themselves were pursuing at home.

Venezuela then (1811) declared herself independent of both the Spanish nation and of the Spanish monarch, and adopted a republican constitution. The promulgation of the Spanish constitution of 1812 further encouraged the spirit of independence in the colonies, but when Ferdinand was restored in 1814, the colonies were still governed in his name, for the revolution of Venezuela, which alone had declared for independence, had been crushed out. Had Ferdinand acted with any moderation or judgment, his American possessions would have been saved to his crown. But the refusal of the colonies, which had now enjoyed practical self-government for several years, to take upon

them without conditions the yoke of absolute authority, was met with the proclamation of a war of reconquest. Reconciliation was thereafter no longer
possible, and independence only a question of time.
By the close of 1815 the revolution had been put down
in all the provinces except La Plata. There it was
never suppressed. For this reason we shall first trace
rapidly the course of the revolution in the south, of
which San Martin was the directing power.

José de San Martin was born in 1778 in Paraguay,
his father being the governor of Misiones. When
eight years of age, his family went to Spain and he
was entered as a pupil in the Seminary of Nobles at
Madrid. At the age of twelve, he joined a regiment
as cadet and saw his first service in Africa. He served
in the Spanish army for more than twenty years, and
won promotion as well as special distinction for bravery. In the battle of Baylen, where a detachment of
Napoleon's disciplined troops was beaten by an army
of recruits inspired by patriotism, San Martin, then a
captain, won a gold medal and a commission as lieu-
tenant-colonel for his conduct. Hearing of the
struggle for liberty in his native land, he resigned his
commission and returned to America. He was almost
unknown personally, but his reputation as a brave soldier and a skilful tactician procured for him immediate
employment. At this time the Argentine Republic had
two armies in the field, the one operating near at home
against the Portuguese in Uruguay and the Spanish
in Montevideo, and the other in Upper Peru (Bolivia)
against the forces sent by the viceroy of Peru to suppress the Argentine revolution. San Martin was
soon given the command of this army in the north,

succeeding General Belgrano. He soon placed his army in an excellent state of discipline and put a check to the advances of the Peruvian army.[30]

On May 16, 1814, the Argentine naval force, under command of an Irishman named Brown, defeated and almost entirely destroyed the Spanish squadron stationed at Montevideo, and that city soon after surrendered to the besieging army of Alvear, San Martin's old comrade in the Spanish army. Alvear, whose political influence was much greater than San Martin's, now aspired to the conquest of Peru, and therefore desired the command in the north. This San Martin willingly relinquished to him. He had other plans in mind, and the state of his health demanded rest. Upper Peru had been the high-road from Peru to Buenos Aires in times of peace, and was, therefore, naturally looked upon as the line of advance for the liberating army. San Martin, however, after a careful study of the question, had become convinced that this was not the strategic line of approach, that the Argentine Republic would never succeed in conquering Peru from this quarter. His idea was to carry the war to the west, to cross the Andes, occupy Chile, and, having secured a naval base there, to attack Peru from the coast, continuing military operations in the north merely as a diversion. The success of this plan depended upon the performance of two apparently impossible tasks—the passage of the Andes and the creation of a navy on the Pacific. San Martin was by far too shrewd a man to advocate such an undertaking before maturing his plans. He, therefore, confided it

---

[30] Mitre, "The Emancipation of South America." Translated by Pilling. London, 1893.

only to a few of his intimate friends, and, taking advantage of his ill health, asked, as a favor for himself, the government of the obscure province of Cuyo, where from its capital of Mendoza he could place himself in communication with the Chilean patriots.

On August 10, 1814, San Martin was appointed governor of Cuyo, and at once devoted himself to the development of the plans which led to the emancipation of half a continent and gave him his place in the world's history. The revolutionary movement in Chile had just been crushed out. It was begun in 1810 and the general course of events had been somewhat similar to the Argentine movement, but it had fallen a victim first to disputes between the Patriot leaders and finally to the troops of the viceroy of Peru. It would require more space than we can give to trace the varying fortunes of the cause in Chile through the stirring events that marked the leadership of Dr. Rosas, of the Carrera brothers, and of Bernardo O'Higgins. After the final collapse, O'Higgins, with a number of other Patriots, fled over the Andes to Mendoza and readily entered into the plans of San Martin. It took the latter two years to organize and equip an army and to convince the government of Buenos Aires of the practicability of his plan.

At length, on January 17, 1817, he began the passage of the Andes with about 5,000 men, 1,600 horses, and 9,000 mules, the latter carrying the field artillery, ammunition, and provisions. The summit of the Uspallata Pass is 12,700 feet above the sea-level, 5,000 feet higher than the Great St. Bernard, by which Napoleon led his army over the Alps. In many other respects San Martin's achievement was more remarkable.   Each piece of artillery had to be carried suspended on a pole between two mules, or, where the road was particularly dangerous, dragged by ropes.   There were chasms that could be crossed only by cable bridges.   The march over the Andes occupied three weeks.   Both men and animals suffered greatly from *soroche,* the illness caused by rarefied atmosphere.

At the foot of the mountain, at Chacabuco, the vanguard of San Martin's army defeated a body of 4,000 Royalists, and thus opened the road to Santiago, which San Martin entered February 14, 1817.   The Chileans chose him Supreme Director of their government, but he declined the office, and O'Higgins was chosen.

San Martin's great object was to crush the colonial power of Spain in its stronghold, Peru.   Having by the successful passage of the Andes and the victory of Chacabuco in a measure justified his plan of campaign, he returned to Buenos Aires for reinforcements.   The Royalists meanwhile retreated to the south. On February 18, 1818, the independence of Chile was proclaimed.   A month later the Patriots were surprised at Cancha-Rayada and almost routed, but within two weeks the army was again ready for action, and on April 5, 1818, encountered the Royalists at Maipo. This battle was a complete victory for the Patriots and decided the fate of Chile.   Only one or two fortresses in the south were now held for Spain.   Five days after the battle of Maipo, San Martin returned once more to Buenos Aires and began organizing an expedition for the liberation of Peru.   Puyrredon, now Supreme Director, supported his undertaking.

While San Martin was soliciting aid from the Argentine Republic, the Chileans were not idle.   They

33

saw that the only way of insuring their independence was by the creation of a navy. Through its agent in London, the Chilean government secured the services of Lord Cochrane, an English naval officer of great distinction and remarkable talents, who by a curious turn of fortune had been brought into unmerited disgrace and dismissed from the British service.[31] He reached Valparaiso in November and hoisted his flag on board the *O'Higgins,* December 22, 1818. During the course of the next year, Cochrane made two attempts to take Callao, the seaport of Peru, but without success beyond harassing the enemy in some of the smaller coast towns. In February, 1820, by a brilliant move, he captured Valdivia, a strongly fortified town still held by the Spaniards in southern Chile.

San Martin returned to Chile in January, 1820, and began to assemble at Valparaiso the army destined for the invasion of Peru. Of the 5,000 men, two-thirds were from Buenos Aires, while nearly all of the officers were Argentine or European volunteers. Of 65 foreign officers, 37 were British and 3 were from the United States. There were, besides, 30 English officers in the Chilean navy. The expedition sailed on August 21, 1820, on board the fleet commanded by Cochrane. San Martin landed his army at Pisco, to the south of Lima, and sent an expedition into the interior under General Arenales, who had served the Patriots for years in Upper Peru. In October, San Martin reembarked his troops and landed them again at Huacho, a point seventy miles north of Lima. Meanwhile the Spanish squadron, completely demoralized by the ap-

---

[31] See Cochrane (Earl Dundonald), " Service in Chili." 2 Vols. London, 1859.

pearance on the Pacific of Lord Cochrane, whose daring exploits were well known, was lying under the guns of Callao Castle. On the night of November 5, 1820, Lord Cochrane led a force of volunteers, consisting of 180 seamen and 100 marines, in open boats right under the batteries of Callao, surprised and overpowered the crew of the *Esmeralda,* the largest Spanish frigate, and, cutting her loose, carried her off to his own squadron.

After Cochrane's exploit at Callao, the moral effect of which was very great, he urged upon San Martin an immediate advance upon Lima, but San Martin had two campaigns before him, the one military, the other political. On first landing at Pisco he had issued an order to his army in which he said, " Remember that you are come not to conquer, but to liberate a people; the Peruvians are our brothers." And in spite of the impatience and restlessness of his officers, he steadily adhered to his plan, to the no small loss of his military prestige and ultimately to his retirement from the scene of activity. His purpose was by the presence of the liberating army to give the people of Peru a chance to rise and throw off the yoke of Spain. To this end he scattered proclamations and addresses of a revolutionary character broadcast through the land and quietly awaited results. The contest in Peru, he said, was not a war of conquest and glory, but entirely of opinion; it was a war of new and liberal principles against prejudice, bigotry, and tyranny.

People ask why I don't march to Lima at once; so I might, and instantly would, were it suitable to my views, which it is not. I do not want military renown; I have no ambition to be the conqueror of Peru; I want solely to liberate the

35

country from oppression. Of what use would Lima be to me if the inhabitants were hostile in political sentiment? How could the cause of independence be advanced by my holding Lima, or even the whole country, in military possession? Far different are my views. I wish to have all men thinking with me, and do not choose to advance a step beyond the gradual march of public opinion. The capital is now ripe for declaring its sentiments, and I shall give them the opportunity to do so in safety. It was in sure expectation of this movement that I have hitherto deferred advancing; and to those who know the full extent of the means which have been put in action, a sufficient explanation is afforded of all the delays that have taken place. I have been gaining, indeed, day by day, fresh allies in the hearts of the people, the only certain allies in such a war. In the secondary point of military strength, I have been, from the same causes, equally successful in augmenting and improving the liberating army; while that of the Spaniards has been wasted by want and desertion. The country has now become sensible of its true interests, and it is right the inhabitants should have the means of expressing what they think. Public opinion is an engine newly introduced into this country; the Spaniards, who are utterly incapable of directing it, have prohibited its use; but they shall now experience its strength and importance.[32]

The campaign of Arenales in the interior was successful. In the presence of the liberating army, the people everywhere rose in revolt. San Martin's method of conducting the campaign was the correct one. Public opinion was soon aroused in the capital itself, and the Royalists finally decided to evacuate Lima. The viceroy retired with his forces to Cuzco in the highlands. In response to an invitation from the city authorities, the Patriots entered Lima July 6, 1821. San Martin himself entered without ceremony

---

[32] Hall's "Journal," Vol. I, p. 181. Report of Conversation with San Martin in Callao Roads.

after dark a few days later. The independence of Peru was proclaimed July 28 with imposing ceremonies in the great square of Lima. San Martin was proclaimed Protector of Peru. He proceeded to organize a civil government, and established the celebrated *Order of the Sun,* distinctively aristocratic in character.

San Martin had played a great part thus far, but he had reached the zenith of his influence and power. Dissensions soon arose. The task he had undertaken was difficult in the extreme. It was much easier to acquire power than to use it. At the time of the evacuation of Lima by the Spaniards, he said to Captain Hall:

For the last ten years I have been unremittingly employed against the Spaniards; or rather in favor of this country, for I am not against any one who is not hostile to the cause of independence. All I wish is that this country should be managed by itself, and by itself alone. As to the manner in which it is to be governed, that belongs not at all to me. I propose simply to give the people the means of declaring themselves independent, and of establishing a suitable form of government; after which I shall consider I have done enough and leave them.[33]

When the time came he kept his word.

While San Martin was leading the army of liberation from the Argentine Republic to Chile, and from Chile to Peru, Simon Bolivar, the liberator of the north, was pursuing his chequered career in Venezuela and Colombia, unfurling the standard of revolution wherever he could get a foothold. He was a man, in every respect, the opposite of San Martin, fiery, im-

[33] Hall's "Journal," Vol. I, p. 194.

petuous, wholly given over to personal ambition, neither a statesman nor a soldier, but one of the greatest revolutionary leaders of any age or country. His ignorance of military affairs led him into undertakings from which an experienced soldier would have held back, but his indomitable pluck carried him safely through all calamities, and his wonderful enthusiasm fired his followers even in the midst of disaster.

This remarkable man, whose reputation in the new world stands second to that of Washington alone, was, like Miranda, a native of Caracas. Sprung from a family of wealth and influence he had, like most young South Americans of his class, received his education abroad, and had for several years led a dissipated life in Paris. At first he held himself aloof from the revolutionary leaders, but after the accomplishment of the revolution of Caracas, April 19, 1810, he was persuaded to join the Patriot cause, and was sent to London to solicit assistance from Great Britain.[34]

The junta of Caracas, like those subsequently formed in the south, professed to act in the name of Ferdinand VII, and fearing the influence of Miranda, then in London, whose advocacy of absolute independence had been open and avowed, they instructed Bolivar and their other agents not to allow him to come to Venezuela. Miranda came in spite of them, however, under an assumed name, and was everywhere received with enthusiasm. Under his influence a congress was elected which, on July 5, 1811, declared Venezuela a republic, free and independent of all foreign dominion. Miranda was appointed Director. This was the first South American declaration of inde-

---

[34] Holstein, "Life of Bolivar." Boston, 1829.

pendence. The formal independence of the Argentine Republic was not declared until July 9, 1816, although the country had been self-governing for several years.

The Patriot cause was ruined, however, by the earthquake of March 25, 1812, which almost destroyed the city of Caracas and several towns of importance. Twenty thousand people are supposed to have perished. As the disaster occurred on Holy Thursday, the clergy were not slow to turn it to political account and to persuade the people that it was a direct chastisement of Heaven upon them for their rebellion against Spain. The cause of the Patriots steadily lost ground until the fall of Porto Cabello, through the inefficiency of Bolivar, caused its complete collapse. Miranda was forced to sign with Monteverde the treaty of Vittoria, July 26, 1812, on the basis of complete submission and a general amnesty. It is hardly necessary to add that the Spanish general did not abide by the terms of the capitulation. Miranda himself was detained by Bolivar, as he was on the point of embarking for England, accused of having received bribes from the Spaniards and of being unwilling to share the fate of his followers, and treacherously handed over to the Spaniards. He was sent to Spain and after languishing for three years in a dungeon at Cadiz, died July 14, 1816. His fate was a sad blot upon the reputation of Bolivar.

The revolution in New Granada, which had been inaugurated July 20, 1810, was still holding out and thither Bolivar proceeded to offer his services to the Patriots of that province. As soon as he had firmly established himself in influence and power, he persuaded the government that their only safety lay in the reconquest of Venezuela. He was provided with troops, and in May, 1813 crossed the frontier and took several important cities. He now assumed a new attitude and became a self-appointed dictator. He proclaimed a war of extermination against Spaniards and adopted a new system of dates: " 3d year of Independence and 1st of the War to the Death." He entered Caracas in triumph August 6, 1813. He proclaimed himself dictator with the title of Liberator. Meanwhile Marino, another Patriot leader, had landed in the eastern part of Venezuela near Cumana and declared himself dictator. There were thus two dictators and no cordiality between them. Before they could come to an agreement the enemy had recovered their position. In December, 1814, the last Patriot force was defeated.

Bolivar and Marino retired once more to New Granada. Bolivar was made captain-general of the forces of New Granada, his title of Liberator was recognized, and another, that of Illustrious Pacificator, bestowed upon him. A second time he undertook the conquest of Venezuela from the west. Dissensions soon arose between Bolivar and the other leaders. He was refused reinforcements and foolishly marched against the Patriot garrison of Cartagena. He was now forced to give up his command, and embarked for Jamaica, May, 1815.

Meanwhile Ferdinand had been restored to the throne of Spain, and an army of 10,000 men, commanded by Marshal Morillo, the ablest Spanish general of the time, had been sent to reduce the provinces on the Main. This expedition reached Cumana in April, 1815, and before the end of the year all the colonies, with the exception of the provinces of the River Plate, were reduced to submission.

Far from giving up hope, however, Bolivar proceeded to Haiti, and from that island, in May, 1816, made a descent upon the eastern part of Venezuela, but was routed by the Spaniards in July, and soon returned to Haiti. A few of the Patriots still kept the field, and towards the close of the year Bolivar's partisans secured his recall. On December 21 he left Haiti with a second expedition for the relief of his native land. He determined now to direct all his efforts, not as hitherto, to the support of the Patriot cause in the capital, but to the holding of the great plains of the Orinoco. With this territory as a base, he carried on, during the year 1817, in conjunction with the Llanero horsemen of General Paez, a desperate struggle with the Spaniards. When the rainy season of 1818 began, Bolivar's army had been cut almost to pieces, he had lost prestige as a general, and his civil authority amounted to nothing. Only the cavalry of Paez maintained the Patriot cause. Still the position of the Spaniards was not much better. Morillo had 12,000 men scattered about, but neither money, arms, nor supplies. He reported to the viceroy of Peru: "Twelve pitched battles, in which the best officers and troops of the enemy have fallen, have not lowered their pride or lessened the vigor of their attacks upon us."

In February, 1819, the second Congress of Venezuela convened at Angostura. The Dictator resigned, but was unanimously elected President and given absolute power in all provinces which were the actual theater of war. The army was reorganized by the accession of foreign troops, in particular the British legion, consisting of 2,000 well equipped men, which achieved much of the success of the next year. Bolivar now conceived the idea of crossing the Cordillera and reconquering New Granada. General Paez was to attract the attention of Morillo on the plains in front, and a demonstration was to be made on the coast near Caracas, while Bolivar marched to the west. This movement changed the whole face of affairs and had a similar effect to the passage of the Andes by San Martin. New Granada was won by the battle of Boyaca, August 7, 1819. Morillo was now isolated in Venezuela. In December, 1819, a congress of delegates from Venezuela and New Granada met and decreed the union of the two provinces in the Republic of Colombia. Bolivar was named provisional President. An armistice was signed by Bolivar and Morillo in November, 1820, which gave the Patriots breathing time. The Spanish troops remaining in Venezuela were defeated by Bolivar in the battle of Carabobo, June 23, 1821. Only a few fortresses on the coast were still held by the Spaniards.

Bolivar entered Caracas once more in triumph and tendered his resignation, an act always considered by him necessary for giving the proper dramatic setting to such occasions. Congress took no notice of it, but drew up a constitution providing for a limited presidential term of four years. The Liberator, " as he feared," was elected President. He repeated his resignation, but added that he would yield if Congress persisted. Congress did persist.

After the battle of Boyaca, Bolivar had sent General Sucre by sea to Guayaquil, nominally to aid the new state against the Royalists, but in reality to induce it to join the Republic of Colombia. Sucre met with reverses, and had to call on San Martin for assistance from Peru. Meanwhile Bolivar was advancing by land. On July 11, 1822, he entered Guayaquil in triumph, and two days later, on his own responsibility, announced its incorporation with Colombia. The junta resigned and took refuge on board the Peruvian squadron in the harbor. On the 25th San Martin arrived by sea, and Bolivar sent two of his aides to welcome him " on Colombian soil." On the following day San Martin went ashore and he and Bolivar met for the first and last time. They had two private interviews, after which San Martin sent his baggage aboard his ship and announced that he would sail after attending the ball to be given that night in his honor. At the public banquet that evening Bolivar rose and proposed a toast: " To the two greatest men of South America—General San Martin and myself." San Martin also proposed a toast: " To the speedy conclusion of the war; to the organization of the different republics of the continent; and to the health of the Liberator of Colombia "—words which well contrasted the personal and political aims of the two men. San Martin and Bolivar had been unable to agree upon any plan for the expulsion of the Spaniards from the highlands of Peru. The self-denying patriot gave way before the man of ambition. To O'Higgins he wrote: " The Liberator is not the man we took him to be."

Upon his return to Peru, San Martin wrote to Bolivar: " My decision is irrevocable. I have convened the first Congress of Peru; the day after its installation I shall leave for Chile, convinced that my presence is the only obstacle which keeps you from coming to Peru with your army." On the 20th of September, 1822, he laid his resignation before the Congress, and issued an address to the nation. "The presence of a fortunate soldier," he said, "however disinterested he may be, is dangerous to a newly founded state. I have proclaimed the independence of Peru. I have ceased to be a public man." These words, whether intentionally so or not, were prophetic of Bolivar's subsequent career. San Martin wrote to O'Higgins: "I am tired of hearing them call me tyrant, that I wish to make myself king, emperor, the devil. On the other hand, my health is broken, this climate is killing me. My youth was sacrificed to the service of Spain; my manhood to my own country. I think I have now the right to dispose of my old age."

Bolivar's jealousy of San Martin prolonged the war, which might have been brought to a close in a few months, for nearly three years. After the withdrawal of San Martin, Bolivar became Dictator of Peru. On December 9, 1824, was fought the last battle for South American independence. On the little plain of Ayacucho, 11,600 feet above the sea, General Sucre defeated and captured the forces of the viceroy. Upper Peru was organized as a separate republic, with the name of Bolivia.

Bolivar had been proclaimed President of Peru for life, but the unpopularity of this measure led him to leave the country in 1826, never to return. That same year he summoned the Congress of Panama, but his plans for the union of South America in one republic failed. San Martin's idea finally triumphed. In 1829 Venezuela separated itself from Colombia and passed a decree of perpetual banishment against Bolivar. In April, 1830, through pressure of public opinion, Bolivar resigned the presidency of Colombia and retired into private life. Congress voted him an annual pension of $30,000. A month later Quito and Guayaquil separated from Colombia and formed the independent state of Ecuador. Even the name Colombia was dropped by the remaining state, and the old name of New Granada adopted. In 1857 the name Colombia was assumed once more.

Bolivar died in a small house near Santa Martha, December 17, 1831, having witnessed the failure of his most cherished plans. San Martin had retired to Europe in 1823 with his only child, a daughter named Mercedes. They lived a retired life in Brussels. Once only, in 1828, he returned to his native land, but was received with such denunciation by the press of Buenos Aires that he quickly turned his face towards Europe again. He died at Boulogne, August 17, 1850. Thirty years later the Argentine people had his remains brought back to his native land. In May, 1880, with imposing ceremonies, they were laid to rest in the Cathedral of Buenos Aires.

Mexico was twice revolutionized. The first struggle began in 1809 and 1810, and was carried on spasmodically until 1817. The second revolution broke out in 1820 on receipt of the news from Spain of the revolution of March, 1820, and the re-adoption of the constitution of 1812. The old revolutionists demanded the proclamation of this constitution in Mexico, but the Viceroy Apodaca opposed them. Augustin de Iturbide, a native Mexican, who in the first revolution had steadfastly adhered to the cause of the king, now defected to the popular side with a large body of troops which the viceroy had entrusted to his command. On February 24, 1821, he issued the celebrated document known as the Plan of Iguala, from the town of that name. In it he proposed the maintenance of the Roman Catholic religion to the exclusion of all others, the independence of Mexico from Spain, and the establishment of a limited monarchy. The Imperial Crown of Mexico was to be offered first to Ferdinand VII; in the event of his declining, to the younger princes of his house; and in the event of their refusal, the duty of naming an emperor was to fall to the representative assembly of Mexico. The personal and property rights of Spaniards in Mexico were carefully guaranteed. In securing the interests of Spaniards and of the clergy, those who had most to lose, this plan differed essentially from the revolutionary policy of the other Spanish colonies. On the other hand, the Creole element was satisfied with the promise of independence and a representative government. The revolutionary army became known as " the Army of the Three Guarantees," these being (1) the maintenance of the religious establishment in its present form, (2) independence, and (3) the union of Americans and Spaniards.[35] This ingenious document received immediately the widest approval.

The Viceroy Apodaca had practically abdicated when his successor, General O'Donaju, arrived from Spain. As the latter had come without troops, there was nothing left but for him to recognize the revolution as an accomplished fact and make the best terms for his country he could. Accordingly he met Iturbide

---

[35] Hall's "Journal," Vol. II, p. 188.

in conference at Cordova, and after a brief discussion signed the treaty bearing that name, August 24, 1821. It was agreed that a provisional junta should be appointed, that O'Donaju should be a member, and that the junta should proceed to carry into effect the plan of Iguala. O'Donaju then persuaded the Royalists to open the gates of the capital, and on September 27, 1821, Iturbide entered. Shortly thereafter O'Donaju died from the yellow fever, thus leaving Iturbide free to carry out his plans. The Spanish government, of course, repudiated the treaty of Cordova.

The Congress, which assembled in pursuance of the program of Iguala, was divided between Imperialists and Republicans. In spite of the opposition of the latter, Iturbide had himself proclaimed emperor and his family ennobled. Congress soon fell into disputes with the emperor, who finally, in October, 1822, dissolved it by force. A few months later Santa Anna inaugurated a counter-revolution from Vera Cruz, which resulted in the abdication of the emperor. Iturbide was allowed to leave the country. He retired to Italy, where he resided until toward the close of 1823, when he went to London. In May, 1824, at the solicitation of certain of his partisans, he sailed again for Mexico,[36] ignorant of the decree of perpetual banishment passed against him by the Congress a few weeks before. He landed at Tampico July 12, but was seized and executed a few days later. The new assembly then in session adopted a constitution, and the Republic of Mexico was launched upon what was to prove, for years to come, a career of turbulence and anarchy.

---

[36] See the statement of Iturbide in regard to his political life published in the *Pamphleteer*, London, 1827.

CHAPTER II

THE RECOGNITION OF THE SPANISH-AMERICAN REPUBLICS

THE struggle of the South American peoples for independence was viewed from the first with feelings of profound satisfaction and sympathy in the United States. From the commencement of the revolution South American vessels were admitted into the ports of the United States under whatever flag they bore. It does not appear that any formal declaration according belligerent rights to the said provinces was ever made, though a resolution to that effect was introduced into the House by committee as early as December 10, 1811.[1] Such formal action was apparently not deemed necessary and, as there was no Spanish minister resident in the United States at that time to protest, our ports were probably thrown open, as a matter of course.[2] The fact that they were accorded full belligerent rights from the first was afterwards stated by President Monroe in his annual messages of 1817 and 1818 and in his special message of March 8, 1822.[3]

At an early date of the revolution commissioners arrived in Washington seeking recognition of independence, and agents were forthwith dispatched to South America to obtain information in regard to

---

[1] Am. St. Papers, For. Rel., Vol. III, p. 538.
[2] Wharton's Digest, Sec. 69, and Moore's Digest of Int. Law, Vol. I, p. 177.
[3] "Messages and Papers of the Presidents," Vol. II, pp. 13, 58, and 116.

48

the state of the revolutionary governments and to watch the movements of England and other European powers. Joel R. Poinsett was sent to Buenos Aires in 1811, and the following year Alexander Scott was sent to Venezuela.[4] In 1817 Cæsar A. Rodney, Theodorick Bland, and John Graham were dispatched as special commissioners to South America. They proceeded to Buenos Aires, where they arrived in February, 1818, and remained until the last of April. Rodney and Graham then returned to the United States while Bland proceeded across the continent to Chile. Their reports were transmitted to Congress November 17, 1818.[5] In 1820 Messrs. J. B. Prevost and John M. Forbes were sent as commercial agents to Chile and Buenos Aires. Reports from them on the state of the revolutions were transmitted to Congress, March 8 and April 26, 1822.[6]

In the meantime a strong sentiment in favor of the recognition of South American independence had arisen in the United States. The struggling colonies found a ready champion in Henry Clay, who, for a period of ten years labored almost incessantly in their behalf, pleading for their recognition first with his own countrymen and then, as secretary of state under the Adams administration, with the governments of Europe. His name became a household word in South America and his speeches were translated and read before the patriot armies.

In spite of the fact that our own political interests were so closely identified with the struggling republics, the President realized the necessity of following a neu-

[4] Lyman, "Diplomacy of the United States." 2 Vols. Boston, 1828, Vol. II, p. 432. Romero, "Mexico and the United States."
[5] Given in full in Am. St. Papers, For. Rel., Vol. IV, pp. 217-270.
[6] Am. St. Papers, For. Rel., Vol. IV, pp. 818-851.

tral course, and in view of the aid the colonies were receiving from citizens of the United States, called upon Congress for the enactment of a more stringent neutrality law. Clay delivered a vigorous speech in opposition to this measure in January, 1817. His greatest effort in behalf of South America, however, was his speech of March 25, 1818, on the general appropriation bill. He moved an amendment appropriating $18,000 for the outfit and year's salary of a minister to the United Provinces of the Plate. Without waiting to hear the report of the three commissioners who had been sent to inquire into the state of the revolutionary governments, he urged that a minister be regularly accredited to Buenos Aires at once. In a speech, three hours in length, he concluded the arguments he had begun the day before. Painting with even more than his usual fire and enthusiasm the beauties and resources of the Southern continent, he said:

> Within this vast region, we behold the most sublime and interesting objects of creation; the loftiest mountains, the most majestic rivers in the world; the richest mines of the precious metals; and the choicest productions of the earth. We behold there a spectacle still more interesting and sublime —the glorious spectacle of eighteen millions of people struggling to burst their chains and be free.[7]

He went on to say that in the establishment of the independence of the South American states the United States had the deepest interest. He had no hesitation in asserting his firm belief that there was no question in the foreign policy of this country, which had ever arisen, or which he could conceive as ever

---

[7] Benton's "Abridgment," Vol. VI, p. 139.

occurring, in the decision of which we had so much at stake. This interest concerned our politics, our commerce, our navigation. There could be no doubt that Spanish America, once independent, whatever might be the form of the governments established in its several parts, those governments would be animated by an American feeling and guided by an American policy. They would obey the laws of the system of the new world, of which they would compose a part, in contradistinction to that of Europe.[8] The House turned a deaf ear to his brilliant rhetoric. The motion was defeated by a vote of 115 to 45, but Clay did not abandon the cause of South America.

Two years later he reopened the question in a direct attack on the policy of the administration, which greatly disturbed President Monroe. On May 20, 1820, he again introduced a resolution declaring it expedient to send ministers to the " governments in South America which have established and are maintaining their independence of Spain." His arraignment of the administration became more violent than ever :

If Lord Castlereagh says we may recognize, we do; if not, we do not. A single expression of the British minister to the present secretary of state, then our minister abroad, I am ashamed to say, has molded the policy of our government toward South America.

A charge of dependence upon Great Britain in affairs of diplomacy was as effective a weapon then as it has been since in matters financial. Clay's resolution passed the House by a vote of 80 to 75, but

---

[8] Benton's " Abridgment," Vol. VI, p. 142.

still the executive arm of the government did not move. In 1817 and 1818 the question of South American independence was continually before the cabinet for discussion. President Monroe seemed strongly inclined toward recognition, but in this he was opposed by Adams and Calhoun, who were unwilling to act in the matter without some understanding with England, and if possible with France. Our relations with Spain in regard to the Indian troubles in Florida were in a very strained condition and any action taken at that time in recognition of South America would have involved us in war with Spain and almost inevitably with other European powers. The President, therefore, as a matter of expediency postponed the action which his sympathy prompted, and, in his annual message of November 16, 1818, expressed his satisfaction at the course the government had hitherto pursued and his intention of adhering to it for the time being.[9] Under the President's direction, however, efforts were made to secure the coöperation of Great Britain and France in promoting the independence of South America.[10]

In 1819 an amicable adjustment of our differences with Spain seemed to have been reached by the negotiation of a treaty providing for the cession of the Floridas to the United States and the settlement of long-standing claims of American citizens against Spain. An unforeseen difficulty arose, however, which proved embarrassing to the administration. The Spanish monarch very shrewdly delayed ratifying the treaty for two years and thus practically tied the

---

[9] " Messages and Papers of the Presidents," Vol. II, p. 44.
[10] " Adams's Diary," September. 1817, to December, 1818, " Letters and Despatches of Castlereagh," Vol. XI, pp. 404 and 458,

hands of the administration during that time as far as the South American question was concerned.

In spite of the awkward position in which the administration found itself, Clay, who was opposed to the treaty on account of its unwarranted surrender of our claims to Texas, continued to plead the cause of South America. Early in the year, 1821, a declaration of interest in the South American struggle, introduced by him, was carried by an overwhelming majority (134 to 12), but the administration held back another year until the *de facto* independence of the colonies no longer admitted of reasonable doubt. Meanwhile the Florida treaty had been ratified. On March 8, 1822, President Monroe, in a special message to Congress, expressed the opinion that the time had come for recognition and asked for the appropriations necessary for carrying it into effect. The President's recommendation was received with approval, and in due course the sum of $100,000 was appropriated for "such missions to the independent nations on the American continent as the President of the United States may deem proper." In accordance with this act Mr. R. C. Anderson of Kentucky was appointed minister to Colombia, Mr. C. A. Rodney of New Jersey to the Argentine Republic, and Mr. H. Allen of Vermont to Chile, in 1824, and Mr. Joel R. Poinsett of South Carolina to Mexico in 1826.

While the United States government was concerning itself with the political interests of the Spanish provinces, Great Britain was quietly reaping all the commercial advantages to be derived from the situation and was apparently well satisfied to let things follow the drift they had taken. By the destruction of the combined fleets of France and Spain at Trafalgar, in 1805, Nelson had won for Great Britain undisputed control of the Atlantic and laid open the route to South America. Ever since the *assiento* of 1713 had placed the slave trade in her hands, Great Britain had realized the possibilities of South American commerce, and the intercourse, which had been kept up with that country after the termination of the slave monopoly by smugglers, now that the danger was removed, became more regular and profitable. During the changes of ministry that followed the death of Pitt, the policy of England in regard to South America was weak and vacillating. We have already called attention to the political indecision that marked the attack upon the provinces of the Plate. With Napoleon's invasion of Spain and the national uprising it occasioned, British policy became once more intelligible. It was wisely deemed of more importance to spare the colonies and to win Spain over to the European alliance against Napoleon, than to take her colonies at the cost of driving her permanently into the arms of France. Meanwhile British commerce with the South American states was steadily growing and that too with the connivance of Spain.

At the close of the Napoleonic wars, Spain, fearing that England, through her desire to keep this trade, would secretly furnish aid to the colonies in their struggle for independence, proposed to the British government to bind itself to a strict neutrality. This England agreed to, and when the treaty was signed, there was, according to Canning, "a distinct understanding with Spain that our commercial intercourse with the colonies was not to be deemed a breach of its stipulations."[11]   Notwithstanding this tacit compact, British commerce suffered greatly at the hands of Spanish privateers and even Spanish war vessels. Numbers of British merchantmen were captured by Spanish ships, carried into the few ports left to Spain on the Main, and condemned as prizes for trading with the insurgent colonies.   Thus at the time of the acknowledgment of South American independence by the United States, a long list of grievances had accumulated in the hands of the British ambassador at Madrid, and in spite of urgent and repeated remonstrances, remained unredressed.

Canning was deterred from making final demands upon the government of Madrid by the consideration that he did not wish to hamper the constitutional government of Spain, which had come into being by the revolution of March, 1820, and against which the other powers of Europe were preparing to act.   The condition of affairs on the Spanish Main was, however, critical and demanded instant redress.   He decided, therefore, to take matters into his own hands without harassing the government of Spain, and to dispatch a squadron to the West Indies to make reprisals.   In a memorandum to the cabinet on this subject, November 15, 1822, in which he outlines his policy, he commends the course of the United States in recognizing the *de facto* independence of the colonies, claiming a right to trade with them and avenging the attempted interruption of that right by making reprisals, as a more straightforward and intelligible course than that of Great Britain, forbearing for the sake of Spain to recognize the colonies, trading with them in faith of

---

[11] Stapleton, " Political Life of Canning," Vol. II, p. 10.

the connivance of Spain and suffering depredations without taking redress. It was not necessary, he thought, to declare war against Spain, for " she has perhaps as little direct and available power over the colonies which she nominally retains as she has over those which have thrown off her yoke. Let us apply, therefore, a local remedy to a local grievance, and make the ships and harbors of Cuba, Porto Rico, and Porto Cabello answerable for the injuries which have been inflicted by those ships, and the perpetrators of which have found shelter in those harbors." In conclusion, he says that the tacit compact, which subsisted for years, by which Spain was to forbear from interrupting British trade with the South American colonies having been renounced by Spain, and the old colonial system having been revived in as full vigor as if she had still a practical hold over her colonies and a navy to enforce her pretensions, " no man will say that under such circumstances our recognition of those states can be indefinitely postponed." [12]

While Great Britain was thus considering the expediency of following the example of the United States in the recognition of Spain's revolted colonies, the powers of central Europe had taken upon them the task of solving the difficulties of that unfortunate country both at home and in America. The restored rule of the Bourbons in Spain had been far from satisfactory to the great mass of the people. In March, 1820, the army which Ferdinand had assembled at Cadiz to be sent against the rebellious colonies, suddenly turned against the government, refused to embark, and demanded the restoration of the constitution

---

[12] Stapleton, " Official Correspondence of Canning," Vol. I, p. 48 ff.

of 1812. The action of the army was everywhere approved and sustained by the mass of the people, and the king was forced to proclaim the constitution and to swear to uphold it. The March revolution in Spain was followed in July by a constitutional movement in Naples, and in August of the same year by a similar movement in Portugal; while the next year saw the outbreak of the Greek struggle for independence. Thus in all three of the peninsulas of Southern Europe the people were struggling for the right of self-government. The movement in Greece was, it is true, of an altogether different character from the others, but it was a revolt against constituted authority and therefore incurred the ill-will of the so-called legitimists. The powers of Europe at once took alarm at the rapid spread of revolutionary ideas and proceeded to adopt measures for the suppression of the movements to which these ideas gave rise. The principle of joint intervention on the part of allied governments in the internal affairs of European states had been developed in the years immediately following the overthrow of Napoleon and was the outcome of the wholly anomalous condition in which he had left the politics of Europe. In the hands of Prince Metternich, the genius of reaction against French revolutionary ideas, this principle had become the most powerful weapon of absolutism and now threatened the subversion of popular institutions throughout Europe.

The rapid development of this doctrine of intervention in the seven years immediately following the second fall of Napoleon not only seriously menaced the liberties of Europe, but also threatened to control the destiny of the new world. At the Congress of Vienna Austria, France, Great Britain, Prussia, and Russia had formed a close union and had signed the treaty upon which the peace of Europe rested for the next half century. The agreement made at Vienna was reaffirmed with some minor changes, after the second overthrow of Napoleon, at Paris, November 20, 1815. France was now practically excluded from the alliance. This treaty undertook especially to guard against any further disturbance of the peace of Europe by Napoleon or France. One of the most significant features of the treaty, or what was to prove so, was the agreement definitely laid down in the sixth article, providing for meetings of the powers at fixed periods.

The first conference held in accordance with this understanding was that at Aix-la-Chapelle in October, 1818. France was readmitted as a member of the alliance and her territory evacuated by the allied armies. The quintuple alliance thus formed declared that it had no other object than the maintenance of peace; that the repose of the world was its motive and its end. The language of the declaration had been in a large measure neutralized to suit the views of the British government. Lord Liverpool had said to Castlereagh before the meeting of the conference: "The Russian must be made to feel that we have a parliament and a public, to which we are responsible, and that we cannot permit ourselves to be drawn into views of policy which are wholly incompatible with the spirit of our government." The members of the British cabinet, except Canning, did not object seriously to the system of congresses at fixed intervals, but to the declarations publicly set forth by them.

Canning, on the other hand, objected to the declarations and to the conferences themselves, " meetings for the government of the world," as he somewhat contemptuously termed them.

It had been generally supposed that the question of the Spanish colonies would come up for discussion at Aix-la-Chapelle. Castlereagh assured the United States, through Bagot, the British minister at Washington, that while England would act with the allied powers at Aix-la-Chapelle in mediation between Spain and her colonies, her mediation would be limited entirely to the employment of her influence and good offices and that she would not take any measures that might assume a character of force.[13]

The revolutions that took place in Spain, Naples, and Portugal in 1820 presented an occasion for another meeting of the allies. In November the representatives of Austria, Russia, and Prussia met in conference at Troppau, and issued a circular setting forth what they had already done for Europe in overthrowing the military tyranny of Napoleon and expressing the determination " to put a curb on a force no less tyrannical and no less detestable, that of revolt and crime." The conference then adjourned to Laybach, where they could, with greater dispatch, order the movements they had decided to take against the revolutionists of Naples. Austria, being more intimately concerned with the political condition of the Italian peninsula than either of the other two powers, was entrusted with the task of suppressing the Neapolitan revolution. The Austrian army entered Naples

---

[13] Bagot to Castlereagh, October 31, 1818. Mem. of a Conversation with Adams. " Letters and Despatches of Castlereagh," Vol. XII, p. 66.

March 23, 1821, overthrew the constitutional government that had been inaugurated, and restored Ferdinand II to absolute power. The revolution which had broken out in Piedmont was also suppressed by a detachment of the Austrian army.

England held aloof from all participation in the proceedings at Troppau and Laybach—though Sir Charles Stuart was present to watch the proceedings. In a circular dispatch of January 21, 1821, the British government expressed its dissent from the principles set forth in the Troppau circular.

The next meeting of the allied powers was arranged for October, 1822, at Verona. Here the affairs of Greece, Italy, and, in particular, Spain came up for consideration. At this Congress all five powers of the alliance were represented. France was uneasy about the condition of Spain, and England had to send a delegate out of self-defense, as her interests were largely involved. Castlereagh was preparing to depart for the congress, when his mind gave way under the stress of work and more remotely of dissipation, and he committed suicide. Canning then became secretary for foreign affairs, and Wellington was sent to Verona.

The congress which now assembled at Verona was devoted largely to a discussion of Spanish affairs. Wellington had been instructed to use all his influence against the adoption of measures of intervention in Spain. When he found that the other powers were bent upon this step and that his protest would be unheeded, he withdrew from the congress. The four remaining powers signed the secret treaty of Verona, November 22, 1822, as a revision, so they declared in the preamble, of the " Treaty of the Holy Alliance." This treaty of the Holy Alliance, signed at Paris, September 26, 1815, by Austria, Russia, and Prussia, is one of the most remarkable political documents extant. It sprang from the erratic brain of the Czar Alexander under the influence of Madame Crudner, who was both an adventuress and a religious enthusiast. Its object was to uphold the divine right of kings and to counteract the spirit of French revolutionary ideas by introducing " the precepts of justice, of charity, and of peace " into the internal affairs of states and into their relations with one another. No one had taken it seriously except the Czar himself and it had been without influence upon the politics of Europe. The agreement reached at Verona gave retrospective importance to the Holy Alliance, and revived the name, so that it became the usual designation of the combined powers. The following alleged text of the secret treaty of Verona soon became current in the press of Europe and America. Although it has never been officially acknowledged and its authenticity has been called in question, it states pretty accurately the motives and aims of the powers. The first four articles are as follows:

The undersigned, specially authorized to make some additions to the Treaty of the Holy Alliance, after having exchanged their respective credentials, have agreed as follows:

ARTICLE I. The high contracting parties being convinced that the system of representative government is equally incompatible with the monarchical principles as the maxim of the sovereignty of the people with the divine right, engage mutually, and in the most solemn manner, to use all their efforts to *put an end* to the system of *representative governments,* in whatever country it may exist in Europe, and to prevent its being introduced in those countries where it is not yet known.

ART. II. As it cannot be doubted that the *liberty of the press* is the most powerful means used by the pretended supporters of the rights of nations, to the detriment of those of Princes, the high contracting parties promise reciprocally to adopt all proper measures to suppress it not only in their own states, but also, in the rest of Europe.

ART. III. Convinced that the principles of religion contribute most powerfully to keep nations in the state of passive obedience which they owe to their Princes, the high contracting parties declare it to be their intention to sustain, in their respective states, those measures which the clergy may adopt, with the aim of ameliorating their own interests, so intimately connected with the preservation of the authority of Princes; and the contracting powers join in offering their thanks to the Pope, for what he has already done for them, and solicit his constant coöperation in their views of submitting the nations.

ART. IV. The situation of Spain and Portugal unites unhappily all the circumstances to which this treaty has particular reference. The high contracting parties, in confiding to France the care of putting an end to them, engage to assist her in the manner which may the least compromise them with their own people and the people of France, by means of a subsidy on the part of the two empires, of twenty millions of francs every year, from the date of the signature of this treaty to the end of the war.

Signed by Metternich for Austria, Chateaubriand for France, Bernstet for Prussia, and Nesselrode for Russia.[14]

Such was the code of absolutism against which England protested and against which President Monroe delivered his declaration.

---

[14] For the Congresses of Aix-la-Chapelle, Troppau, Laybach, and Verona, see " Letters and Despatches of Castlereagh," Vol. XII; " Life of Lord Liverpool," Vol. III; " Political Life and Official Correspondence of Canning "; Chateaubriand's " Congrès de Verone," and W. A. Phillips, " The Confederation of Europe, 1813-1823." The text of the treaty of Verona is published in Niles' Register, August 2, 1823, Vol. 24, p. 347, and in Elliot's " American Diplomatic Code," Vol. II, p. 179.

The Congress broke up about the middle of December, and the following April, the Duc d'Angoulême led a French army across the Pyrenees. By October the constitutional party had been overthrown and absolutism reigned supreme once more in western Europe. In England alone was there still any semblance of constitutional government.

The Congress of Verona was the last of the joint-meetings of the powers for the discussion of the internal affairs of states. It marked the final withdrawal of England from the European alliance. Henceforth she took up a position distinctly hostile to the principles advocated by her former allies and her policy in relation to Spanish America practically coincided with that of the United States.

The great majority of the English people sympathized deeply with the constitutional movement in Spain and were ready to take up arms in support of the Spanish people. The protest of England having been disregarded by the powers at Verona, it became necessary for the cabinet, in view of the preparations going on in France for the invasion of the Peninsula, to say what they contemplated doing. In February, 1823, Lord Liverpool circulated among his colleagues a minute prepared by Canning, which gave at length the reasons, military and other, why it would be unwise for England to undertake the defense of Spain. In the first place, the war against Spain was unpopular in France, and if Great Britain should take part in the war, the French government would avail itself of the fact to convert it into an English war and thus render it popular. Second, England would have to undertake the defense of Spain against invasion by land, and her naval superiority would not materially aid the Spaniards or baffle the French. Third, the continental powers were committed to the support of France. Fourth, there was a possibility that the invasion of Spain would be unsuccessful. Fifth, on the other hand, it might meet with success, in which event France might assist Spain to recover her American colonies. Here, he says, England's naval superiority would tell, "and I should have no difficulty in deciding that we ought to prevent, by every means in our power, perhaps Spain from sending a single Spanish regiment to South America, after the supposed termination of the war in Spain, but certainly France from affording to Spain any aid or assistance for that purpose." Sixth, in case of the invasion of Portugal by France and Spain, he thought England would be in honor bound to defend her, in case she asked for aid. The military defense of Portugal would not be so difficult as a land war in Spain.[15]

In accordance with this determination Canning dispatched a letter to Sir Charles Stuart, British ambassador at Paris, March 31, 1823, in which he spoke of recognition of the colonies as a matter to be determined by time and circumstances, and, disclaiming all designs on the part of the British government on the late Spanish provinces, intimated that England, although abstaining from interference in Spain, would not allow France to acquire any of the colonies by conquest or cession. To this note the French government made no reply and England took this silence as a tacit agreement not to interfere with the colonies.

[15] "Life of Lord Liverpool," Vol. III, p. 231. "Official Correspondence of Canning," Vol. I, p. 85.

The British government continued, however, to watch closely the movements of France.[16]

As the invasion of Spain drew near to a successful termination, the British government had reason to suspect that the allied powers would next direct their attention to the Spanish colonies with a view to forcing them back to their allegiance or of otherwise disposing of them, that is, by cession to some other European power. It was already in contemplation to call another European congress for the discussion and settlement of this question. As this was a subject of vital interest to the United States, Canning invited the American minister, Mr. Rush, to a conference, August 16, 1823, in which he suggested the expediency of an understanding on this question between England and the United States. He communicated to Mr. Rush the substance of his dispatch of March 31 to Sir Charles Stuart. Mr. Rush said he understood the import of this note to be that England would not remain passive to any attempt on the part of France to acquire territory in Spanish America. Mr. Canning then asked what the United States would say to going hand in hand with England in such a policy. Mr. Rush replied that his instructions did not authorize him to give an answer, but that he would communicate the suggestion informally to his government. At the same time he requested to be enlightened as to England's policy in the matter of recognizing the independence of the colonies. Mr. Canning replied that England had taken no steps in the matter of recognition whatever, but was considering the question of sending commissioners to the colonies to inquire into

---

[16] Stapleton, " Political Life of Canning," Vol. II, p. 18.

the condition of affairs. For the present these commissioners would be sent to Mexico alone.[17]

Mr. Stapleton in his "Life of Canning" simply says that as Mr. Rush was not authorized to enter into any formal agreement, Canning thought the delay of communicating with Washington would render such proceeding of no effect, and so the matter was dropped.[18] This, however, we learn from Mr. Rush's dispatches, is not the whole truth. Several communications passed between them after the conversation above given, which throw a totally different light upon the affair.

In an unofficial and confidential letter to Mr. Rush, dated August 20, 1823, Canning asked again if the moment had not arrived when the two governments might come to an understanding in regard to the Spanish-American colonies. He stated the views of England as follows: (1) That the recovery of the colonies by Spain was hopeless; (2) That the question of their recognition as independent states was one of time and circumstances; (3) That England was not disposed, however, to throw any obstacle in the way of an arrangement between the colonies and the mother-country by amicable negotiation; (4) That she aimed at the possession of no portion of the colonies for herself; and (5) That she could not see the transfer of any portion of them to any other power with indifference. He added "that if the United States acceded to such views, a declaration to that effect on their part, concurrently with England, would be the most effectual and least offensive mode of

---

[17] Rush's " Residence at the Court of London," p. 406.
[18] " Political Life of Canning," Vol. II, p. 24.

making known their joint disapprobation of contrary projects; that it would at the same time put an end to all jealousies of Spain as to her remaining colonies, and to the agitation prevailing in the colonies themselves by showing that England and the United States were determined not to profit by encouraging it." [19]

Prior to the formal recognition of South America, the United States had repeatedly expressed the wish to proceed in the matter hand in hand with Great Britain,[20] but that act placed the United States on an altogether different footing from England. Canning seemed to forget in the wording of his proposal that the United States had already, in the most formal manner, acknowledged the independence of the Spanish colonies. In reply Mr. Rush reminded him of this fact and of the desire of the United States to see the colonies recognized by England. In other respects, he believed that the views unfolded by Mr. Canning in his note were shared by the United States, but he added that he had no authority to avow these principles publicly in the manner suggested.

As soon as Rush's first dispatch was received President Monroe realized fully the magnitude of the issue presented by the proposal of an Anglo-American alliance. Before submitting the matter to his cabinet he transmitted copies of the dispatch to ex-Presidents Jefferson and Madison and the following interesting correspondence took place. In his letter to Jefferson of October 17th, the President said:

I transmit to you two despatches which were receiv'd from Mr. Rush, while I was lately in Washington, which

---

[19] Rush's " Residence at the Court of London," p. 412.
[20] " Letters and Despatches of Castlereagh," Vol. XI, p. 458. Bagot's reports of interviews with Adams.

involve interests of the highest importance. They contain two letters from Mr. Canning, suggesting designs of the holy alliance, against the Independence of S°. America, & proposing a co-operation, between G. Britain & the U States, in support of it, against the members of that alliance. The project aims, in the first instance, at a mere expression of opinion, somewhat in the abstract, but which, it is expected by Mr. Canning, will have a great political effect, by defeating the combination. By Mr. Rush's answers, which are also enclosed, you will see the light in which he views the subject, & the extent to which he may have gone. Many important considerations are involved in this proposition. 1st Shall we entangle ourselves, at all, in European politicks, & wars, on the side of any power, against others, presuming that a concert, by agreement, of the kind proposed, may lead to that result? 2^{d} If a case can exist in which a sound maxim may, & ought to be departed from, is not the present instance, precisely that case? 3^{d} Has not the epoch arriv'd when G. Britain must take her stand, either on the side of the monarchs of Europe, or of the U States, & in consequence, either in favor of Despotism or of liberty & may it not be presum'd that, aware of that necessity, her government has seiz'd on the present occurrence, as that, which it deems, the most suitable, to announce & mark the commenc'ment of that career.

My own impression is that we ought to meet the proposal of the British govt. & to make it known, that we would view an interference on the part of the European powers, and especially an attack on the Colonies, by them, as an attack on ourselves, presuming that, if they succeeded with them, they would extend it to us. I am sensible however of the extent & difficulty of the question, & shall be happy to have yours, & Mr. Madison's opinions on it.[21]

Jefferson's reply dated Monticello, October 24th, displays not only a profound insight into the international situation, but a wide vision of the possibilities involved. He said:

---

[21] Hamilton, "Writings of James Monroe," Vol. VI, pp. 323-325.

SPANISH-AMERICAN REPUBLICS

The question presented by the letters you have sent me, is the most momentous which has ever been offered to my contemplation since that of Independence. That made us a nation, this sets our compass and points the course which we are to steer through the ocean of time opening on us. And never could we embark on it under circumstances more auspicious. Our first and fundamental maxim should be, never to entangle ourselves in the broils of Europe. Our second, never to suffer Europe to intermeddle with cis-Atlantic affairs. America, North and South, has a set of interests distinct from those of Europe, and peculiarly her own. She should therefore have a system of her own, separate and apart from that of Europe. While the last is laboring to become the domicil of despotism, our endeavor should surely be, to make our hemisphere that of freedom. One nation, most of all, could disturb us in this pursuit; she now offers to lead, aid, and accompany us in it. By acceding to her proposition, we detach her from the bands, bring her mighty weight into the scale of free government, and emancipate a continent at one stroke, which might otherwise linger long in doubt and difficulty. Great Britain is the nation which can do us the most harm of any one, or all on earth; and with her on our side we need not fear the whole world. With her then, we should most sedulously cherish a cordial friendship; and nothing would tend more to knit our affections than to be fighting once more, side by side, in the same cause. Not that I would purchase even her amity at the price of taking part in her wars. But the war in which the present proposition might engage us, should that be its consequence, is not her war, but ours. Its object is to introduce and establish the American system, of keeping out of our land all foreign powers, of never permitting those of Europe to intermeddle with the affairs of our nations. It is to maintain our own principle, not to depart from it. And if, to facilitate this, we can effect a division in the body of the European powers, and draw over to our side its most powerful member, surely we should do it. But I am clearly of Mr. Canning's opinion, that it will prevent instead of provoking war. With Great Britain withdrawn from their scale and shifted into that of

our two continents, all Europe combined would not undertake such a war. For how would they propose to get at
either enemy without superior fleets? Nor is the occasion
to be slighted which this proposition offers, of declaring our
protest against the atrocious violations of the rights of
nations, by the interference of any one in the internal affairs
of another, so flagitiously begun by Bonaparte, and now
continued by the equally lawless Alliance, calling itself
Holy.[22]

Madison not only agreed with Jefferson as to the
wisdom of accepting the British proposal of some
form of joint action, but he went even further and
suggested that the declaration should not be limited
to the American republics, but that it should express
disapproval of the late invasion of Spain and of any
interference with the Greeks, who were then struggling
for independence from Turkey.[23]   Monroe, it appears, was strongly inclined to act on Madison's suggestion, but his cabinet took a different view of the
situation.   From the diary of John Quincy Adams,
Monroe's secretary of state, it appears that almost the
whole of November was taken up by cabinet discussions on Canning's proposals and on Russia's aggres-
sions in the northwest.   Adams stoutly opposed any
alliance or joint declaration with Great Britain.   The
composition of the President's message remained in
doubt until the 21st, when the more conservative views
of Adams were, according to his own statement of
the case, adopted.   He advocated an independent
course of action on the part of the United States, without direct reference to Canning's proposals, though
substantially in accord with them.   Adams defined his

---

[22] Ford, " Writings of Thomas Jefferson," Vol. X, pp. 277-278.
[23] Hamilton, " Writings of James Madison," Vol. IX, pp. 161-162.

position as follows: "The ground that I wish to take is that of earnest remonstrance against the interference of the European powers by force with South America, but to disclaim all interference on our part with Europe; to make an American cause and adhere inflexibly to that." [24] Adams's dissent from Monroe's position was, it is claimed, due partly to the influence of Clay, who advocated a Pan American system, partly to the fact that the proposed coöperation with Great Britain would bind the United States not to acquire some of the coveted parts of the Spanish possessions, and partly to the fear that the United States as the ally of Great Britain would be compelled to play a secondary part. He probably carried his point by showing that the same ends could be accomplished by an independent declaration, since it was evident that the sea power of Great Britain would be used to prevent the reconquest of South America by the European powers. Monroe, as we have seen, thought that the exigencies of the situation justified a departure from the sound maxim of political isolation, and in this opinion he was supported by his two predecessors in the presidency.

The opinions of Monroe, Jefferson, and Madison in favor of an alliance with Great Britain and a broad declaration against the intervention of the great powers in the affairs of weaker states in any part of the world, have been severely criticised by some historians and ridiculed by others, but time and circumstances often bring about a complete change in our point of view. Since our entrance into the great world conflict several writers have raised the question

---

[24] W. C. Ford, "Genesis of the Monroe Doctrine," in *Mass. Hist. Soc. Proceedings*, second series, Vol. XV, p. 392.

as to whether the three elder statesmen were not right and Adams and Clay wrong.[25] If the United States and England had come out in favor of a general declaration against intervention in the concerns of small states and established it as a world-wide principle, the course of human history during the next century might have been very different, but Adams's diary does not tell the whole story. On his own statement of the case he might be justly censured by posterity for persuading the President to take a narrow American view of a question which was world-wide in its bearing. / An important element in the situation, however, was Canning's change of attitude between the time of his conference with Rush in August and the formulation of the President's message. Two days after the delivery of his now famous message Monroe wrote to Jefferson in explanation of the form the declaration had taken: " Mr. Canning's zeal has much abated of late." It appears from Rush's correspondence that the only thing which stood in the way of joint action by the two powers was Canning's unwillingness to extend immediate recognition to the South American republics. On August 27th, Rush stated to Canning that it would greatly facilitate joint action if England would acknowledge at once the full independence of the South American colonies. In communicating the account of this interview to his government Mr. Rush concluded:

Should I be asked by Mr. Canning, whether, in case the recognition be made by Great Britain without more delay, I am on my part prepared to make a declaration, in the name of my government, that it will not remain inactive under

---

[25] See especially G. L. Beer, " The English-Speaking Peoples," p. 79.

an attack upon the independence of those states by the Holy Alliance, the present determination of my judgment is that I will make such a declaration explicitly, and avow it before the world."[26]

About three weeks later Canning, who was growing restless at the delay in hearing from Washington, again urged Rush to act without waiting for specific instructions from his government. He tried to show that the proposed joint declaration would not conflict with the American policy of avoiding entangling alliances, for the question at issue was American as much as European, if not more. Rush then indicated his willingness to act provided England would " immediately and unequivocally acknowledge the independence of the new states." Canning did not care to extend full recognition to the South American states until he could do so without giving unnecessary offense to Spain and the allies, and he asked if Mr. Rush could not give his assent to the proposal on a promise of future recognition. Mr. Rush refused to accede to anything but immediate acknowledgment of independence and so the matter ended.[27] As Canning could not come to a formal understanding with the United States, he determined to make a frank avowal of the views of the British cabinet to France and to this end he had an interview with Prince Polignac, the French ambassador at London, October 9, 1823, in which he declared that Great Britain had no desire to hasten recognition, but that any foreign interference, by force, or by menace, would be a motive for immediate recognition; that England " could not go

[26] Rush's " Residence at the Court of London," p. 419.
[27] Ibid., pp. 429, 443.

73

into a joint deliberation upon the subject of Spanish
America upon an equal footing with other powers,
whose opinions were less formed upon that question."
This declaration drew from Polignac the admission
that he considered the reduction of the colonies by
Spain as hopeless and that France " abjured in any
case, any design of acting against the colonies by
force of arms." [28]   This admission was a distinct victory for Canning, in that it prepared the way for
ultimate recognition by England, and an account of
the interview was communicated without delay to
the allied courts.   The interview was not communicated to Rush until the latter part of November, and
therefore had no influence upon the formation of
Monroe's message of December 2.[29]

Before the close of the year the British government
appointed consuls to the South American states, and
about the time of their departure, an invitation was
sent to the courts of St. Petersburg, Paris, and Vienna
to a conference to be held at Paris to " aid Spain in
adjusting the affairs of the revolted colonies."   A copy
of this invitation was also handed to the British ambassador at Madrid, but in such a form as to leave
him in doubt as to whether his government was invited
to the conference or not.[30]   While the discussion as
to the proposed conference was going on and before
Canning had announced what action his government
would take in the matter, President Monroe's message arrived in Europe.

Spanish America was not the only part of the western continent threatened at this time by European

[28] " Political Life of Canning," Vol. II, p. 26.
[29] Rush's " Residence at the Court of London," p. 448.
[30] " Political Life of Canning," Vol. II, p. 33.

aggression. On the 4th of September, 1821, the emperor of Russia had issued an ukase, in which he claimed the northwestern coast of North America down to the 51st degree. This claim was incompatible with the pretensions of both England and the United States, and was stoutly opposed by them. This was a part of the territory known as the Oregon country, which continued in dispute between England and the United States until 1846. In July, 1823, Adams declared to Baron Tuyll, the Russian minister to the United States, "that we should contest the right of Russia to any territorial establishment on this continent, and that we should assume distinctly the principle that the American continents are no longer subjects for any new European colonial establishments." This language was incorporated substantially in the President's message.

The Monroe Doctrine is comprised in two widely separated paragraphs that occur in the message of December 2, 1823. The first, relating to Russia's encroachments on the northwest coast, and occurring near the beginning of the message, was an assertion to the effect that the American continents had assumed an independent condition and were no longer open to European colonization. This may be regarded as a statement of fact. No part of the continent at that time remained unclaimed. The second paragraph relating to Spanish America and occurring near the close of the message, was a declaration against the extension to the American continents of the system of intervention adopted by the Holy Alliance for the suppression of popular government in Europe.

UNITED STATES AND LATIN AMERICA

The language used by President Monroe is as follows:

1. At the proposal of the Russian Imperial Government, made through the minister of the emperor residing here, a full power and instructions have been transmitted to the minister of the United States at St. Petersburg to arrange by amicable negotiation the respective rights and interests of the two nations on the northwest coast of this continent. A similar proposal had been made by His Imperial Majesty to the government of Great Britain, which has likewise been acceded to. The government of the United States has been desirous by this friendly proceeding of manifesting the great value which they have invariably attached to the friendship of the emperor and their solicitude to cultivate the best understanding with his government. In the discussions to which this interest has given rise and in the arrangements by which they may terminate, the occasion has been judged proper for asserting, as a principle in which the rights and interests of the United States are involved, that the American continents, by the free and independent condition which they have assumed and maintain, are henceforth not to be considered as subjects for future colonization by any European powers.[31]

2. In the wars of the European powers in matters relating to themselves we have never taken any part, nor does it comport with our policy so to do. It is only when our rights are invaded or seriously menaced that we resent injuries or make preparation for our defense. With the movements in this hemisphere we are of necessity more immediately connected, and by causes which must be obvious to all enlightened and impartial observers. The political system of the allied powers is essentially different in this respect from that of America. This difference proceeds from that which exists in their respective governments; and to the defense of our own, which has been achieved by the loss of so much blood and treasure, and matured by the wisdom of their most enlightened citizens, and under which

---

[31] " Messages and Papers of the Presidents," Vol. II, p. 209.

we have enjoyed unexampled felicity, this whole nation is devoted. We owe it, therefore, to candor and to the amicable relations existing between the United States and those powers to declare that we should consider any attempt on their part to extend their system to any portion of this hemisphere as dangerous to our peace and safety. With the existing colonies or dependencies of any European power we have not interfered and shall not interfere. But with the governments who have declared their independence and maintained it, and whose independence we have, on great consideration and on just principles, acknowledged, we could not view any interposition for the purpose of oppressing them, or controlling in any other manner their destiny, by any European power in any other light than as the manifestation of an unfriendly disposition toward the United States. In the war between those new governments and Spain we declared our neutrality at the time of their recognition, and to this we have adhered, and shall continue to adhere, provided no change shall occur which, in the judgment of the competent authorities of this government, shall make a corresponding change on the part of the United States indispensable to their security.[32]

The President's message reached England while the discussion in regard to the proposed congress at Paris was still going on. It was received with enthusiasm by the liberal members of Parliament. Lord Brougham said:

The question with regard to South America is now, I believe, disposed of, or nearly so; for an event has recently happened than which none has ever dispersed greater joy, exultation, and gratitude over all the free men of Europe; that event, which is decisive on the subject, is the language held with respect to Spanish America in the message of the President of the United States.

---

[32] " Messages and Papers of the Presidents," Vol. II, p. 218.

Sir James Mackintosh said:

> This coincidence of the two great English commonwealths
> (for so I delight to call them; and I heartily pray that they
> may be forever united in the cause of justice and liberty)
> cannot be contemplated without the utmost pleasure by
> every enlightened citizen of the earth.[33]

They evidently had reference to the second clause
alone, the one relating to Spanish America. The
other clause, the one against European colonization
in America, seems not to have attracted much attention. Canning, however, saw the bearing of it and
objected to the principle it set forth, which was
directed against England as much as against the
allies. He was evidently a little taken aback at the
turn his proposal had taken. The President's message really settled the question before Canning had
announced what action his government would take.
Some little chagrin is apparent in the tone of his
letter to Sir William à Court, British minister at
Madrid, December 21, 1823.

> While I was yet hesitating [he says], what shape to give
> to the declaration and protest which ultimately was conveyed
> in my conference with P. de Polignac, and while I was more
> doubtful as to the effect of that protest and declaration, I
> sounded Mr. Rush (the American minister here) as to his
> powers and disposition to join in any step which we might
> take to prevent a hostile enterprise on the part of the Euro-
> pean powers against Spanish America. He had no powers;
> but he would have taken upon himself to join with us if
> we would have begun by recognizing the Spanish-Ameri-
> can states. This we could not do, and so we went on with-
> out. But I have no doubt that his report to his government
> of this *sounding*, which he probably represented as an over-

---

[33] "Wharton's Digest," Sec. 57, Vol. I, p. 276.

ture, had a great share in producing the explicit declaration of the President.[34]

The conference with Prince Polignac here referred to was that of October 9th quoted above. It was not until after the receipt of President Monroe's message in Europe that Canning framed his answer to the Spanish communication informing him of the proposed meeting in Paris for the discussion of the South American question. In that reply he stated to the Spanish government very fully his views upon the question at issue. He said that while England did not wish to precede Spain in the matter of recognition, yet she reserved to herself the privilege of recognizing the colonies when she deemed it best for her interests and right to them. He said that these views had been communicated fully from time to time to the powers invited to the congress and he concluded with the statement: " It does not appear to the British cabinet at all necessary to declare that opinion anew, even if it were perfectly clear (from the tenor of M. Ofalia's instruction) that Great Britain was in fact included in the invitation to the conference at Paris." [35]

While Canning and Monroe acted independently of each other, the expression that each gave to the views of his government was rendered more emphatic and of more effect by the knowledge of the other's attitude in the matter. Another point to be noted is that Monroe's message was made public, while Canning's answer was for some time known only to the diplomatic corps.

The determination of both England and the United

34 " Wharton's Digest," Sec. 57, Vol. I, p. 272.
35 " Political Life of Canning," Vol. II, p. 42.

States to oppose the intervention of the allies in South America had the desired effect. Conferences in answer to the invitation of Spain were held in Paris, but they were participated in only by the ordinary representatives of the powers invited, resident in that capital, and their only result was to advise Spain not to listen to the counsels of England.

All further discussion that took place between England and Spain in reference to recognition of the colonies by Great Britain was confined to the status of the revolutionary governments, and upon this point their views were so divergent that Canning finally announced to the Spanish government that, "His Majesty would, at his own time, take such steps as he might think proper in respect to the several states of Spanish America without further reference to the court of Madrid; but at the same time without any feeling of alienation towards that court, or of hostility towards the real interests of Spain." [36]

The French troops continuing to occupy Spain after the time stipulated by treaty, Canning sought an explanation from France, but without satisfactory results. He therefore determined at a cabinet meeting held December 14, 1824, to recognize Mexico and Colombia forthwith. On January 1, 1825, after the ministers had left England with instructions and full powers, the fact of recognition was communicated officially to the diplomatic corps and two days later it was made public. That this recognition was a retaliatory measure to compensate England for the French occupation of Spain was understood at the time and was distinctly avowed by Canning two years

---

[36] "Political Life of Canning," Vol. II, p. 54.

later.[37]   In a speech delivered December 12, 1826, in defense of his position in not having arrested the French invasion of Spain, he said:

I looked another way—I sought for compensation in another hemisphere. Contemplating Spain, such as our ancestors had known her, I resolved that, if France had Spain, it should not be Spain *with the Indies*. I called the New World into existence to redress the balance of the Old.

In spite of the great indebtedness of South America to Canning, this boast falls somewhat flat when we remember that the Spanish colonies had won their independence by their own valor and had been recognized as independent governments by the United States two years before Great Britain acted in the matter.

Mr. Stapleton, Canning's private secretary and biographer, says that the recognition of Spanish-American independence was, perhaps, the most important measure adopted by the British cabinet while Canning was at the head of the foreign office.   He sums up the reasons and results of the act as follows:

First, it was a measure essentially advantageous to British interests; being especially calculated to benefit our commerce. Next, it enabled this country to remain at peace, since it compensated us for the continued occupation of Spain by a French force, a disparagement to which, otherwise, it would not have become us to submit.   Lastly, it maintained the balance between conflicting principles; since it gave just so much of a triumph to popular rights and privileges, as was sufficient to soothe the irritation felt by their advocates at the victory, which absolute principles had obtained by the over-

[37] "Official Corresp. of Canning," Vol. II, p. 242. Letter to Granville. On the general question of recognition, see "Life of Lord Liverpool," Vol. III, pp. 297-304.

throw of the constitutions of Spain, Portugal, and Naples; and it dealt a death-blow to the Holy Alliance, by disabusing its members of the strange fancy, with which they were prepossessed, that the differences between them and the British ministers (where they did differ) were merely feints on the part of the latter to avoid a conflict with public opinion.[38]

The United States government did not relax its efforts in behalf of the South American states with the recognition of England, but continued to exert itself in order to secure the acknowledgment of their independence by the other powers of Europe, particularly Spain.[39]   Mr. Clay tried to get the other members of the alliance, especially the emperor of Russia, to use their good offices with Spain for the purpose of inducing her to recognize her late colonies, but the emperor of Russia, the head of the alliance, continued to preach to Spain "not only no recognition of their independence, but active war for their subjugation."   To the request of the United States he replied that, out of respect for " the indisputable titles of sovereignty," he could not prejudge or anticipate the determination of the king of Spain.[40]   It was some ten years before Spain could be persuaded to renounce her ancient claims.

---

[38] " Political Life of Canning," Vol. II, p. 1.
[39] Am. St. Papers, For. Rel., Vol. V, pp. 794-796, and Vol. VI, pp. 1006-1014.
[40] Am. St. Papers, For. Rel., Vol. V, p. 850 ff.

CHAPTER III

The Diplomacy of the United States in Regard to Cuba

The Cuban question had its origin in the series of events that have been narrated in the two preceding chapters—the Napoleonic invasion of Spain and the resulting paralysis of Spanish power in America. The declaration of President Monroe, enforced by the well-known attitude of England, dealt the death-blow to Spanish hopes of recovering the Southern continent. Hence the islands of Cuba and Porto Rico, which had remained loyal to the king, were clung to with all the greater tenacity as the sole remains of the imperial possessions over which the successors of Ferdinand and Isabella had ruled for three centuries. The " Everfaithful Island of Cuba " was rewarded for her loyalty by the concession of certain liberties of trade and invited to send representatives to the Spanish Cortes—a privilege which was subsequently withdrawn. Spain was now too weak to protect her two West Indian dependencies—the remains of her former glory, but her very weakness secured their possession to her. The naval and commercial importance of Cuba, " the pearl of the Antilles," made it a prize too valuable to be acquired by any one of the great maritime powers without exciting the jealousy and opposition of the others. Henceforth, to borrow the figure of a contemporary journalist, Cuba was to be the trans-Atlantic Turkey, trembling to its fall, but sustained by the jealousies of those who were eager to share the spoils.

The strategic importance of Cuba, commanding to a large extent the commerce of the West Indies and of the Central American states, and, what was of vital interest to us, the traffic of the Mississippi valley, attracted at an early period the attention of American as well as of European statesmen. In a letter to President Madison in 1809, Jefferson, in speaking of Napoleon's policy in regard to the Spanish-American colonies, said:

That he would give up the Floridas to withhold intercourse with the residue of those colonies cannot be doubted. But that is no price; because they are ours in the first moment of the first war; and until a war they are of no particular necessity to us. But, although with difficulty, he will consent to our receiving Cuba into our Union, to prevent our aid to Mexico and the other provinces. That would be a price, and I would immediately erect a column on the southern-most limit of Cuba, and inscribe on it a *ne plus ultra* as to us in that direction.[1]

President Madison expressed his views on the Cuban question in a letter to William Pinkney, October 30, 1810:

The position of Cuba gives the United States so deep an interest in the destiny, even, of that island, that although they might be an inactive, they could not be a satisfied spectator at its falling under any European government, which might make a fulcrum of that position against the commerce and security of the United States.[2]

[1] H. A. Washington, " Writings of Thomas Jefferson," Vol. V, p. 443.
[2] " Madison's Works," Vol. II. p. 488.

This was the first statement in the evolution of a Cuban policy consistently adhered to by the United States until the successes of the Mexican war super-induced larger ideas of the mission and destiny of the Union.

As early as 1817 fears as to the fate of Cuba were raised in the minds of the American public by news-paper reports to the effect that England had proposed a relinquishment of her claim against Spain for the maintenance of the British army during the Peninsular campaign, amounting to £15,000,000, in return for the cession of the island.[3] Reports of this nature were circulated for several months on both sides of the Atlantic, but the question did not assume any very great importance until 1819, when the treaty for the cession of the Floridas to the United States was being negotiated with Spain. It was then insisted by the British press that the acquisition of the Floridas would give the United States such a preponderating influence in West Indian affairs as to render necessary the occupation of Cuba by Great Britain as the natural and only off-set.[4] The Florida treaty was ratified after some delay, which, however, does not appear to have been caused by the British government, as was supposed at the time. The British papers, neverthe-less, continued to condemn in strong terms the treaty as well as the inaction of their government in not mak-ing it a pretext for the seizure of Cuba.

As the preparations of France for the invasion of Spain in 1823 progressed the fate of Cuba became a

[3] Niles's " Register," under date November 8, 1817.
[4] For a full discussion of the question see the pamphlet by J. Freeman Rattenbury, entitled, " The Cession of the Floridas to the United States of America and the Necessity of Acquiring the Island of Cuba by Great Britain." London, 1819.

question of absorbing interest in America. There was little hope that the island would continue a dependency of Spain. It was rumored that Great Britain had engaged to supply the constitutional government of Spain with money in her struggle with France and would occupy Cuba as a pledge for its repayment. Both Spanish and French journals spoke of British occupation of Cuba as a matter no longer to be doubted, and the presence in the West Indies of a large British squadron, sent nominally for the purpose of suppressing piracy, seemed to lend color to the reports.[5] The British press was clamoring for the acquisition of Cuba. The *Packet* declared: " The question then comes to this, shall England occupy Cuba, or by permitting its acquisition by the United States (which they have long desired) sacrifice her whole West India trade? There can be no hesitation as to the answer."

The British government, however, officially disclaimed all designs upon Cuba, but this disclaimer did not fully reassure the American government, and our representatives abroad were instructed to exercise a close scrutiny upon all negotiations between Spain and England. In the spring of 1823 Mr. Forsyth was succeeded by Mr. Nelson at the court of Madrid. In his instructions to the new minister, which went much beyond the usual length and were occupied almost exclusively with a discussion of the Cuban question, John Quincy Adams used the following remarkable words:

" In looking forward to the probable course of events for the short period of half a century, it seems scarcely possible to resist the conviction that the an-

---

[5] Niles's " Register," March and April, 1823.

nexation of Cuba to our Federal Republic will be indispensable to the continuance and integrity of the Union itself." We were not then prepared for annexation, he continued, " but there are laws of political as well as physical gravitation; and if an apple, severed by the tempest from its native tree, cannot choose but fall to the ground, Cuba, forcibly disjoined from its own unnatural connection with Spain, and incapable of self-support, can gravitate only towards the North American Union, which, by the same law of nature, cannot cast her off from its bosom." [6]

President Monroe consulted Jefferson on the subject of Spanish-American affairs and the entanglements with European powers likely to arise therefrom. Jefferson replied, June 11, 1823:

Cuba alone seems at present to hold up a speck of war to us. Its possession by Great Britain would indeed be a great calamity to us. Could we induce her to join us in guaranteeing its independence against all the world, except Spain, it would be nearly as valuable as if it were our own. But should she take it, I would not immediately go to war for it; because the first war on other accounts will give it to us, or the island will give itself to us when able to do so. [7]

During the summer of 1825 a large French squadron visited the West Indies and hovered for several weeks about the coasts of Cuba. This action on the part of the French government, without explanation, excited the alarm of both England and the United States and drew forth strong protests from Mr. Canning and from Mr. Clay. Canning wrote to Gran-

---

[6] " H. Ex. Doc. No. 121, Thirty-second Cong., First Sess.; also Brit. and For. St. Pap., Vol. XLIV, pp. 114-236.
[7] H. A. Washington, " Writings of Jefferson," Vol. VII, p. 288.

ville, the British minister at Paris, that he could not consent to the occupation of Havana by France, even as a measure of protection against possible attacks from Mexico and Colombia.[8] Again some two months later he wrote:

As to Cuba you cannot too soon nor too amicably, of course, represent to Villèle the impossibility of our allowing France (or France us, I presume) to meddle in the internal affairs of that colony. We sincerely wish it to remain with the mother-country. Next to that I wish it independent, either singly or in connection with Mexico. But what cannot or must not be, is that any great maritime power should get possession of it. The Americans (Yankees, I mean) think of this matter just as I do.[9]

The expressions of the United States, as to the designs of France, were as emphatic as those of England. Mr. Clay declared " that we could not consent to the occupation of those islands by any other European power than Spain under any contingency whatever." [10]

In this connection Canning wished to bring about the signature, by England, France, and the United States, of " ministerial notes, one between France and the United States, and one between France and Great Britain, or one tripartite note signed by all, disclaiming each for themselves, any intention to occupy Cuba, and protesting against such occupation by either of the others." [11] The government of the United States held this proposal under advisement, but on France declining, it was dropped.[12] In 1826 when an attack

---

[8] " Official Corresp. of Canning," Vol. I, p. 265.
[9] *Ibid.*, Vol. I, p. 275.
[10] Am. St. Pap., For. Rel., Vol. V, p. 855. Also " Wharton's Digest," Sec. 60.
[11] Stapleton, " Political Life of Canning." Vol. III, p. 154.
[12] Mr. Clay to Mr. King, October 25, " Wharton's Digest," Sec. 60.

upon Portugal was feared Canning advised, in case of such an attack, the immediate seizure of Cuba by Great Britain as more effective than half a dozen Peninsular campaigns.[13]

The Cuban question was involved in the long debate on the proposal of the executive of the United States to send delegates to the congress of Spanish-American republics assembled at Panama in 1826. This debate occupied the attention of Congress during the winter and spring of 1826, and was engaged in with great earnestness. One of the chief objections to the proposed mission was the fact that the question of Cuba and Porto Rico would come up and that the United States government had already committed itself to the foreign powers on that subject. The report of the Senate committee on foreign relations declared that,

The very situation of Cuba and Porto Rico furnishes the strongest inducement to the United States not to take a place at the contemplated congress, since, by so doing, they must be considered as changing the attitude in which they hitherto have stood as impartial spectators of the passing scenes, and identifying themselves with the new republics.[14]

The Southern members were united in their opposition to the Panama mission, and in fact to any closer alliance with the new republics, for the reason that the latter had adopted the principle of emancipation and any further extension of their influence would jeopardize the institution of slavery in the United States. For the same reason they were opposed to the transfer of Cuba to any other European power. If a change from its connection with Spain were neces-

---

[13] Canning to Earl of Liverpool, October 6, 1826.
[14] Am. St. Pap., For. Rel., Vol. V, p. 863.

sary they favored annexation by the United States, and meantime they were strongly opposed to the government entering into any engagement with foreign powers or in any way committing itself on the Cuban question.[15]

The declaration of Mr. Clay against the interference of England and France in the affairs of Cuba was consistently adhered to under the administrations of Jackson and Van Buren.

In 1838-39, the British government dispatched special commissioners to Cuba and Porto Rico to report on the condition of the slave trade. The presence of these agents in Cuba gave rise to reports that Great Britain contemplated revolutionizing the island, or at least occupying it for the purpose of suppressing the slave trade. The United States gave Spain to understand that we would not consent to British control in whatever way it might be brought about. Mr. Forsyth wrote to Mr. Vail, our representative at Madrid, July 15, 1840:

You are authorized to assure the Spanish government, that in case of any attempt, from whatever quarter, to wrest from her this portion of her territory, she may securely depend upon the military and naval resources of the United States to aid her in preserving or recovering it.[16]

Again, Mr. Webster in January, 1843, wrote to Mr. Campbell, United States consul at Havana:

The Spanish government has long been in possession of the policy and wishes of this government in regard to Cuba,

---

[15] Benton's "Abridgment," Vol. VIII, pp. 427, 428, and Vol. IX, pp. 90-218.
[16] H. Ex. Doc. No. 121, Thirty-second Cong., First Sess.; also "Wharton's Digest," Sec. 60.

which have never changed, and has repeatedly been told that the United States never would permit the occupation of that island by British agents or forces upon any pretext whatever; and that in the event of any attempt to wrest it from her, she might securely rely upon the whole naval and military resources of this country to aid her in preserving or recovering it.[17]

A copy of this letter was also sent to Washington Irving, our representative at Madrid to make such use of as circumstances might require.[18]

During the first period of our Cuban diplomacy the efforts of this government were directed toward preventing the acquisition of the island, or the establishment of a protectorate over it, by Great Britain or France. With the Mexican war, however, and the growing conviction of " manifest destiny," our foreign policy assumed a much bolder and more aggressive character, and during the next fifteen years all manner of schemes for the southward extension of our territory were suggested and many of them actually undertaken. Cuba became an object of desire, not only in the eyes of the slave-holding population of the South as an acquisition to slave territory, but of a large part of the nation, because of its strategic importance in relation to the inter-oceanic transit routes of Central America, which seemed the only feasible line of communication with our rapidly developing interests in California. Consequently various attempts were made to annex the island to the United States, both by purchase from Spain and forcibly by filibustering expeditions.

---

[17] " Wharton's Digest," Sec. 60.
[18] Mr. Upshur, who succeeded Mr. Webster as secretary of state, wrote to Mr. Irving to the same effect, October 10, 1843.

In June, 1848, under the administration of President Polk, Mr. Buchanan, secretary of state, wrote to our minister at Madrid, directing him to open negotiations with the Spanish government for the purchase of Cuba. After referring to the dangers of British occupation and to the advantages of annexation, he said: " Desirable, however, as this island may be to the United States, we would not acquire it except by the free will of Spain. Any acquisition not sanctioned by justice and honor would be too dearly purchased." He stated that the President would stipulate for the payment of $100,000,000, as a maximum price.[19] This offer was rejected by the Spanish government. The minister of state after several months' delay finally replied " that it was more than any minister dare to entertain any such proposition; that he believed such to be the feeling of the country, that sooner than see the island transferred to any power, they would prefer seeing it sunk in the ocean."

Under the Whig administration of Taylor and Fillmore no effort was made for the purchase of Cuba. On August 2, 1849, Mr. Clayton wrote to Mr. Barringer that the government did not desire to renew the negotiation for the purchase of Cuba made by the late administration, since the proposition had been considered by the Spanish government as a national indignity; that should Spain desire to part with Cuba, the proposal must come from her.

About this time active preparations were going on for the invasion of Cuba by an armed expedition under the Cuban patriot Narciso Lopez. On August

---

[19] Mr. Buchanan to Mr. Saunders, June 17, 1848, H. Ex. Doc. No. 121, Thirty-second Cong., First Sess.; also Brit. and For. St. Pap., Vol. XXVI.

11, 1849, President Taylor issued a proclamation warning all citizens of the United States against taking part in such expedition and saying, " No such persons must expect the interference of this government in any form on their behalf, no matter to what extremities they may be reduced in consequence of their conduct." [20] A few days later the entire force of Lopez was arrested by the United States marshal just as it was on the point of leaving New York.

Nothing daunted, Lopez traveled through the southern and southwestern states secretly enlisting men and making arrangements for their transportation to Cuba. Many men of prominence at the South were in open and avowed sympathy with the enterprise. In the spring of 1850, Lopez called upon Gen. John A. Quitman, governor of Mississippi, who had served with great distinction in the Mexican war, and offered him, in the name of his compatriots, the leadership of the revolution and the supreme command of the army. Quitman's sympathies were thoroughly enlisted in the movement, but he declined the honor on account of the serious aspect of political affairs, particularly what he considered the encroachments of the federal government upon the rights of the states. He made liberal contributions of money, however, and gave Lopez sound advice about his undertaking, insisting that he must have an advance column of at least 2,000 men to maintain a footing on the island until reinforcements could go to their aid.[21]

---

[20] "Messages and Papers of the Presidents," Vol. V, p. 7.
[21] J. F. H. Claiborne, " Life and Corresp. of John A. Quitman," Vol. II, pp. 55-56, and Appendix, p. 385.
In June the Grand Jury of the United States Circuit Court at New Orleans found a bill against John A. Quitman, John Henderson, Governor of Louisiana, and others, for setting on foot the invasion of Cuba. Quitman's

Unfortunately for Lopez he did not follow the advice of Quitman. A company of volunteers altogether inadequate for the successful accomplishment of the enterprise was collected at New Orleans. There Lopez chartered a steamer, the *Creole,* and two barks, the *Georgiana* and the *Susan Loud.* Three-fourths of the volunteers had served in the Mexican war. The first detachment comprising 250 men left New Orleans in the bark *Georgiana,* April 25, 1850, under the command of Col. Theodore O'Hara. They proceeded to the island of Contoy off the coast of Yucatan in the territory of Mexico. There they were joined three weeks later by Lopez and 450 followers in the *Creole.* The entire command, with the exception of the crews of the two barks and a few others to guard the stores, embarked in the *Creole* and effected a landing at Cardenas, but the natives did not come to the aid of Lopez and after holding the town for twelve hours he reluctantly reëmbarked and headed for Key West. The *Creole* was pursued by the *Pizarro,* a Spanish war vessel, which steamed into the harbor just as she cast anchor. For a few moments the Spaniards seemed to be on the point of preparing to open fire on the *Creole,* but when they saw the United States custom-house of-

---

view of state sovereignty did not admit the right of the United States Courts to proceed against the chief executive of a sovereign state. He sought the advice of friends throughout the South as to what course he should pursue. None of them admitted the right of the United States Courts to indict him and several of them advised him that it was his duty to assert the principle of state sovereignty even to the point of calling out the state militia to protect him against arrest. Others advised him to submit under protest so as to avoid an open breach. This course was finally adopted, and when the United States marshal appeared on the 3rd of February, 1851, to take him into custody, he yielded, causing at the same time an address to be issued to the people of Mississippi, in which he resigned the office of governor. After proceedings which lasted two months. Henderson was acquitted and the charges against Quitman and the others dismissed.

ficers take possession of her they changed their minds and left the harbor.

The two barks, which had been left with a small guard at the island of Contoy, were captured by Spanish warships, taken to Havana, condemned as prizes and the men put on trial for participation in the Lopez expedition. As these men had committed no act of hostility against Spain, and had, moreover, been seized on neutral territory, the United States government at once issued its protest and demanded their release. The Spanish government replied that these men had been described as pirates by the President of the United States in his proclamation warning citizens against joining the expedition and were, therefore, beyond the pale of the protection of the United States. After heated negotiations which lasted several months and seriously threatened the peace of the two countries, the prisoners were released, but it was declared to be an act of grace on the part of the Queen and not a concession to the demands of the United States.[22]

Lopez was prosecuted by the United States government for violation of the neutrality laws, but escaped conviction and at once set about organizing another expedition. On August 3, 1851, the third and last expedition of Lopez, consisting of over 400 men, left New Orleans. After touching at Key West the steamer proceeded to the coast of Cuba and landed the expedition at Bahia Honda. The main body under Lopez proceeded into the country where they had been led to expect a general uprising of the Cubans. Col. W. S. Crittenden, who had served with bravery in the Mexican war, was left in command of a smaller

[22] Sen. Ex. Doc. No. 41, Thirty-first Cong., Second Sess.

body to bring up the baggage. This detachment was attacked on the 13th and forced to retreat to the place where they had landed, where about fifty of them obtained boats and tried to escape. They were, however, intercepted off the coast, taken to Havana, sentenced before a military court, and executed on the 16th.

The main body under Lopez was overcome and dispersed by Spanish troops on the 24th. Lopez was taken prisoner, tried, and executed. Many of his followers were killed or died of hunger and fatigue and the rest made prisoners. Upon receipt of this news Commodore Parker was at once ordered to proceed in a frigate to Havana to inquire into the charges against the prisoners executed, and the circumstances of their capture, trial, and sentence. To these inquiries the captain-general replied that he considered those executed as pirates, that they had been so denounced by the President of the United States in his proclamation, that he was not at liberty to furnish a copy of the court records, but would send them to Madrid and to the Spanish minister at Washington.[23]

When the news of the executions at Havana reached New Orleans the excitement was intense. The office of the Spanish consul was broken into, portraits of the Queen and Captain-General of Cuba defaced, the Spanish flag torn in pieces, and the consul burned in effigy in LaFayette Square. The consul had to flee from the city for safety and the property of certain Spaniards residing in New Orleans was destroyed. A long correspondence ensued between the two governments. The United States agreed to pay an indemnity

[23] H. Ex. Doc. No. 1, Thirty-second Cong., First Sess.; also 2d Annual Message of Fillmore, December 2, 1851. "Messages and Papers of the Presidents" Vol. V, p. 113.

for injuries to the public property of Spain, but not for the destruction of property belonging to Spanish residents, who were entitled only to the same protection afforded our own citizens.[24]

A few weeks after the last Lopez expedition the British and French representatives at Washington notified our government that orders had been issued to their squadrons in the West Indies to repel by force any attempts at the invasion of Cuba from any quarter. Our government replied that such action on the part of England and France could " not but be regarded by the United States with grave disapproval, as involving on the part of European sovereigns combined action of protectorship over American waters." [25]

In order to allay the uneasiness caused by the attempts of filibusters, supposed to be encouraged or at least connived at by the government of the United States, the Spanish government requested Great Britain and France, in January, 1852, to secure the signature by the American government in conjunction with them of an abnegatory declaration with respect to Cuba.[26] Accordingly in April, 1852, the British and French ministers at Washington brought the subject to the attention of this government in notes of the same date, suggesting a tripartite convention for the guarantee of Cuba to Spain.[27]

To this proposal Mr. Webster replied in part as follows :

[24] H. Ex. Doc. No. 1, Thirty-second Cong., First Sess.

[25] Mr. Crittenden to Comte de Sartiges, October 22, 1851. See also Pres. Fillmore to Mr. Webster and Mr. Webster's reply. 2 Curtis's " Life of Webster," p. 551.

[26] Brit. and For. St. Pap., Vol. XLIV, Lord Howden to Earl Granville, January 9, 1852.

[27] Comte de Sartiges to Mr. Webster, April 23, 1852. Sen. Ex. Doc. No. 13, Thirty-second Cong., Second Sess.

It has been stated and often repeated to the government of Spain by this government, under various administrations, not only that the United States have no design upon Cuba themselves, but that, if Spain should refrain from a voluntary cession of the island to any other European power, she might rely on the countenance and friendship of the United States to assist her in the defense and preservation of that island. At the same time it has always been declared to Spain that the government of the United States could not be expected to acquiesce in the cession of Cuba to an European power.

He reminded them, furthermore, that " the policy of the United States has uniformly been to avoid, as far as possible, alliances or agreements with other states, and to keep itself free from national obligations, except such as affect directly the interests of the United States themselves." [28]

The matter was again urged upon the United States by the British and French governments in notes to Mr. Webster, dated July 9, 1852, in which the indefeasibility of the Spanish title to the island and its bearings upon the neutrality of the proposed Central American canals were dwelt upon. The death of Mr. Webster postponed for some time the answer of the United States, but the proposal was finally rejected in a notable dispatch prepared by Webster's successor, Edward Everett.

With the growth of the slavery conflict, which had now become paramount to all other questions, the annexation of Cuba had become a party issue, and the return of the Democratic party to power, in 1853, was hailed by the southern extremists as a signal for the

---

[28] Mr. Webster to Comte de Sartiges, April 29, 1852. To Mr. Crampton, same date, to same effect.

acquisition of the long coveted prize. This expectation was further heightened by the declaration of President Pierce, in his inaugural address, that the policy of his administration would " not be controlled by any timid forebodings of evil from expansion," and that the acquisition of certain possessions not within our jurisdiction was " eminently important for our protection, if not in the future essential for the preservation of the rights of commerce and the peace of the world."

William L. Marcy, of New York, was appointed secretary of state and for the mission to Spain the President selected Pierre Soulé of Louisiana, a Frenchman by birth and education, who had been exiled for political reasons. His appointment under the circumstances created unfavorable comment both in this country and in Europe, and his sojourn of several days at Paris on the way to his post at Madrid caused the French government some annoyance. Louis Napoleon advised the court of Madrid not to receive him, as his views on the Cuban question were well known to be of a radical character.

In his instructions to Mr. Soulé, July 23, 1853, Mr. Marcy emphasized the importance of our relations with Spain in view of the rumors of contemplated changes in the internal affairs of Cuba and of the recent interposition of England and France. He directed him to try to negotiate a commercial treaty with Spain favorable to our trade with Cuba, and pointed out the urgent necessity of allowing a " qualified diplomatic intercourse between the captain-general of that island and our consul at Havana, in order to prevent difficulties and preserve a good understanding between the two countries." [29]   The difficulty of set-tling disputes arising in Cuba had been the subject of frequent remonstrances on the part of the United States. The captain-general was clothed with almost " unlimited powers for aggression, but with none for reparation." He exercised no diplomatic functions and was in no way subject to the authority of the Spanish minister at Washington.

Upon the arrival of Mr. Soulé in Spain, he found that Mr. Calderon, the head of the cabinet, was strongly opposed to any commercial treaty or agree-ment which would promote intercourse between the United States and the dependencies of Spain, and equally averse to allowing the captain-general any dip-lomatic powers.[30]   Mr. Soulé was by nature hot-headed and impetuous and could suffer anything sooner than enforced inactivity. Whatever may have been the intentions of the executive in sending him, he had come to Madrid for the purpose of consum-mating the long cherished scheme of acquiring Cuba. Accordingly, on February 23, 1854, he wrote to Mr. Marcy that the affairs of the Spanish government were about to reach a crisis, that a change of ministry was imminent, and that contingencies involving the fate of Cuba were likely to arise which might be of great in-terest to the United States. He, therefore, asked for definite instructions. Relying upon these representa-tions and upon Mr. Soulé's judgment, Mr. Marcy transmited in due time the necessary powers, author-izing him to negotiate with Spain for the purchase of Cuba, or for its independence, if such an arrange-

---

[29] H. Ex. Doc. No. 93, Thirty-third Cong., Second Sess., p. 3.
[30] Mr. Soulé to Mr. Marcy, November 10, and December 23, 1853, and January 20, 1854.

ment would be more agreeable to Spanish pride, in which event the United States would be willing to contribute substantial aid to the result.

In the meantime, however, the *Black Warrior* affair had strained the relations of the two countries almost to the point of rupture. This case, involving the seizure of an American steamer by Spanish officials at Havana for an unintentional violation or neglect of custom-house regulations, was of an unusually exasperating character.

As soon as the department at Washington was fully informed of this outrage, Mr. Marcy forwarded all the documents in the case to Mr. Soulé and directed him to demand of the Spanish government a prompt disavowal of the act and the payment of an indemnity to the owners of the vessel and of the cargo, the extent of the injury being estimated at $300,000. On April 8 Mr. Soulé presented a formal demand on the part of his government. No answer to this note having been received, on the 11th he repeated his demands much more emphatically, calling for an indemnity of $300,000, insisting that all persons, whatever their rank or importance, who were concerned in the perpetration of the wrong, be dismissed from her majesty's service, and finally declaring that non-compliance with these demands within forty-eight hours would be considered by the government of the United States as equivalent to a declaration that her majesty's government was determined to uphold the conduct of its officers.

Mr. Calderon replied, on the 12th, that whenever her majesty's government should have before it the authentic and complete data, which it then lacked, a reply would be given to the demand of the United States conformable to justice and right; that the peremptory tone of Mr. Soulé's note suggested to the government of her majesty " a suspicion that it was not so much the manifestation of a lively interest in the defense of pretended injuries, as an incomprehensible pretext for exciting estrangement, if not a quarrel between two friendly powers." To this note Mr. Soulé replied that the suggestion made as to the motives of the United States in seeking redress was " but little creditable to the candor of her Catholic majesty's government, and comes in very bad grace from one who, like your excellency, cannot but be aware that the records of this legation, as well as those of her Catholic majesty's department of state, are loaded with reclamations bearing on grievances most flagrant, which have never been earnestly attended to and were met at their inception with precisely the same dilatory excuses through which the present one is sought to be evaded."

Meanwhile the aspects of the case were altogether changed by a private agreement between the Havana officials and the owners of the *Black Warrior,* by which the ship and her cargo were released. Mr. Soulé continued, however, according to instructions from Washington, to demand compensation for the damages sustained by the owners and passengers not compensated for by the return of the ship and cargo, and also reparation for the insult to the United States flag. The Spanish government, however, refused to recognize any ground for reparation after the restitution of the ship and cargo, and persisted in contradicting, without the support of any evidence whatever, the facts as presented by the United States, although they were all certified to in proper legal form.

On June 24 Mr. Marcy wrote that the President was far from satisfied with the manner in which our demands were treated by the Spanish government, but that before resorting to extreme measures he was determined to make a final appeal to Spain for the adjustment of past difficulties and for the guarantee of more friendly relations in the future. Although satisfied with the spirited manner in which Mr. Soulé had performed the duties of his mission, the President was considering the expediency of reinforcing the demands of the United States by the appointment of an extraordinary commission of two distinguished citizens to act in conjunction with him. He instructed him, therefore, not to press the affair of the *Black Warrior,* but to wait until the question of the special commission could be laid before Congress.

During the summer there was a change of ministry in the Spanish government, which, as was not infrequently the case, was attended with more or less serious disorders. In August Mr. Marcy wrote that in view of the unsettled condition of affairs in Spain and for other reasons not stated, the purpose of sending a special mission had, for the present at least, been abandoned. Without pressing matters Mr. Soulé was, nevertheless, to avail himself of any opportunity which might be presented, of settling the affairs in dispute and of negotiating for the purchase of Cuba.

Under the same date he proposed to Mr. Soulé the plan of consulting with Mr. Mason and Mr. Buchanan, our ministers at Paris and London, for the purpose of overcoming any obstacles that England and France might interpose. This suggestion led to the celebrated meeting at Ostend and the so-called manifesto.

In accordance with the instructions of the President, Messrs. Soulé, Mason, and Buchanan proceeded to make arrangements for the proposed conference, which was held at Ostend, in Belgium, October 9, 10, 11, 1854. They then adjourned to Aix-la-Chapelle for a week, where the reports of their proceedings were prepared.

The greater part of the report is taken up with an enumeration of the advantages that would accrue to the United States from the acquisition of Cuba, and an elaborate exposition of the ways in which the interests of Spain would be promoted by the sale. The only specific recommendation of the report was that a proposal should be made through the proper diplomatic channel to the Supreme Constituent Cortes about to assemble, to purchase Cuba from Spain, the maximum price to be $120,000,000. The report then proceeds to discuss the question, what ought to be the course of the American government should Spain refuse to sell Cuba? The ministers declared:

After we shall have offered Spain a price for Cuba far beyond its present value, and this shall have been refused, it will then be time to consider the question, does Cuba, in the possession of Spain, seriously endanger our internal peace and the existence of our cherished Union?

Should this question be answered in the affirmative, then, by every law, human and divine, we shall be justified in wresting it from Spain if we possess the power; and this upon the very same principle that would justify an individual in tearing down the burning house of his neighbor if there were no other means of preventing the flames from destroying his own home.

The report also recommended that all proceedings in reference to the negotiations with Spain " ought to be open, frank, and public." This recommendation, together with the general character of the report, indicates that its authors were rather bent on making political capital of the affair at home than on seriously furthering negotiations at Madrid. As a matter of fact the Ostend Manifesto made Buchanan an acceptable presidential candidate to the southern wing of the Democratic party and played no small part in securing for him the nomination in 1856.[31]

The objectionable features of the report were politely but firmly repudiated by the administration in Marcy's reply to Soulé and Soulé promptly resigned his mission. This fact was generally overlooked at the time, while the unfortunate publicity given to the proceedings at Ostend brought endless censure upon President Pierce and Secretary Marcy.

In spite of the " jingo " policy attributed to the Pierce administration, the complications arising out of the seizure of the *Black Warrior* were not made a *casus belli*, as might easily have been done. After Mr. Soulé's return to the United States the negotiations were continued by his successor. The conduct of the officials concerned in the seizure was disavowed, and the indemnity claimed by the American citizens concerned was paid. The administration closed on terms of comparative friendship with Spain, although there were numbers of claims still unadjusted. The Cuban question figured conspicuously in the campaign of 1856. The platform of the Democratic party was

[31] The correspondence relating to the *Black Warrior* case and to the Ostend conference is contained in H. Ex. Doc. No. 93, Thirty-third Cong., Second Sess.

strongly in favor of acquisition, while the new Republican platform stigmatized the Ostend manifesto as the highwayman's plea.

Until the Buchanan administration all negotiations for the purchase of Cuba had been undertaken on the authority of the executive alone. An effort was now made to get the two houses of Congress to concur in an appropriation for this purpose. It was thought that united action on the part of the legislative and executive branches of the government would produce some impression on Spain. Accordingly, in his second, third and fourth annual messages, President Buchanan brought the matter to the attention of Congress, but his appeal met with little encouragement. In January, 1859, Senator Slidell, the chairman of the Senate Committee on Foreign Relations, reported a bill carrying $30,000,000, to be placed at the disposal of the President as a preliminary sum for the purchase of Cuba.[32]

This report created violent opposition, and in February the bill was withdrawn by Mr. Slidell at the urgent request of his friends.

The annexationist and filibustering schemes of the decade immediately preceding the War of Secession were prompted by two motives. The one was the extension of slave territory, or at least the thwarting of the schemes of emancipation for Cuba which Great Britain was urging upon the Spanish government. The other was to secure, by the occupation of this strong strategic position, undisputed control over the proposed interoceanic canal routes of Central America and communication by this means with the new states on the Pacific coast. These motives for annexation

[32] Sen. Report No. 351, Thirty-fifth Cong., Second Sess., Vol. I.

were removed, the one by the abolition of slavery in the United States, and the other by the construction of the great transcontinental railroads which established direct overland communication with the Pacific states. During the period following the civil war, therefore, our policy was mainly concerned in urging upon the Spanish government the abolition of slavery in Cuba, the establishment of a more liberal form of government through independence or autonomy, and the promotion of more untrammelled commercial intercourse with the United States.

The abolition of slavery in the southern states left the Spanish Antilles in the enjoyment of a monopoly of slave labor, which in the production of sugar, especially, gave them advantages which overcame all competition. This led to the formation of a strong Spanish party, for whom the cause of slavery and that of Spanish dominion were identical. These were known as Peninsulars on Spanish immigrants. They were the official class, the wealthy planters and slave-owners and the real rulers of Cuba. On the other hand there was a party composed of Creoles, or native Cubans, whose cry was "Cuba for the Cubans!" and who hoped to effect the complete separation of the island from Spain, either through their own efforts or through the assistance of the United States. Not infrequently in the same family, the father, born and brought up in the Peninsula, was an ardent loyalist, while the son, born in Cuba, was an insurgent at heart, if not actually enlisted in the ranks.

The Spanish revolution of September, 1868, was the signal for an uprising of the native or Creole party in the eastern part of the island. This movement was not at first ostensibly for independence, but for the revolution in Spain, the cries being "Hurrah for Prim!" "Hurrah for the Revolution!" Its real character was, however, apparent from the first and its supporters continued for a period of ten years, without regard to the numerous vicissitudes through which the Spanish government passed—the provisional government, the regency, the elective monarchy, the republic, and the restored Bourbon dynasty—to wage a dogged, though desultory warfare against the constituted authorities of the island. This struggle was almost coterminous with President Grant's administration of eight years.

At an early stage of the contest the Spanish authorities conceived it to be necessary to issue certain decrees which were contrary to public law and, in so far as they affected citizens of the United States, in violation of treaty obligations. On March 24, 1869, the captain-general issued a decree authorizing the capture on the high seas of vessels carrying men, arms, munitions, or effects in aid of the insurgents, and declaring that "all persons captured in such vessels without regard to their number will be immediately executed." [33] By another decree the estates of American citizens suspected of sympathy with the insurgents were confiscated.[34] Secretary Hamilton Fish protested against these decrees so far as they affected citizens of the United States, as they were in violation of the provisions of the treaty of 1795.

On July 7, 1869, the captain-general issued another decree closing certain ports, declaring voyages with

[33] Sen. Ex. Doc. No. 7, Forty-first Cong., Second Sess.
[34] Ibid.

arms, ammunition, or crew for the insurgents illegal, and directing cruisers on the high seas to bring into port all vessels found to be enemies. On July 16 Mr. Fish called the attention of the Spanish minister to this decree, saying that it assumed powers over the commerce of the United States that could be permitted only in time of war; that the United States would not yield the right to carry contraband of war in time of peace, and would not permit their vessels to be interfered with on the high seas except in time of war; that if Spain was at war she should give notice to the United States to that effect, and that a continuance of the decree or any attempt to enforce it would be regarded as a recognition by Spain of a state of war in Cuba. This declaration produced a prompt modification of the decree so far as it concerned the search of vessels on the high seas.

As our commercial interests at large, as well as the interests of individual citizens, were deeply affected by the condition of the island, President Grant determined at the beginning of his administration to offer to mediate between Spain and the insurgents. General Daniel E. Sickles was appointed minister to Spain and his instructions, under date of June 29, 1869, directed him to offer to the cabinet at Madrid the good offices of the United States for the purpose of bringing to a close the civil war then ravaging the island and establishing the independence of Cuba. Mr. Fish instructed General Sickles to explain to the Spanish government that he used the term civil war advisedly, not as implying any public recognition of belligerent rights, but a condition of affairs that might not justify withholding much longer those rights from the insurgents.[35] In reply Spain agreed to accept the good offices of the United States, but on conditions that were impracticable and unsatisfactory. At the same time the Spanish government allowed the purport of General Sickles's note tendering the good offices of the United States to get out, and it was accepted by the press as indicating the purpose of the United States to recognize the Cubans as belligerents if its offer of mediation were refused. No Spanish cabinet could possibly endure the odium of having made a concession to the Cubans under a threat from an outside power. The Spanish government therefore requested the withdrawal of the American note.

After the rejection of the offer of mediation President Grant decided to recognize the Cuban insurgents and in August, 1869, while on his way from New York to New England on the Fall River boat he signed a proclamation of Cuban belligerency which he forwarded to Washington with a note to Secretary Fish, requesting him to sign, seal, and issue it. Mr. Fish disapproved of this step, and while he affixed the seal and signed the document, he did not issue it, but kept it in a safe place to await further developments. Grant's attention was diverted by Wall Street speculations in gold and the crisis that followed on " Black Friday." He failed to notice at the time that the secretary of state did not carry out his instructions, and later he thanked Mr. Fish for having saved him from a serious mistake.[36]

For some time the United States had been urging upon Spain the importance of abolishing slavery in

[35] House Ex. Doc. No. 160, Forty-first Cong., Second Sess.
[36] C. F. Adams, " The Treaty of Washington," in " Lee at Appomattox and Other Papers," p. 119.

Cuba as a necessary condition to the complete pacification of the island. During the fall of 1869 Spain gave repeated assurances to the United States of her readiness to effect emancipation in Cuba as soon as hostilities should cease, but the Spanish government could never be brought to enter into any definite engagement on the subject. In fact as regarded the slavery question the cabinet of Madrid found itself unable to choose between the horns of the dilemma. The United States and Great Britain were urging the immediate abolition of slavery, while the most influential upholders of Spanish rule in Porto Rico as well as in Cuba were the slaveholders themselves. The insurgents on the other hand had abolished slavery by a decree of the assembly of February 26, 1869, promising indemnity to the owners in due time and providing for the enrolment of liberated slaves in the army.[37] On January 26, 1870, Mr. Fish wrote to General Sickles:

It becomes more apparent every day that this contest cannot terminate without the abolition of slavery. This government regards the government at Madrid as committed to that result. . . . You will, therefore, if it shall appear that the insurrection is regarded as suppressed, frankly state that this government, relying upon the assurances so often given, will expect steps to be taken for the emancipation of the slaves in the Spanish colonies.

The British representative at Madrid, Mr. Layard, was instructed to second the suggestions of the United States minister in regard to the abolition of slavery in the Spanish colonies.

---

[37] Sen. Ex. Doc. No. 113, Forty-first Cong., Second Sess.

From the outbreak of the insurrection the Cuban patriots had the sympathy of the great mass of the American people, and that of the administration, although the latter was kept within the bounds of public law and treaty obligation, so as to avoid giving offense to Spain. The government did all that treaty obligations demanded of it to prevent the violation of the neutrality laws. Numbers of filibustering expeditions did, however, escape from American ports, and those that were arrested at the instance of the Spanish government through its representatives in this country usually escaped conviction in our courts for want of evidence.

In June, 1870, the question of granting belligerent rights to the Cubans was brought before Congress in the form of a joint resolution introduced into the House. Personally General Grant sympathized with the Cubans and was disposed to grant them the rights of belligerents, but his judgment was again overruled by the counsels of Mr. Fish. On June 13, during the heat of the debate on the question of belligerency, the President sent to Congress a message embodying the views of the executive. At Mr. Fish's instance the message took the ground that the facts did not justify the recognition of a state of war, although Mr. Fish himself had made use of the term civil war in his instructions to General Sickles. The Secretary had almost to force the President to sign this message, though General Grant was afterwards satisfied as to the wisdom of the measure.[38] The message said in part:

---

[38] Private journal of Mr. Fish, quoted by Prof. J. B. Moore in the *Forum,* May, 1896.

The question of belligerency is one of fact not to be decided by sympathies with or prejudices against either party. The relations between the parent state and the insurgents must amount, in fact, to war in the sense of international law. Fighting, though fierce and protracted, does not alone constitute war; there must be military forces acting in accordance with the rules and customs of war—flags of truce, cartels, exchange of prisoners, etc.,—and to justify belligerency there must be, above all, a *de facto* political organization of the insurgents sufficient in character and resources to constitute it, if left to itself, a state among nations capable of discharging the duties of a state, and of meeting the just responsibilities it may incur as such toward other powers in the discharge of its international duties.

This message provoked a long and animated discussion in the House next day and sharp criticism on the part of the Cuban sympathizers of the President's conduct in thus " intruding himself into the House for the purpose of controlling their deliberations." The debate continued until June 16, when the resolution passed the House by a vote of 80 to 68.[39] It was taken up by the Senate, discussed and amended, but finally lost.

The conclusion of an agreement on February 12, 1871, for the submission to a mixed commission of claims of American citizens arising in Cuba,[40] took away all our pressing grievances against Spain and for more than two years our diplomatic relations were on a comparatively friendly basis. Good feeling between the two countries was further promoted by the proclamation of the Spanish republic in 1873 and by

---

[39] Congressional Globe, Forty-first Cong., Second Sess., p. 4438.
[40] " Treaties and Conventions of the United States " (Malloy's Ed.), Vol. II, p. 1661.

the prompt action of General Sickles in extending to it the recognition of the United States. After striving in vain for more than two years to reconcile and unite the contending factions of Spain, King Amadeus on February 11, 1873, abdicated the royal authority and returned to the nation the powers with which he had been intrusted. The Cortes at once proclaimed a republic. General Sickles had on January 30 telegraphed to Washington for instructions in case the republicans should succeed in their efforts. On the day after the abdication, he received directions to recognize the republican government when it was fully established and in possession of the power of the nation. Three days later, in the uniform of a major-general of the United States army he was given an audience by the president of the assembly and formally recognized the republic.

On March 6, Congress by joint resolution, in behalf of the American people, tendered its congratulations to the people of Spain. It seemed at last as if our relations with Spain were on a good footing. General Sickles urged upon the new republican government the abolition of slavery and the concession of self-government to Cuba.

But such cordial relations did not long continue. On October 31, 1873, the steamer *Virginius,* sailing under American colors and carrying a United States registry, was captured on the high seas by the *Tornado,* a Spanish war vessel, and on the afternoon of the first of November taken into the port of Santiago de Cuba. The men and supplies she bore were bound for the insurgents, but the capture did not occur in Cuban waters. General Burriel, the commandant of the city, summoned a court-martial, and in spite of the protests of the American consul, condemned to death at the first sitting four of the passengers, General W. A. C. Ryan, an Irish patriot and three Cubans. They were shot on the morning of November 4. On the 7th twelve other passengers were executed and on the 8th, Captain Fry and his entire crew, numbering thirty--six, making the total number of executions fifty-three. As soon as news of the capture reached Madrid, General Sickles called upon President Castelar and represented to him the difficulties that might arise in case the ship had been taken on the high seas bearing United States colors. Upon General Sickles's suggestion the President of the Spanish republic at once telegraphed to the captain-general to await orders before taking any steps in regard to the captured vessel and crew.

In accordance with instructions from Mr. Fish, General Sickles on November 14 protested by note against these executions as brutal and barbarous and stated that ample reparation would be demanded. The next day he received from the minister of state an ill-tempered reply, rejecting the protest as inadmissible when neither the cabinet at Washington nor that of Madrid had sufficient data upon which to ground a complaint. On the day this reply was received General Sickles, following out telegraphic instructions from Washington, made a formal demand by note for the restoration of the *Virginius,* the surrender of the survivors, a salute to the United States flag, and the punishment of the guilty officials. In case of a refusal of satisfactory reparation within twelve days, General Sickles was instructed by his government, at the expiration of that period, to close the legation and leave Madrid.

The formal reply to General Sickles's demand for reparation was received November 18. The Spanish government declared that it would make no reparation until satisfied that an offense had been committed against the flag of the United States, and that when so convinced through her own sources of information or by the showing of the United States, due reparation would be made.

The representations made at Washington by the Spanish minister were of a much more satisfactory character than those made to General Sickles at Madrid. Mr. Fish, therefore, instructed General Sickles to remain at his post until the 26th, and if no accommodation were reached by that time he could demand his passports. By the time this dispatch reached Madrid General Sickles had already asked for his passports, but had not received the reply of the Spanish government. On the 26th he received a note from the Spanish minister asking for a postponement to December 25 and promising that if by that time Spain could not show that she had the right on her side—i.e., that the *Virginius* was not entitled to sail under the United States flag—she would comply with the demands of the United States. General Sickles replied that he could not accept such a proposal, but that he would inform his government of it and take the responsibility of deferring his departure.

Meanwhile the Spanish minister at Washington had proposed arbitration, but Mr. Fish declined to submit to arbitration the question of an indignity to the United States flag. The minister then asked for a delay, but Mr. Fish told him that delay was impossible in view of the approaching meeting of Congress. Unless settled beforehand the question would have to be referred to Congress. This firm stand brought the Spanish minister to time and on November 27 a proposition was submitted and accepted by Mr. Fish, by the terms of which Spain stipulated to restore the vessel forthwith, to surrender the survivors of her passengers and crew, and on the 25th of December to salute the flag of the United States. If, however, before that date Spain should prove to the satisfaction of the United States that the *Virginius* was not entitled to carry the flag of the United States, the salute should be dispensed with, but in such case the United States would expect a disclaimer of intent of indignity to its flag.

The Spanish envoy submitted to the state department a large number of documents and depositions to show that the *Virginius* had no right to sail under the United States flag. These were referred to the attorney-general, and on December 17 he gave his opinion that the evidence was conclusive that the *Virginius,* although registered in New York on September 26, 1870, in the name of one Patterson, who made oath as required by law that he was the owner, was in fact the property of certain Cubans and was controlled by them. In conclusion the attorney-general said:

Spain, no doubt, has a right to capture a vessel, with an American register, and carrying the American flag, found in her own waters assisting, or endeavoring to assist, the insurrection in Cuba, but she has no right to capture such a vessel on the high seas upon an apprehension that, in violation of the neutrality or navigation laws of the United States, she was on her way to assist said rebellion. Spain may defend her territory and people from the hostile attacks of what is, or appears to be, an American vessel; but she has no jurisdiction whatever over the question as to whether or not such vessel is on the high seas in violation of any law of the United States. Spain cannot rightfully raise that question as to the *Virginius,* but the United States may, and, as I understand the protocol, they have agreed to do it, and, governed by that agreement and without admitting that Spain would otherwise have any interest in the question, I decide that the *Virginius,* at the time of her capture, was without right, and improperly carrying the American flag."[1]

This decision was communicated to the Spanish authorities and, according to the agreement, the salute to the United States flag was dispensed with, and on January 3, 1874, the Spanish minister, on behalf of his government, expressed a disclaimer of an intent of indignity to the flag of the United States. Spain later paid indemnities to Great Britain and the United States for the families of those who had been executed.

Meanwhile General Sickles offered his resignation by cable in consequence of certain reports that his conduct had been disapproved. Mr. Fish replied that such reports were unauthorized, that no dissatisfaction had been expressed or intimated and that it was deemed important that he remain at his post. Ten days later, General Sickles requested that the telegram tendering his resignation and the reply be published. Mr. Fish declined to do so, as the resignation was hypothetical. On December 20, General Sickles again tendered his resignation and it was accepted.

After the settlement of the *Virginius* affair the gov-

---

[1] The correspondence relating to the case of the *Virginius* is in Foreign Relations for the years 1874, 1875, and 1876.

ernment of the United States addressed itself once more to the task of forcing a settlement of the Cuban question in general. In his instructions to Mr. Cushing, who succeeded General Sickles, Secretary Fish expressed the policy of the administration at considerable length. After reviewing the main facts of the insurrection which had then lasted more than five years, with little or no change in the military situation, and after referring to the rejection by Spain of the offers of mediation made by the United States at an early day of the trouble, he said:

In these circumstances, the question what decision the United States shall take is a serious and difficult one, not to be determined without careful consideration of its complex elements of domestic and foreign policy, but the determination of which may at any moment be forced upon us by occurrences either in Spain or in Cuba.

Withal the President cannot but regard independence, and emancipation, of course, as the only certain, and even the necessary, solution of the question of Cuba. And, in his mind, all incidental questions are quite subordinate to those, the larger objects of the United States in this respect.

It requires to be borne in mind that, in so far as we may contribute to the solution of these questions, this government is not actuated by any selfish or interested motive. The President does not meditate or desire the annexation of Cuba to the United States, but its elevation into an independent republic of freemen, in harmony with ourselves and with the other republics of America.[42]

For some months Mr. Cushing was occupied with the settlement of the indemnities in the *Virginius* case. After nearly two years had elapsed since the instructions above quoted, the Grant administration deter-

---

[42] Foreign Relations, 1874-75, p. 859.

mined, in view of the unchanged condition of the Cuban struggle, to bring matters to an issue and to force, if need be, the hand of the Spanish government. On November 5, 1875, Mr. Fish addressed a long letter of instruction to Mr. Cushing. After reviewing the course of the insurrection, the interests of the United States affected thereby, the numerous claims arising therefrom, many of them still unsettled, the persistent refusal of Spain to redress these grievances and the general neglect on her part of treaty obligations, he concluded:

In the absence of any prospect of a termination of the war, or of any change in the manner in which it has been conducted on either side, he (the President) feels that the time is at hand when it may be the duty of other governments to intervene, solely with a view to bringing to an end a disastrous and destructive conflict, and of restoring peace in the island of Cuba. No government is more deeply interested in the order and peaceful administration of this island than is that of the United States, and none has suffered as the United States from the condition which has obtained there during the past six or seven years. He will, therefore, feel it his duty at an early day to submit the subject in this light, and accompanied by an expression of the views above presented, for the consideration of Congress.

Mr. Cushing was instructed to read this note to the Spanish minister of state. At the same time a copy was sent to General Robert C. Schenck, United States minister at London, with instructions to read the same to Lord Derby, and to suggest to him that it would be agreeable to the United States if the British government would support by its influence the position assumed by the Grant administration. In the course of a few days copies of this note were sent to our representatives at Paris, Berlin, Vienna, Rome, Lisbon, and St. Petersburg, with instructions to communicate its purport orally, or by reading the note, to the governments to which they were accredited and to ask their intervention with Spain in the interests of terminating the state of affairs existing in Cuba.

As the result of Mr. Cushing's friendly representations and in view of the President's message discountenancing recognition of either independence or belligerency, the Spanish minister, Mr. Calderon, received the communication of November 5 threatening intervention, in good part, and expressed his intention of answering it after he should have had time to consider it carefully.

The reply of Great Britain was given to General Schenck in an interview with Lord Derby on January 25, 1876. It was in substance that he was convinced that Spain would not listen to mediation, and that the British government was not prepared to bring pressure to bear upon her in case she refused; that the Spanish government hoped to finish the Carlist war in the spring and would then be in a position to put forth its whole military strength for the reduction of Cuba; in conclusion, therefore, Lord Derby thought " that if nothing were contemplated beyond an amicable interposition, having peace for its object, the time was ill-chosen and the move premature." The answers of the other powers were unsatisfactory or evasive, none of them being willing to bring pressure to bear upon the government of young Alfonso, while the Carlist war was on his hands.

The answer of Spain was finally given in the form

of a note dated February 3, 1876, addressed to the representatives of Spain in other countries, including the United States, communicated to Mr. Cushing February 19. This answer, written by Mr. Calderon was in good temper. He stated that the insurrection was supported and carried on largely by negroes, mulattoes, Chinese, deserters, and adventurers; that they carried on a guerrilla warfare from their mountain retreats, that Spain had sufficient forces in the island to defeat them in the field; that the triumph of Spain would soon be followed by the total abolition of slavery and the introduction of administrative reforms. The number of vessels of war and troops in Cuba was enumerated to show that Spain was putting forth a reasonable effort to bring the rebellion to a close, and statistics were quoted to show that the trade between Cuba and the United States, as well as the general trade of the island, had actually increased largely since the outbreak of the insurrection. Finally he declared that while individual foreigners had suffered, Spain had done justice to all claims presented.

In conversation with Mr. Cushing, Mr. Calderon intimated that Spain, although she would resist to the uttermost armed intervention, might be willing under certain circumstances to accept the mediation of the United States in Cuba, and he invited a frank statement of what the United States would advise or wish Spain to do with regard to Cuba. In reply to this suggestion, Mr. Fish, after disclaiming on the part of the United States all intention of annexing Cuba, stated the following points as the wish of his government:

(1) The mutual and reciprocal observance of treaty

obligations, and a full, friendly, and liberal understanding and interpretation of all doubtful treaty provisions, wherever doubt or question might exist.

(2) Peace, order, and good government in Cuba, which involved prompt and effective measures to restore peace, and the establishment of a government suited to the spirit and necessities of the age.

(3) Gradual but effectual emancipation of slaves.

(4) Improvement of commercial facilities and the removal of the obstructions then existing in the way of trade and commerce.

In reply to these suggestions Mr. Calderon handed Mr. Cushing a note, dated April 16, 1876, in which he represented that his majesty's government was in full accord with Mr. Fish's suggestions.

This assurance on the part of the Spanish government completely thwarted Mr. Fish's plans, and, together with Lord Derby's reply, put all further attempts at intervention out of the question.

The substance of Mr. Fish's note threatening intervention appeared unofficially in the press of Europe and America in December, 1875, and attracted such general attention that in January the House asked for the correspondence. In reply Mr. Fish submitted to the President for transmission the note of November 5, together with a few carefully chosen extracts from the correspondence between himself and Mr. Cushing,[43] but nothing was given that might indicate that the United States had appealed to the powers of Europe to countenance intervention. As rumors to this effect had, however, appeared in the press, the House called the next day for whatever correspon-

---

[43] House Ex. Doc. No. 90, Forty-fourth Cong., First Sess.

dence had taken place with foreign powers in regard to Cuba. Mr. Fish replied that "no correspondence has taken place during the past year with any European government, other than Spain, in regard to the island of Cuba," but that the note of November 5 had been orally communicated to several European governments by reading the same.[44] This was putting a very strict and a very unusual construction upon the term "correspondence," to say the least. The dispatches, notes, and telegrams that pass between a government and its representatives abroad are the generally recognized means of communicating with foreign powers, and are always spoken of as the correspondence with those powers. The whole affair reveals a curious lack of candor and of courage on the part of Mr. Fish. He was trying to shield either the administration or himself, and did not wish the American public to know that he had reversed the time-honored policy of the state department by appealing to the powers of Europe to intervene in what had been uniformly treated, from the days of John Quincy Adams and Henry Clay, as a purely American question.

This correspondence was suppressed for twenty years. On March 24, 1896, the Senate called for "copies of all dispatches, notes, and telegrams in the department of state, from and after the note from Secretary Fish to Mr. Cushing of November 5, 1875, and including that note, until the pacification of Cuba in 1878, which relate to mediation or intervention by the United States in the affairs of that island, together with all correspondence with foreign governments relating to the same topic." On April 15 President

[44] House Ex. Doc. No. 100, Forty-fourth Cong., First Sess.

124

Cleveland transmitted the "correspondence" called for, which forms a document of 137 pages.[45]

The Cuban struggle continued for two years longer. In October, 1877, several leaders surrendered to the Spanish authorities and undertook the task of bringing over the few remaining ones. Some of these paid for their efforts with their lives, being taken and condemned by court-martial by order of the commander of the Cuban forces. Finally, in February, 1878, the terms of pacification were made known. They embraced representation in the Spanish Cortes, oblivion of the past in respect of political offenses committed since the year 1868, and the freedom of slaves in the insurgent ranks.[46] In practice, however, the Cuban deputies were never truly representative, but were men of Spanish birth designated usually by the captain-general. By gradual emancipation slavery ceased to exist in the island in 1885. The powers of the captain-general, the most objectionable feature of Spanish rule, continued uncurtailed.

In February, 1895, the final insurrection against Spanish rule in Cuba began, and soon developed the same features as the "Ten Years' War." The policy of Maximo Gomez, the insurrectionary chief, was to fight no pitched battles but to keep up incessant skirmishes, to destroy sugar plantations and every other source of revenue with the end in view of either exhausting Spain or forcing the intervention of the United States. With the opening of the second year of the struggle, General Weyler arrived in Havana as governor and captain-general, and immediately in-

---

[45] Sen. Ex. Doc. No. 213, Fifty-fourth Cong., First Sess.
[46] Sen. Ex. Doc. No. 79, Forty-fifth Cong., Second Sess.

augurated his famous " Reconcentration " policy. The inhabitants of the island were directed by proclamation to assemble within a week in the towns occupied by Spanish troops under penalty, if they refused, of being treated as rebels. The majority of those who obeyed the proclamation were women and children who, as a result of being cooped up in crowded villages under miserable sanitary conditions and without adequate food, died by the thousands.[47] In the province of Havana alone 52,000 perished.

Public opinion in the United States was thoroughly aroused by the execution of policies which not only excited sympathy for the unfortunate inhabitants of Cuba, but which paralyzed the industries of the island and destroyed its commerce. American citizens owned at least fifty millions of property in the island, and American commerce at the beginning of the insurrection amounted to one hundred millions annually. Furthermore, numbers of persons claiming American citizenship were thrown into prison by Weyler's orders. Some of them were native Americans, but the majority were Cubans who had sought naturalization in the United States in order to return to Cuba and claim American protection.

Other Cubans, including many who were still Spanish subjects, established themselves in American ports and furnished the insurgents with arms and supplies. On June 12, 1895, President Cleveland issued a proclamation calling attention to the Cuban insurrection and warning all persons within the jurisdiction of the United States against doing any of the acts prohibited by the American neutrality laws. Notwithstanding

---

[47] Sen. Doc. No. 25, p. 125, Fifty-eighth Cong., Second Sess.

all the efforts of the administration, illegal expeditions were continually being fitted out in the United States, and while the great majority of them were stopped by port officials or intercepted by the navy, some of them succeeded in reaching the coasts of Cuba. President Cleveland's proclamation recognized insurgency as a status distinct from belligerency. It merely put into effect the neutrality laws of the United States. It did not recognize a state of belligerency and therefore did not bring into operation any of the rules of neutrality under international law. President Cleveland consistently refused to recognize the Cubans as belligerents. In February, 1896, Congress passed a joint resolution, by a vote of 64 to 6 in the Senate and 246 to 27 in the House, recognizing a state of war in Cuba, and offering Spain the good offices of the United States for the establishment of Cuban independence. Notwithstanding the overwhelming majority which this resolution had received, the President ignored it, for it is a well recognized principle that Congress has no right to force the hand of the President in a matter of this kind. It amounted merely to an expression of opinion by Congress.

In April, 1896, Secretary Olney addressed a note to the Spanish minister in which the United States offered to mediate between Spain and the insurgents for the restoration of peace on the basis of autonomy. Spain rejected this offer, claiming that Cuba already enjoyed " one of the most liberal political systems in the world," and suggesting that the United States could contribute greatly to the pacification of the island by prosecuting " the unlawful expeditions of some of its citizens to Cuba with more vigor than in the past." [48]   In his last annual message to Congress, President Cleveland reviewed the Cuban situation at length and, in conclusion, declared:

When the inability of Spain to deal successfully with the insurgents has become manifest and it is demonstrated that her sovereignty is extinct in Cuba for all purposes of its rightful existence, and when a hopeless struggle for its reëstablishment has degenerated into a strife which means nothing more than the useless sacrifice of human life and the utter destruction of the very subject-matter of the conflict, a situation will be presented in which our obligations to the sovereignty of Spain will be superseded by higher obligations, which we can hardly hesitate to recognize and discharge.

The McKinley administration, which began March 4, 1897, soon directed its attention to the Cuban question.   It was unfortunate that with this question rapidly approaching a crisis the State Department was in feeble hands.   John Sherman, the veteran senator from Ohio, was appointed secretary of state by McKinley in order to make a place in the Senate for Mark Hanna, who had so successfully conducted Mc-Kinley's campaign.   General Woodford was sent to Madrid to succeed Hannis Taylor, and he was instructed to tender again the good offices of the United States, to remind Spain of the resolution passed by the previous Congress, and to warn her that another Congress was soon to assemble.[49]   Six days after the receipt of General Woodford's note the Spanish ministry resigned, and on October 14 the liberal ministry of Sagasta assumed office.   Its first act was to recall

---

[48] Spanish Dipl. Corresp. and Docs. (translation, Washington, 1905), pp. 7, 8.
[49] Foreign Relations, 1898, p. 568.

General Weyler, and to appoint General Blanco to succeed him as governor and captain-general of Cuba. The new ministry promised to grant autonomy to Cuba, and President McKinley in his message of December 6, 1897, declared his intention of allowing time for the new policy to be tested.

It was soon evident that the grant of autonomy had come too late. The Cubans would no longer be satisfied with anything short of independence. On January 13, 1898, there was serious rioting in Havana, deliberately planned as a demonstration against the autonomy scheme, and Consul-General Fitzhugh Lee cabled his government that it was evident that autonomy would prove a failure, that he doubted whether Blanco could control the situation, and that it might be necessary to send warships for the protection of Americans in Havana. The suggestion as to warships met with a prompter response than General Lee had expected. The United States battleship *Maine* was immediately dispatched to Havana, where she arrived January 25 and was assigned an anchorage by the port officials.[60] While she was lying quietly at anchor in Havana harbor, attention was suddenly diverted from Cuba to Washington by the Dupuy de Lôme incident. On February 9, 1898, the New York *Journal* published in facsimile a letter from the Spanish minister at Washington to a friend in Cuba which severely criticized President McKinley's policy and referred to him as " a would-be politician who tries to leave a door open behind him while keeping on good terms with the jingoes of his party." The letter was genuine, though surreptitiously acquired, and was of such a character

---

[60] Foreign Relations, 1898, p. 1025.

that it could not be overlooked. When called on for an explanation, Señor de Lôme admitted having written the letter but questioned the accuracy of the translation. He claimed that the language which he had used was permissible under the seal of private correspondence. When General Woodford, acting under instructions from Washington, informed the Spanish minister of foreign affairs that the President expected the immediate recall of Señor de Lôme, he was informed that the latter's resignation had already been accepted by cable.[51]

Before the excitement over this incident had subsided, the battleship *Maine* was suddenly blown up in Havana harbor on the night of February 15, and two of her officers and two hundred and fifty-eight of her crew were killed. After a careful examination of witnesses and of the wreck, an American naval court of inquiry reported that the destruction of the ship was due to a submarine mine.[52] A Spanish board of inquiry, after examining a number of witnesses who had seen or heard the explosion, made a brief report the following day to the effect that the ship had been destroyed by an explosion in the forward magazine. It is generally admitted that the American report was correct, but the responsibility for the mine has never been disclosed.

As soon as the report of the court of inquiry was made public, the American people, who had displayed great self-control, threw aside all restraint and the country witnessed an outburst of patriotic fervor such as had not been seen since 1861. "Remember the

[51] Foreign Relations, 1898, pp. 1007-1020.
[52] Sen. Doc. No. 207, Fifty-fifth Cong., Second Sess.

Maine" became a watchword, and the demand for war was overwhelming. President McKinley decided, however, to make one more effort at a diplomatic settlement. He proposed an armistice between Spain and the insurgents pending negotiations for a permanent adjustment through the friendly offices of the President of the United States. In reply the Spanish government made counter-propositions to the effect that the questions arising out of the destruction of the *Maine* be submitted to arbitration and that the pacification of the island be left to a Cuban parliament. Meanwhile, the governor-general would be authorized to accept a suspension of hostilities, provided the insurgents should ask for it and agree to disarm. This was simply an invitation to the insurgents to submit, in which case Spain would consider what degree of autonomy was needed or practicable. The President considered the Spanish reply as a rejection of his proposal and determined to submit the entire question to Congress.[53] This meant war, for public feeling in America was at the highest pitch of excitement, the " yellow " press was clamoring for war, and it was with the greatest difficulty that the President, who really wanted peace, had held Congress in check. The message to Congress was held back a few days in consequence of a telegram from General Lee, who urged that he be given time to get Americans safely out of Havana. During this period of delay the representatives of Germany, Austria-Hungary, France, Great Britain, Italy, and Russia made a formal appeal to the President for peace, and the Pope persuaded the Queen of Spain to authorize General Blanco to sus-

[53] Foreign Relations, 1898, p. 731.

pend hostilities. This concession did not meet fully the American ultimatum and seemed too much like another play for time. The Spanish minister was, therefore, simply informed that the President would notify Congress of this latest communication. President McKinley was later severely criticized for not giving greater consideration to this note and for merely alluding to it in his message instead of transmitting it in full. Had he given it greater consideration, war might have been delayed a few months, but it would not have been averted, for Spain was not willing to make concessions that the Cubans at this late date would have regarded as satisfactory.

In his message to Congress of April 11, 1898, President McKinley referred to the *Maine* only incidentally as " a patent and impressive proof of a state of things in Cuba that is intolerable." He suggested forcible intervention as the only solution of the question and declared that it was justified, not only on grounds of humanity, but as a measure for the protection of the lives and property of American citizens in Cuba, and for the purpose of putting a stop to a conflict which was a constant menace to our peace.[54] Two days later the House passed a resolution by vote of 324 to 19, directing the President to intervene at once to stop the war in Cuba with the purpose of " establishing by the free action of the people thereof a stable and independent government of their own in the island." On the same day the Senate Committee on Foreign Relations reported a resolution demanding the immediate withdrawal of Spain from the Island of Cuba, but the minority report urging in addition the immediate rec-

---

[54] Richardson, " Messages and Papers of the Presidents," Vol. X, p. 147.

ognition of the Cuban republic as then organized was at first embodied in the Senate resolution by a vote of 67 to 21. It was feared by members of the Senate that if we liberated Cuba without first recognizing the so-called republic of Cuba, the island would inevitably be annexed by the United States. After two days of hot debate, the Senate reconsidered, and the House resolution prevailed. On April 19, the anniversary of the battle of Lexington and of the first bloodshed of the Civil War in the streets of Baltimore, the fateful resolutions were adopted in the following terms:

Resolved by the Senate and House of Representatives of the United States in Congress assembled,

First, That the people of the island of Cuba are, and of right ought to be, free and independent.

Second, That it is the duty of the United States to demand, and the Government of the United States does hereby demand, that the Government of Spain at once relinquish its authority and government in the island of Cuba, and withdraw its land and naval forces from Cuban waters.

Third, That the President of the United States be, and he hereby is, directed and empowered to use the entire land and naval forces of the United States, and to call into the actual service of the United States the militia of the several States to such extent as may be necessary to carry these resolutions into effect.

Fourth, That the United States hereby disclaims any disposition or intention to exercise sovereignty, jurisdiction, or control over said island except for the pacification thereof, and asserts its determination, when that is accomplished, to leave the government and control of the island to its people.[55]

As soon as these resolutions were approved by the President, the Spanish minister asked for his pass-

[55] " U. S. Statutes at Large," Vol. XXX, p. 738.

ports, thus severing diplomatic relations, and Woodford was directed to leave Madrid. The North Atlantic Squadron, then at Key West under command of Rear-Admiral William T. Sampson, was immediately ordered to blockade the northern coast of Cuba, and Commodore George Dewey was ordered from Hong Kong to Manila Bay for the purpose of capturing or destroying the Spanish fleet. During the war that followed, foreign public opinion, outside of England, was decidedly hostile to the United States, but in the face of the victories of Santiago and Manila Bay this sentiment underwent a marked change, and Spain abandoned whatever hopes she had cherished of European intervention. By the end of July, 1898, the American as well as the European press was beginning to ask why the war should not be brought to a close.

After the surrender of Santiago General Miles embarked for Porto Rico with a force of 16,000 men, and in a two-weeks' campaign overran most of that island with the loss of three killed and forty wounded. A large number of troops had also been sent to the Philippines. It was evident, therefore, that while the war had been undertaken for the liberation of Cuba, the United States did not feel under any obligation to confine its military operations to that island. Having met all the demands of honor, Spain asked the French government to authorize the French ambassador at Washington to arrange with the President of the United States the preliminary terms of peace. The negotiations begun on July 26 resulted in the protocol of August 12, in which Spain agreed to the following demands: first, the immediate evacuation of Cuba and the relinquishment of Spanish sovereignty; second, the cession of Porto Rico and one of the Ladrones by way of indemnity; and third, the occupation by the United States of "the city, bay and harbor of Manila pending the conclusion of a treaty of peace which shall determine the control, disposition, and government of the Philippines." [56]

By the terms of the protocol Paris was selected as the place of meeting for the peace commissioners, and here negotiations were opened on October 1. The United States delegation was composed of William R. Day, who resigned the office of Secretary of State to head the mission; Cushman K. Davis, Chairman of the Senate Committee on Foreign Relations; William P. Frye, President *pro tem* of the Senate; Senator George Gray of Delaware; and Whitelaw Reid, editor of the New York *Tribune;* with John Bassett Moore, Assistant Secretary of State, as Secretary. An entire month was taken up with the Cuban question, the Spanish commissioners striving in vain to saddle the Cuban debt either on the United States or on the people of Cuba. The Philippine question occupied most of the next month. When the commissioners were appointed, President McKinley had not fully made up his mind on this important question. His first intention seems to have been to retain the bay and city of Manila as a naval base and a part or possibly the whole of Luzon. Public sentiment in the United States in favor of acquiring the whole group made rapid headway, and after an extended trip through the South and West, during which he sounded opinion on this question, the President instructed the

---

[56] Spanish Dipl. Corresp. and Docs., p. 206; Foreign Relations, 1898, p. 819.

commissioners to demand the entire group. The commissioners were later authorized to offer $20,000,000 for the cession. This offer, which was recognized by the Spanish commissioners as an ultimatum, was finally accepted under protest. On other points the United States secured what had been demanded in the protocol, and the treaty was signed December 10, 1898.[57]

The treaty was submitted to the Senate January 4, 1899, and precipitated a memorable debate which lasted until February 6. The principal opposition came from Senator Hoar of Massachusetts, who declared that the proposal to acquire and govern the Philippine Islands was in violation of the Declaration of Independence, the Constitution, and the whole spirit of American institutions. The treaty could not be ratified without the aid of Democrats, and the result was in doubt when Bryan went to Washington and advised his friends in the Senate to vote for ratification, saying that the status of the Philippines could be determined in the next presidential campaign. The outbreak of hostilities between the Filipinos and the American troops occupying Manila put an end to the debate, and on February 6 the treaty was ratified.

When the United States demanded the withdrawal of Spain from Cuba, it was with the declaration that " The United States hereby disclaims any disposition or intention to exercise sovereignty, jurisdiction, or control over said island except for the pacification thereof, and asserts its determination, when that is accomplished, to leave the government and control of the island to its people." Never has a pledge made by

---

[57] Senate Doc. No. 62, Fifty-Fifth Cong., Third Sess.

a nation under such circumstances been more faithfully carried out. The administration of Cuba during the period of American military occupation was a model of its kind. General Leonard Wood, the military governor, and his associates found the cities and towns crowded with refugees and reconcentrados, and governmental affairs in a state of the utmost confusion. They established order, relieved distress, organized hospitals and charitable institutions, undertook extensive public works, reorganized the system of public schools, and put Havana, Santiago, and other cities in a sanitary condition. In a hospital near Havana Major Walter Reed, a surgeon in the United States army, demonstrated the fact that yellow fever is transmitted by the bite of a mosquito. This discovery was at once put to the test in Havana, and the city was rendered free from yellow fever for the first time in one hundred and forty years.[58]

In the organization of a government for the island, the first step was to take a census of the inhabitants, determine the proper basis of suffrage, and hold municipal elections for the purpose of organizing local government. This work having been successfully accomplished, a constitutional convention, summoned by General Wood, convened in the city of Havana, November 5, 1900. By February 21, 1901, the convention had agreed upon a constitution modelled in general after that of the United States. The new constitution provided for the recognition of the public debts contracted by the insurgent government, but was silent on the subject of future relations with the United States. This subject had been brought to the

---

[58] Report of the Military Governor of Cuba, 8 vols., 1901.

attention of the convention early in February by General Wood, who had submitted for incorporation in the constitution certain provisions which had been drafted in Washington. The convention objected to these proposals on the ground that they impaired the independence and sovereignty of the island, and that it was their duty to make Cuba " independent of every other nation, the great and noble American nation included."

The United States, however, had no intention of withdrawing from the island until this matter was satisfactorily adjusted. A provision, known as the Platt Amendment, was therefore inserted in the army appropriation bill of March 2, 1901, directing the President to leave the control of the island to its people so soon as a government should be established under a constitution which defined the future relations with the United States substantially as follows:

I. That the government of Cuba shall never enter into any treaty or other compact with any foreign power or powers which will impair or tend to impair the independence of Cuba, nor in any manner authorize or permit any foreign power or powers to obtain by colonization or for military or naval purposes or otherwise, lodgment in or control over any portion of said island.

II. That said government shall not assume or contract any public debt, to pay the interest upon which, and to make reasonable sinking fund provision for the ultimate discharge of which, the ordinary revenues of the island, after defraying the current expenses of government shall be inadequate.

III. That the government of Cuba consents that the United States may exercise the right to intervene for the preservation of Cuban independence, the maintenance of a government adequate for the protection of life, property, and individual liberty, and for discharging the obligations with respect to Cuba imposed by the treaty of Paris on the United States, now to be assumed and undertaken by the government of Cuba.

IV. That all acts of the United States in Cuba during its military occupancy thereof are ratified and validated, and all lawful rights acquired thereunder shall be maintained and protected.

V. That the government of Cuba will execute, and as far as necessary extend, the plans already devised or other plans to be mutually agreed upon, for the sanitation of the cities of the island. . . .

VI. That the Isle of Pines shall be omitted from the proposed constitutional boundaries of Cuba, the title thereto being left to future adjustment by treaty.

VII. That to enable the United States to maintain the independence of Cuba, and to protect the people thereof, as well as for its own defense, the government of Cuba will sell or lease to the United States lands necessary for coaling or naval stations at certain specified points, to be agreed upon with the President of the United States.

VIII. That by way of further assurance the government of Cuba will embody the foregoing provisions in a permanent treaty with the United States.[59]

These articles, with the exception of the fifth, which was proposed by General Leonard Wood, were carefully drafted by Elihu Root, at that time Secretary of War, discussed at length by President McKinley's cabinet, and entrusted to Senator Platt of Connecticut, who offered them as an amendment to the army appropriation bill. In order to allay doubts expressed by members of the convention in regard to the third article, General Wood was authorized by Secretary Root to state officially that the intervention described in this article did not mean intermeddling in the af-

---

[59] U. S. Statues at Large, Vol. XXXI, p. 897.

fairs of the Cuban government, but formal action on the part of the United States, based upon just and substantial grounds. With this assurance the convention adopted the Platt amendment June 12, 1901, and added it as an appendix to the constitution.

On May 20, 1902, Tomas Estrada Palma was inaugurated as first president of the Republic of Cuba, and General Wood handed over to him the government of the island.[60] The Americans left a substantial balance in the Cuban treasury. The total receipts for the entire period were $57,197,140.80, and the expenditures $55,405,031.28. The customs service, which furnished the principal part of the revenues during the period of military occupation, was ably administered by General Tasker H. Bliss.[61]

While the Platt amendment determined the political relations that were to exist between Cuba and the United States, there had been no agreement on the subject of commercial relations. The sugar industry, which had been almost destroyed by the insurrection, was dependent upon the willingness of the United States to arrange for a reduction of its tariff in favor of the Cuban product. Otherwise Cuban sugar could not compete with the bounty-fed beet sugar of Europe or with the sugars of Porto Rico and Hawaii, which were now admitted to the American market free of duty. President Roosevelt had hoped to settle this question before the withdrawal of American troops, and he had urged upon Congress the expediency of providing for a substantial reduction in tariff duties on

---

[60] Documentary History of the Inauguration of the Cuban Government, in Annual Report of the Secretary of War, 1902, Appendix A.
[61] Documentary History of the Inauguration of the Cuban Government, in Annual Report of the Secretary of War, 1902, Appendix B.

Cuban imports into the United States, but a powerful opposition, composed of the beet-sugar growers of the North and West and of the cane-sugar planters of Louisiana, succeeded in thwarting for two years the efforts of the administration to do justice to Cuba. All attempts to get a bill through Congress failed.[62]

In the meantime a reciprocity convention was agreed upon in the ordinary diplomatic way December 11, 1902, under which Cuban products were to be admitted to the United States at a reduction of twenty per cent. As the Senate failed to act on this treaty before the 4th of March, 1903, President Roosevelt convened an extra session of the Senate which ratified the treaty with amendments, and with the very unusual provision that it should not go into effect until approved by Congress. As the House was not then in session, this meant that the treaty had to go over until the fall. The Cuban situation grew so bad that the President finally convened Congress in extra session November 9, 1903. In a special message he urged prompt action on the treaty on the ground that the Platt amendment had brought the island of Cuba within our system of international policy, and that it necessarily followed that it must also to a certain degree come within the lines of our economic policy. The House passed the bill approving the treaty November 19 by the overwhelming vote of 335 to 21, but the Senate, although it had already ratified the treaty, permitted the extra session to expire without passing the measure which was to give the treaty effect. When the new session began December 7, the Cuban treaty bill was made the special order in the

[62] Senate Docs. Nos. 405 and 679, Fifty-Seventh Cong., First Sess.

Senate until December 16, when the final vote was taken and it passed. Under the reciprocity treaty commercial relations with Cuba were established on a firm basis and the volume of trade increased rapidly.

In August, 1906, President Palma was reëlected for another term, but the Cubans had not learned the primary lesson of democracy, submission to the will of the majority, and his opponents at once began an insurrectionary movement which had for its object the overthrow of his government. About the middle of September President Roosevelt sent Secretary Taft to Havana for the purpose of reconciling the contending factions, but Mr. Taft's efforts proved unavailing and President Palma resigned. When the Cuban Congress assembled, it was found impossible to command a quorum. Under these circumstances Secretary Taft assumed control of affairs on September 29 and proclaimed a provisional government for the restoration of order and the protection of life and property. A body of United States troops under command of General Franklin Bell was sent to Cuba to preserve order and to uphold the provisional government. On October 3, 1906, Secretary Taft was relieved of the duties of provisional governor in order that he might resume his duties in Washington, and Charles E. Magoon was appointed to take his place at Havana.[63] In his message to Congress December 3, 1906, President Roosevelt declared that while the United States had no desire to annex Cuba, it was " absolutely out of the question that the island should continue independent " if the " insurrectionary habit "

---

[63] Secretary Taft's report on the Cuban situation was sent to Congress December 17, 1906.

should become " confirmed." The second period of American occupation lasted a little over two years, when the control of the government was again restored to the people of the island and the American troops were withdrawn.

CHAPTER IV

The Diplomatic History of the Panama Canal

The cutting of the isthmus between North and South America was the dream of navigators and engineers from the time when the first discoverers ascertained that nature had neglected to provide a passage. Yet the new continent which so unexpectedly blocked the way of Columbus in his search for the Indies opposed for centuries an insurmountable barrier to the commerce of the East and the West. The piercing of the isthmus always seemed a perfectly feasible undertaking, but the difficulties in the way proved greater than at first sight appeared. There were (1) the physical or engineering problems to be solved, and (2) the diplomatic complications regarding the control of the canal in peace and its use in war. The weakness of the Spanish-American states, whose territories embraced the available routes, and their recognized inability either to construct or protect a canal made what might otherwise have been merely a question of domestic economy one of grave international import. In this respect, as in others, the problem presented the same features as the Suez canal. To meet these difficulties three plans were successively developed during the nineteenth century: (1) a canal constructed by a private corporation under international control, (2) a canal constructed by a private corporation under the exclusive control of the United States, and (3) a canal constructed, owned, operated, and controlled by the United States as a government enterprise. The Clayton-Bulwer treaty provided for the construction of a canal in accordance with the first plan; several unsuccessful attempts were made to raise the necessary capital under the second plan; while the third plan was the one under which the gigantic task was actually accomplished.

The comparative merits of the Nicaragua and Panama routes long divided the opinion of experts. American engineers generally favored that through Nicaragua. The length of the Nicaragua route, from Greytown on the Atlantic to Brito on the Pacific by way of the San Juan river and through Lake Nicaragua, is about 170 miles. The elevation of the lake above the sea is about 110 feet. Its western shore is only twelve miles from the Pacific, with an intervening divide 154 feet above the sea. From the southeast corner of the lake flows the San Juan river, 120 miles to the Atlantic, with an average fall of about 10 inches to the mile. The serious objections to this route are: (1) the lack of harbors at the terminals, Brito being a mere indentation on the coast, rendering the construction of immense breakwaters necessary, while at Greytown the San Juan broadens out into a delta that would require extensive dredging; and (2) the enormous rainfall at Greytown, exceeding that known anywhere else on the western continent—nearly 25 feet.

The Panama route from Colon on the Atlantic to Panama on the Pacific is about 50 miles in length, with a natural elevation nearly double that of Nicaragua. There are natural harbors at each end which are capacious and able to accommodate the heaviest shipping. The Panama Railroad, built along the line of the proposed canal, in 1850-55, gave this route an additional advantage. There were, however, certain disadvantages: (1) the unhealthfulness of the vicinity, rendering labor scarce and inefficient; (2) the heavy rainfall, 10 to 12 feet at Colon; and (3) the treacherous character of the geologic structure, due to its volcanic origin, through which the cut had to be made. The impossibility of making even approximate estimates of the cost of the work in such a deadly climate and through such an uncertain geologic formation was one of the greatest difficulties to be overcome. The De Lesseps plan provided for an open cut throughout at the sea-level, at an estimated cost of $170,000,-000. The work was begun in 1884 and prosecuted until 1888, when the gigantic scheme collapsed, after the company had expended about $300,000,000 and accomplished less than one-third of the work.

Great as the engineering problems of the various canal schemes have been shown to be, the importance to the world's commerce of the object in view would, in all probability, have led to their solution and to the construction of a canal long before the United States undertook the Panama enterprise, had it not been for difficulties of an altogether different character, complications arising out of the question as to the status of the canal in international law. The diplomatic difficulties in the case of an interoceanic canal are very great. It cannot be regarded as a natural strait, like the Dardanelles, the Danish Belts, or the Straits of Magellan, which were for a long time held under exclusive jurisdiction, but are now free to all nations. Nor, on the other hand, could an isthmian canal be compared to the Kiel canal, which is within the territory of Germany, and which, although open to commerce, was specially designed to meet the needs of the German navy. Such canals as this are built by the capital of the country through which they pass, and are protected and controlled by its government.

No one of the republics to the south of us, through whose territory it was proposed to build a canal, could raise the capital for its construction or insure its protection when completed. No company chartered by one of these governments could have raised the necessary capital without some further guarantee. Hence it was that all companies organized for this purpose had to secure their charters from some more powerful nation, such as the United States or France, and their concessions from one of the Central American states. This rendered necessary a treaty between the state granting the concession or right to construct a canal through its territory and the state chartering the company. The claims of other states to equality of treatment in the use of such a canal constituted another element that had to be considered.

With the establishment of the independence of the Spanish-American republics the question of the construction of a ship canal across the isthmus became a matter of general interest, and it was one of the proposed subjects of discussion at the Congress of American Republics summoned by Bolivar to meet at Panama in 1826. In the instructions to the United States commissioners to that congress, Mr. Clay authorized them to enter into the consideration of that subject, suggesting that the best routes would likely be found in the territory of Mexico or of the Central Republic. As to the diplomatic status of the canal, he said:

If the work should ever be executed so as to admit of the passage of sea vessels from ocean to ocean, the benefits of it ought not to be exclusively appropriated to any one nation, but should be extended to all parts of the globe upon the payment of a just compensation or reasonable tolls.[1]

In 1835, and again in 1839, the United States Senate passed resolutions authorizing the President to enter into negotiations with other nations, particularly Central America and New Granada, for the purpose of protecting by treaty either individuals or companies who might undertake to open communication between the two oceans, and of insuring " the free and equal navigation of the canal by all nations." Presidents Jackson and Van Buren both commissioned agents with a view to carrying out these resolutions, but without success.

While a prisoner at Ham in 1845, Prince Louis Napoleon Bonaparte secured from the government of Nicaragua a concession granting him power to organize a company for the construction of a waterway to be known as " Le Canale Napoléon de Nicaragua." After his escape from Ham, he published in London a pamphlet entitled " The Canal of Nicaragua, or a Project for the Junction of the Atlantic and Pacific Oceans by means of a Canal." [2]

Although the United States government was a party to endless negotiations in regard to an inter-oceanic canal, there were only three treaties of any practical

---

[1] Report of International American Conference, Vol. IV (Hist. App.), p. 143.
[2] Snow: " Treaties and Topics in American Diplomacy," p. 328.

importance prior to the close of the nineteenth century, by which it acquired rights and assumed obligations on that account.[3] These were (1) the treaty with New Granada (Colombia) of 1846; (2) the Clayton-Bulwer treaty with England of 1850; and (3) the treaty with Nicaragua of 1867. We shall proceed to examine these in detail.

The treaty with New Granada was signed at Bogota, December 12, 1846, and ratified by both governments in 1848. It did not differ materially from the general draft of treaties, except in the thirty-fifth article, which was of a special character and related to the Isthmus of Panama. By this article " the government of New Granada guarantees to the government of the United States that the right-of-way or transit across the Isthmus of Panama, upon any modes of communication that now exist or that may be hereafter constructed, shall be open and free to the government and citizens of the United States," for the transportation of all articles of lawful commerce upon the same terms enjoyed by the citizens of New Granada.

And in order to secure to themselves the tranquil and constant enjoyment of these advantages, and for the favors they have acquired by the 4th, 5th, and 6th articles of this treaty, the United States guarantee positively and efficaciously to New Granada, by the present stipulation, the perfect neutrality of the before-mentioned isthmus, with the view that the free transit from the one to the other sea may not be interrupted or embarrassed in any future time while this treaty exists; and, in consequence, the United States also guarantee, in the same manner, the rights of sovereignty and

[3] Our treaties with Mexico and Honduras, although covering the case of canal constructions, were of no practical importance, as the routes through these countries were not feasible.

property which New Granada has and possesses over the said territory.[4]

This treaty was to remain in force for twenty years, and then, if neither party gave notice of intended termination, it was to continue in force, terminable by either party at twelve months' notice. This treaty was in full force when the Panama revolution of 1903 took place. Under the protection of this treaty the Panama Railroad Company, composed mainly of citizens of the United States, secured a charter from New Granada, and between 1850 and 1855 constructed a railroad across the isthmus along the line of the proposed Panama canal. In consequence of the riot at Panama in 1856, efforts were made by the United States to modify this treaty so as to give the United States greater control and power to protect the means of transit, but without success.[5] Other attempts to modify it in 1868 and 1870 likewise failed.[6]

In 1862 the Granadian government, through its representative at Washington, notified the United States that a revolutionary chief, who was then trying to subvert the Granadian confederation, had sent an armed force to occupy the Isthmus of Panama, and the government of Granada called upon the United States to enforce its guarantee. Simultaneously the same information was received from the United States consul at Panama, and the President instructed the United States naval commander at that port to protect at all hazards and at whatever cost the safety of the railroad transit across the isthmus.

---

[4] Correspondence in relation to the Proposed Interoceanic Canal, the Clayton-Bulwer Treaty, and the Monroe Doctrine. Government Printing Office, 1885, p. 5. Referred to hereafter as "Collected Correspondence."
[5] *Ibid.*, pp. 23-27.
[6] *Ibid.*, pp. 27 and 40.

The Granadian government, however, was not satisfied with this action, and urged the United States to land a body of troops at Panama, suggesting that it consist of 300 cavalry. Under the circumstances, President Lincoln hesitated to take such action without consulting Great Britain and France, and Mr. Seward instructed our representatives at London and Paris to seek an understanding with those governments in regard to the matter. He declared:

This government has no interest in the matter different from that of other maritime powers. It is willing to interpose its aid in execution of its treaty and for the benefit of all nations. But if it should do so it would incur some hazard of becoming involved in the revolutionary strife which is going on in that country. It would also incur danger of misapprehension of its object by other maritime powers if it should act without previous consultation with them.[7]

In a conference between Mr. Adams and Lord John Russell, the latter declared that he did not consider that the contingency had arisen which called for intervention; that so far as he could learn, no attempt had been made to obstruct the free transit across the isthmus. The French government took substantially the same view.[8] In questions of a similar nature that arose later, the attorney-general of the United States expressed the opinion that the guarantee by the United States of Granadian sovereignty and property in the territory of the isthmus was only against foreign governments, and did not authorize the United States to take sides with one or the other party in the intestine troubles of that nation.

---

[7] Seward to Adams, July 11, 1862.
[8] " Collected Correspondence," pp. 7 and 8

In April, 1885, the Colombian government, which was embarrassed by civil war, called upon the United States for the fulfillment of the treaty of 1846, to secure the neutrality and sovereignty of the isthmus. President Cleveland at once sent a body of troops to the isthmus with instructions to confine their action to preventing the transit and its accessories from being interrupted or embarrassed. As soon as peace was reëstablished, the troops of the United States were withdrawn.[9]

Four years after the signature of the above treaty with Colombia, and two years after its ratification by the Senate, the United States and Great Britain executed what is popularly known as the Clayton-Bulwer treaty. It is of great importance to understand clearly the circumstances under which this treaty was negotiated.

For very obvious reasons, the Isthmus of Panama was for many years the objective point of all canal schemes, but as the engineering difficulties of this route began to be fully appreciated, attention was directed more and more to that through Nicaragua. The occupation by Great Britain, under the assumption of a protectorate, of the territory about the mouth of the San Juan river, which belonged to Nicaragua and Costa Rica, and in which the Atlantic terminus of the canal would fall, was a source of no little uneasiness and perplexity to the United States. In June, 1849, Mr. Hise, chargé d'affaires of the United States in Central America, negotiated without the authorization or knowledge of his government, a treaty with

---

[9] Mr. Scruggs to Mr. Bayard, April 16, 1885, For. Rel., also " Messages and Papers of the Presidents," Vol. VIII, p. 326.

Nicaragua which gave the United States exclusive rights in the construction of a canal through the territory of that state.[10] This treaty was not submitted to the Senate, but was made use of in the negotiations that were opened shortly thereafter with Great Britain for the purpose of ousting her from her position of control over the mouth of the San Juan. A few months later, September 28, 1849, Mr. Squier signed with Honduras a treaty which ceded Tiger Island, in the Bay of Fonseca, to the United States, thus giving us a naval station on the Pacific side of the isthmus. This treaty, like that negotiated by Mr. Hise, was unauthorized and never submitted to the Senate.[11] Both treaties were used, however, in bringing England to the signature of the Clayton-Bulwer treaty. This activity in treaty-making was occasioned by the acquisition of California and the rush to the gold fields by way of the isthmus.

During the period that elapsed between Mr. Bancroft's withdrawal from London and Mr. Lawrence's arrival as the representative of the United States, Mr. Clayton instructed Mr. Rives, who was on his way to Paris, to stop in London and hold a conference with Lord Palmerston on the Central American question. At this date the United States was striving simply for equal rights in any waterway that might be opened through the isthmus and not for any exclusive rights. Mr. Rives declared to Lord Palmerston " that citizens of the United States had entered into a contract with the state of Nicaragua to open, on certain conditions, a communication between the Atlantic and Pacific

---

[10] " Collected Correspondence," p. 94.
[11] *Ibid.*, p. 14.

oceans by the river San Juan and the Nicaragua lake; that the government of the United States, after the most careful investigation of the subject, had come undoubtedly to the conclusion that upon both legal and historical grounds the state of Nicaragua was the true territorial sovereign of the river San Juan as well as of the Nicaragua lake, and that it was, therefore, bound to give its countenance and support, by all proper and reasonable means, to rights lawfully derived by their citizens under a grant from that sovereign." He further said:

That the United States would not, if they could, obtain any exclusive right or privilege in a great highway, which naturally belonged to all mankind, for they well knew that the possession of any such privilege would expose them to inevitable jealousies and probable controversies which would make it infinitely more costly than advantageous; that while they aimed at no exclusive privilege for themselves, they could never consent to see so important a communication fall under the exclusive control of any other great commercial power; that we were far from imputing to Her Britannic Majesty's government any views of that kind, but Mosquito possession at the mouth of the San Juan could be considered in no other light than British possession, and his lordship would readily comprehend that such a state of things, so long as it was continued, must necessarily give rise to dissatisfaction and distrust on the part of other commercial powers.[12]

The negotiations thus opened by Mr. Rives were continued by Mr. Lawrence upon his arrival in England, but were shortly thereafter transferred to Washington, where Mr. Clayton succeeded in arranging with Sir Henry Lytton Bulwer the terms of a convention which was signed April 19, 1850. The inten-

---

[12] "Collected Correspondence," pp. 11 and 12.

tion of the two governments, as declared in the preamble, was to set forth "their views and intentions with reference to any means of communication by ship canal which may be constructed between the Atlantic and Pacific oceans by the way of the river San Juan de Nicaragua, and either or both of the lakes of Nicaragua or Managua, to any port or place on the Pacific ocean."

By the first article Great Britain and the United States bound themselves never to obtain or maintain any exclusive control over the said ship canal; never to erect or maintain any fortifications commanding the same or in the vicinity thereof, or to colonize or exercise dominion over Nicaragua, Costa Rica, the Mosquito coast, or any part of Central America; and never to make use of any alliance, connection or influence with any of these states to obtain any unequal advantages in regard to commerce or navigation through the said canal.

The second article provided for the neutralization of the canal in the event of war between the contracting parties. The third guaranteed protection for the persons and property of the parties legally undertaking the construction of the canal. The fourth related to gaining the consent of the states whose territory the canal should traverse. The fifth article provided for the neutralization and protection of the canal so long as it was managed without discrimination against either of the contracting parties, and stipulated that neither of them would withdraw its protection without giving the other six months' notice. In the sixth article the contracting parties promised to invite every state with which they were on terms of friendly intercourse to accede to this convention. In the seventh article the contracting parties agreed to lend their support and encouragement to the first company offering to construct the canal in accordance with the spirit and intention of this convention. The eighth article was of special importance. It declared that "the governments of the United States and Great Britain having not only desired, in entering into this convention, to accomplish a particular object, but also to establish a general principle, they hereby agree to extend their protection, by treaty stipulations, to any other practicable communication, whether by canal or railway, across the isthmus which connects North and South America, and especially to the interoceanic communications, should the same prove practicable, whether by canal or railway, which are now proposed to be established by the way of Tehuantepec or Panama." [13]

Such are the main stipulations of the celebrated Clayton-Bulwer treaty, which remained in force until 1901, and which during that period probably called forth more discussion than any treaty which the United States had ever signed.

In after years a large number of people on this side of the Atlantic, forgetting the object and aim of the treaty and the circumstances under which it was negotiated, thought that the United States conceded too much and violated the principle of the Monroe Doctrine in giving England a position and interest in America which she did not before possess. This opinion was held by some prominent statesmen at the time the treaty was negotiated, notably by Buchanan, who poured forth severe criticism and ridicule upon

---

[13] "Collected Correspondence," p. 99.

it. While it was before the Senate for ratification, he wrote to a friend:

> If Sir Henry Bulwer can succeed in having the two first provisions of this treaty ratified by the Senate, he will deserve a British peerage. The consideration for our concessions is the relinquishment of the claim to the protectorate of the Mosquito shore—so absurd and unfounded that it has been ridiculed even by the London *Times*. Truly Sir Henry has brought this claim to a good market when he found a purchaser in Mr. Clayton. The treaty altogether reverses the Monroe Doctrine, and establishes it against ourselves rather than European governments.[14]

Let us see what the interests of the two signatory powers were at that time in Central America. The United States had recently acquired California by the treaty of Guadalupe Hidalgo, and the rapid development of the Pacific states made the canal a question of greater importance to the United States than ever before. The great transcontinental railroads, which some fifteen years later established direct overland communication with the Pacific states, were then hardly thought of.

England's interest in the canal, on the other hand, was rather a prospective one, but farsighted as usual, she had provided for future contingencies by occupying several years before, under the guise of a protectorate over the Mosquito Indians, Greytown at the mouth of the San Juan river, the Atlantic terminus of the canal. In addition to the Mosquito coast, England at this time held the Bay Islands and Belize, or British Honduras. The United States, it is true, had

[14] Mr. Buchanan to Hon. John A. McClernand, April 2, 1850, "American Hist. Rev.," Oct., 1899.

never recognized the claims of Great Britain to dominion over the Mosquito coast. These claims, which dated back to the eighteenth century, when British wood-cutters in search of mahogany, and smugglers entered the territory occupied by the Mosquito Indians and established cordial relations with them, had been abandoned by the treaty of 1786 with Spain, but were revived in 1841, when a ship of war was sent to San Juan del Norte to announce the protection of England over the lands of the Mosquito king and to raise the Mosquito flag.[15] In 1848 the English and Indians drove the Nicaraguans out of the town and changed the name to Greytown.

The United States uniformly denied the rights of the Mosquito king to sovereignty over the district, and consequently the pretensions of the inhabitants of Greytown to political organization or power derived in any way from the Mosquitos. In his instructions to Mr. Hise soon after the occupation of Greytown, Secretary Buchanan said:

The object of Great Britain in this seizure is evident from the policy which she has uniformly pursued throughout her history, of seizing upon every available commercial point in the world whenever circumstances have placed it in her power. Her purpose probably is to obtain control of the route for a railroad or canal between the Atlantic and Pacific oceans by way of Lake Nicaragua. . . . The government of the United States has not yet determined what course it will pursue in regard to the encroachment of the British government. . . . The independence as well as the interests of the nations on this continent require that they should maintain an American system of policy entirely distinct from that which prevails in Europe. To suffer any interference on the part of the European governments with the domestic concerns of the American republics, and to permit them to establish new colonies upon this continent, would be to jeopard their independence and ruin their interests. These truths ought everywhere throughout this continent to be impressed upon the public mind; but what can the United States do to resist such European interference whilst the Spanish-American republics continue to weaken themselves by civil divisions and civil war, and deprive themselves of doing anything for their own protection.

Whatever the rights of the case, Great Britain was in actual possession of the Atlantic terminus of the proposed canal, and the United States was not prepared forcibly to oust her, even if such a course had been deemed advisable. The United States had no rights in the case at this time by treaty with Nicaragua or otherwise, none of the statesmen of that day having been broad enough in their views or bold enough to consider the territory of Nicaragua as "a part of the coast-line of the United States." All that could be opposed to England's *de facto* possession was the Monroe Doctrine, and England held that her claim antedated the declaration of that principle of American diplomacy. Mr. Clayton cannot, therefore, be justly charged with a violation of the Monroe Doctrine, for the effect of the treaty was to leave England weaker territorially on this continent than she was before.

The Clayton-Bulwer treaty left open several minor questions that required adjustment before the canal enterprise could be pushed forward with success. Chief among these were the dispute between Nicaragua and Costa Rica in regard to their boundary line and the controversy between Great Britain and Nicaragua in regard to the territory claimed by the

Mosquito Indians. In April, 1852, Mr. Webster and Sir John Crampton agreed upon a basis for the settlement of Central American affairs, and drew up and signed a proposal to be submitted to Nicaragua and Costa Rica.[16] This proposed basis for a treaty was rejected by Nicaragua, which left the questions involved in the same unsettled position.

A much more serious obstacle to the accomplishment of the objects of the Clayton-Bulwer treaty than the failure of the above proposal arose from the wide divergence of opinion between the British and American governments in regard to its interpretation. The discussion involved two principal points: (1) Whether the abnegatory clauses of the first article were merely prospective in character and directed against future acquisitions in Central America, or whether they required Great Britain to abandon her protectorate over the Mosquito coast at once; and (2) whether the Bay Islands came within the purview of the treaty. It was expressly stipulated that Belize or British Honduras was not included in Central America and therefore not affected by the treaty one way or the other. A declaration to this effect was filed at the state department by the British minister, Sir Henry Bulwer. In reply, Mr. Clayton, after conference with the chairman of the Senate committee on foreign relations, acknowledged that British Honduras did not come within the scope of the treaty, but at the same time carefully refrained from affirming or denying the British title to that settlement or its alleged dependencies.[17] This left open the question as to whether the

---

[16] " Collected Correspondence," p 102.
[17] *Ibid.*, p. 234, also Wharton's Digest, Vol. II, p. 190.

Bay Islands were dependencies of Belize or of the Republic of Honduras.

Shortly after the failure of the Crampton-Webster proposals, Great Britain took advantage of the uncertainty that existed in regard to the status of the Bay Islands and by a formal proclamation, issued July 17, 1852, converted her settlements on those islands into " The Colony of the Bay Islands." When the United States government expressed its surprise at this proceeding, the British government replied that the Bay Islands were dependencies of Her Majesty's settlement at Belize and therefore, by explicit agreement, not within the scope of the Clayton-Bulwer treaty.[18]

In 1856 an effort was made to terminate the difficulties arising out of the different constructions put upon the Clayton-Bulwer treaty by the negotiation of a supplementary convention. On October 17 of that year a treaty was signed in London by the American minister and Lord Clarendon, known as the Dallas-Clarendon treaty. It provided (1) for the withdrawal of the British protectorate over the Mosquito Indians; (2) it regulated the boundaries of the Belize settlements on the basis of a compromise; and (3) it provided for a cession of the Bay Islands to Honduras, upon condition of the ratification of a treaty already negotiated between Great Britain and Honduras, which virtually erected an independent state of the islands, exempt in many particulars from the sovereignty of Honduras, and under the protectorate of Great Britain.

The first two clauses were acceptable to the United

---

[18] " Collected Correspondence," p. 248.

States Senate, but it was deemed proper to amend the third by striking out all that part of it which contemplated the concurrence of the United States in the British treaty with Honduras, and simply to provide for a recognition by the two governments of the sovereignty of Honduras over the islands in question.[19] Great Britain rejected this amendment and the Dallas-Clarendon treaty fell through. Great Britain and the United States were thus thrown back upon the Clayton-Bulwer treaty with its conflicting interpretations.

In October, 1857, the President was notified informally that the British government had decided to dispatch Sir Wm. Ouseley, a diplomatist of well-recognized authority and experience, to Central America to make a definite settlement of all matters in dispute between the United States and England; that the efforts of the new plenipotentiary would be directed to those objects which had been dealt with in the Dallas-Clarendon treaty of 1856, viz., the cession of the Bay Islands to Honduras, the substitution of the sovereignty of Nicaragua for the protectorate of England over the Mosquitos and the regulation of the frontiers of Belize; that it was the intention of Her Majesty's government to carry the Clayton-Bulwer treaty into execution according to the general tenor of the interpretation put upon it by the United States, but to do so by separate negotiation with the Central American republics, in lieu of a direct engagement with the federal government.[20]

President Buchanan replied that he would be satis-

[19] " Collected Correspondence," p. 286.
[20] *Ibid.*, p. 262-263.

fied with this course and that upon receiving an official assurance to that effect, he would change the character of the message he had already prepared for Congress. On the 30th of November, 1857, the British government submitted to the United States the alternative of referring the Clayton-Bulwer treaty to the arbitration of any European power which the United States might prefer to select or of adjusting matters by negotiations with the Central American republics, as already outlined in Sir William Ouseley's prospective mission.[21]

At this stage of the negotiations matters were further complicated (1) by the negotiation of the Cass-Yrissari treaty of November 16, 1857, between the United States and Nicaragua for protection of the transit route and (2) by the invasion of Nicaraguan territory by a band of filibusters under General Walker, bent on the subversion of the lawful government of the country. The treaty was not ratified, however, and the Walker expedition was arrested by the interposition of the United States navy.

The United States government not having given any definite answer to the British proposal to submit the treaty to arbitration, the British government delayed dispatching Sir William Ouseley on his mission. In the negotiations which took place during this delay the question of the abrogation of the Clayton-Bulwer treaty was discussed between the two governments. In his message of December 8, 1857, President Buchanan had suggested the abrogation of the treaty by mutual consent as the wisest course that could be pursued in view of the increasing complica-

---

[21] *Ibid.*, p. 276.

tions to which the varying constructions of it were giving rise. The British government took up this suggestion and expressed its willingness to concur in such a course, but also expressed the opinion that the initiative should be taken by the government which was dissatisfied with its provisions.

The British minister was, however, directed by his government to make it perfectly clear to the government of the United States, that to abrogate the treaty was to return to the *status quo ante* its conclusion in 1850; that Great Britain had no kind of jealousy respecting American colonization in Central America, and did not ask or wish for any exclusive privileges whatever in that quarter.[22] Finally, Sir William Ouseley was dispatched on his mission and during the years 1859 and 1860 succeeded in negotiating treaties with Guatemala, Honduras, and Nicaragua, the provisions of which were in substantial accord with the rejected Dallas-Clarendon treaty.[23]

The treaty with Nicaragua signed at Managua, January 28, 1860, though restoring to that republic nominal sovereignty over the Mosquito territory, reserved to the Indians the right of retaining their own customs, assigned boundaries to that reservation in all probability greatly beyond its true limits, and confirmed grants of land previously made in that territory. Notwithstanding these facts, in his annual message of December 3, 1860, President Buchanan declared that the United States government was satisfied with the final settlement. His words were:

---

[22] " Collected Correspondence," p. 280.
[23] *Ibid.*, pp. 294-302.

The discordant constructions of the Clayton-Bulwer treaty between the two governments, which at different periods of the discussion bore a threatening aspect, have resulted in a final settlement entirely satisfactory to this government.[24]

The Clayton-Bulwer treaty was negotiated with the expectation that the construction of a ship canal would rapidly follow, but the unfortunate entanglements that grew out of the variant constructions put upon that treaty by the contracting powers deferred to an indefinite period the accomplishment of the object it was designed to promote. By the time these differences were adjusted the attention of the American public was centered upon the first throes of the gigantic struggle of the war of secession and the canal question was for several years completely overshadowed. The government of the United States emerged from that struggle with larger ideas of its position among the powers of the world and with broader views of national policy. Mr. Seward gave expression to that feeling in the purchase of Alaska, in his interposition in Mexico and in his efforts to secure a position for the United States in the West Indies. In order to strengthen the position of the United States he wished to purchase Tiger Island, a possession of Honduras in Fonseca bay on the Pacific coast. As this island lay in Central America, Mr. Seward could not take any steps in the matter without the consent of Great Britain, on account of the renunciatory clause with respect to that territory in the Clayon-Bulwer treaty. He, therefore, directed Mr. Adams, April 25, 1866, to sound Lord Clarendon as to the disposition of the British government toward the United States acquir-

---

[24] "Messages and Papers of the Presidents," Vol. V, p. 639.

ing a coaling station in Central America. In this dispatch we find the first suggestion of a repudiation of the Clayton-Bulwer treaty on the ground that it was a special and not a general contract, and that the work for which it had been negotiated had never been undertaken. Mr. Seward uses these words:

At the time the treaty was concluded there was every prospect that that work would not only soon be begun, but that it would be carried to a successful conclusion. For reasons, however, which it is not necessary to specify, it never was even commenced, and at present there does not appear to be a likelihood of its being undertaken. It may be a question, therefore, supposing that the canal should never be begun, whether the renunciatory clauses of the treaty are to have perpetual operation. Technically speaking, this question might be decided in the negative. Still, so long as it should remain a question, it would not comport with good faith for either party to do anything which might be deemed contrary to even the spirit of the treaty.[26]

The subject was brought to the attention of Lord Clarendon in a casual way by Mr. Adams, but it was not pressed and Mr. Seward refrained from disregarding the renunciatory clause of the treaty.

In 1867, a treaty between the United States and Nicaragua, covering the case of an interoceanic canal, was negotiated and ratified by both parties. It granted to the United States the right of transit between the Atlantic and Pacific oceans on any lines of communication, natural or artificial, by land or by water, then existing, or that might thereafter be constructed, upon equal terms with the citizens of Nicaragua, and the United States agreed to extend its protection to all

---

[26] " Collected Correspondence," p. 303.

such routes of communication, and "to guarantee the neutrality and innocent use of the same." The United States further agreed to employ its influence with other nations to induce them to guarantee such neutrality and protection.[26]

This treaty, like the treaty with Colombia of 1846 and the Clayton-Bulwer treaty, contemplated the neutralization of the canal. It in no way infringed our engagements with England under the Clayton-Bulwer treaty, but in providing for the joint guarantee of other powers, was in accord with the provisions of that treaty.

In 1873, Mr. Hamilton Fish directed General Schenck to remonstrate, if upon investigation he found it to be necessary, against British encroachments upon the territory of Guatemala as an infringement of the Clayton-Bulwer treaty.[27]

In spite of the doubts expressed by Mr. Seward in the dispatch to Mr. Adams above quoted, as to the perpetual character of the obligations imposed by the Clayton-Bulwer treaty, the obligatory force of that instrument after the readjustment of 1860 was not seriously questioned until interest in the canal question was suddenly aroused anew by the concession granted by Colombia to Lieutenant Wyse in 1878, and the subsequent organization of a French construction company under the presidency of Ferdinand de Lesseps, the promoter of the Suez canal.

The prospect of the speedy construction of a canal under French control, for which De Lesseps' name seemed a sufficient guarantee, produced a sudden and

---

[26] "Collected Correspondence," p. 132.
[27] *Ibid.*, pp. 310-12.

radical change of policy on the part of the United States. In a special message to Congress, March 8, 1880, President Hayes made the following statement of what he conceived to be the true policy of this country in regard to a Central American canal:

The policy of this country is a canal under American control. The United States cannot consent to the surrender of this control to any European power, or to any combination of European powers. If existing treaties between the United States and other nations, or if the rights of sovereignty or property of other nations stand in the way of this policy—a contingency which is not apprehended—suitable steps should be taken by just and liberal negotiations to promote and establish the American policy on this subject, consistently with the rights of the nations to be affected by it.

The capital invested by corporations or citizens of other countries in such an enterprise must, in a great degree, look for protection to one or more of the great powers of the world. No European power can intervene for such protection without adopting measures on this continent which the United States would deem wholly inadmissible. If the protection of the United States is relied upon, the United States must exercise such control as will enable this country to protect its national interests and maintain the rights of those whose private capital is embarked in the work.

An interoceanic canal across the American isthmus will essentially change the geographical relations between the Atlantic and Pacific coasts of the United States, and between the United States and the rest of the world. It will be the great ocean thoroughfare between our Atlantic and our Pacific shores, and virtually a part of the coast-line of the United States. Our merely commercial interest in it is greater than that of all other countries, while its relation to our power and prosperity as a nation, to our means of defense, our unity, peace, and safety, are matters of paramount concern to the people of the United States. No other great power would, under similar circumstances, fail to assert a rightful control over a work so closely and vitally affecting its interests and welfare.

Without urging further the grounds of my opinion, I repeat, in conclusion, that it is the right and the duty of the United States to assert and maintain such supervision and authority over any interoceanic canal across the isthmus that connects North and South America as will protect our national interests. This I am quite sure will be found not only compatible with, but promotive of, the widest and most permanent advantage to commerce and civilization.[28]

The message itself was accompanied by a report from the secretary of state, Mr. Evarts, in which he called attention to the mutual engagements entered into between the United States and Colombia by the treaty of 1846 in reference to a transit route across the isthmus and declared that the guarantee of the neutrality of the isthmus and of the sovereignty of Colombia over the same would be a very different thing when the isthmus should be opened to the interests and ambitions of the great commercial nations.[29]

President Garfield, in his inaugural address, approved the position taken by his predecessor on the canal question,[30] and very soon after assuming the portfolio of state, Mr. Blaine outlined the new policy to our representatives in Europe, cautioning them, however, against representing it as the development of a new policy and affirming that it was " nothing more than the pronounced adherence of the United States to principles long since enunciated by the highest authority of the government."

[28] " Messages and Papers of the Presidents," Vol. VII, p. 585.
[29] " Collected Correspondence," p. 313.
[30] " Messages and Papers of the Presidents," Vol. VIII, p. 11.

This dispatch of Mr. Blaine is remarkable for several reasons, but chiefly for the fact that it completely ignores the existence of the Clayton-Bulwer treaty, there being no allusion to that celebrated convention either open or implied. Aside from this there are three points to be noted. In the first place Mr. Blaine calls attention to the rights and duties devolving upon the United States from the treaty with Colombia of 1846, and states that in the judgment of the President the guarantee there given by the United States requires no reënforcement, or accession, or assent from any other power; that the United States in more than one instance had been called upon to vindicate the neutrality thus guaranteed; and that there was no contingency, then foreseen or apprehended, in which such vindication would not be within the power of the nation.

In the second place, Mr. Blaine declared with emphasis that during any war to which the United States of America or the United States of Colombia might be a party, the passage of armed vessels of a hostile nation through the canal of Panama would be no more admissible than would the passage of the armed forces of a hostile nation over the railway lines joining the Atlantic and Pacific shores of the United States, or of Colombia. This declaration was in direct opposition to the second article of the Clayton-Bulwer treaty. Mr. Blaine then proceeded to expatiate upon the remarkable development of our Pacific slope and the importance of the canal in facilitating communication between our Atlantic and Pacific states, alluding to the canal in this connection, in the very apt phrase of President Hayes, as forming a part of the *coast-*

line of the United States. It does not appear to have occurred to Mr. Blaine that the same arguments applied with equal force to Great Britain's American possessions to the north of us, which likewise extended from the Atlantic to the Pacific, and were likewise entering upon a period of unusual development.

The third point to be noted in the dispatch is the statement that the United States would object to any concerted action of the European powers for the purpose of guaranteeing the canal or determining its status.[31] This declaration was supposed to be nothing more than a reaffirmation of the Monroe Doctrine.

A copy of this document was left by Mr. Lowell at the British foreign office on the 12th of July, 1881. No formal notice of the dispatch was taken by the British government until November, when Lord Granville replied that, as Mr. Blaine had made the statement that the government of the United States had no intention of initiating any discussion upon this subject, he did not propose to enter into a detailed argument in reply to Mr. Blaine's observations. He wished, however, merely to point out that the position of Great Britain and the United States with reference to the canal, irrespective of the magnitude of the commercial relations of the former power, was determined by a convention signed between them at Washington on the 19th of April, 1850, commonly known as the Clayton-Bulwer treaty, and her majesty's government relied with confidence upon the observance of all the engagements of that treaty.[32]

Before this reply reached Washington, Mr. Blaine

---

[31] "Collected Correspondence," pp. 322-326.
[32] *Ibid.*, p. 326.

had again taken up the question of the canal in a special dispatch of November 19, 1881. In this dispatch he addressed himself specifically to a consideration of the Clayton-Bulwer treaty, and urged upon the consideration of the British government modifications of such a radical character as to amount to a complete abrogation of the treaty. The grounds of objection to the treaty were stated in full. In the first place it was declared that the treaty had been made more than thirty years before under exceptional and extraordinary conditions, which were at least temporary in their nature and had long since ceased to exist. The remarkable development of the United States on the Pacific coast since that time had created new duties and responsibilities for the American government which required, in the judgment of the President, some essential modifications in the treaty. The objections to the perpetuity of the treaty were then stated in full. First and foremost was the objection that the treaty by forbidding the military fortification of the proposed canal practically conceded its control to Great Britain by reason of her naval superiority. The military power of the United States in any conflict on the American continent was irresistible, yet the United States was restrained from using this power for the protection of the canal, while no restrictions could be placed upon the natural advantages that England enjoyed in this regard as a great naval power. A more serious objection to the treaty, however, was urged in the statement that it embodied a misconception of the relative positions of Great Britain and the United States with respect to interests on this continent. The United States would not consent to perpetuate any treaty that impeached " our right and long-established claim to priority on the American continent."

In the third place, at the time the convention was agreed upon, Great Britain and the United States were the only nations prominent in the commerce of Central and South America. Since that time other nations not bound by the prohibitions of that treaty had become interested in Central America, and the republic of France had become sponsor for a new canal scheme. Yet by the treaty with England the United States was prevented from asserting its rights and the privileges acquired through treaty with Colombia anterior to the Clayton-Bulwer treaty.

In the fourth place, the treaty had been made with the implied understanding that British capital would be available for the construction of a canal. That expectation had never been realized, and the United States was now able to construct a canal without aid from outside resources.

In conclusion, Mr. Blaine proposed several modifications of the treaty which would leave the United States free to fortify the canal and to hold political control of it in conjunction with the country in which it might be located.[33]

A few days after the dispatch was written, Lord Granville's answer to Mr. Blaine's first dispatch reached Washington, and on the 29th of November, Mr. Blaine wrote a second dispatch equally voluminous with the one of November 19. In this he reviewed the discussions which had taken place between 1850 and 1860 in regard to the treaty with a view to

[33] " Collected Correspondence," pp. 327-332.

showing that it had never been satisfactory to the United States and had been the cause of serious misunderstanding. He failed, however, to make mention of the settlement of 1860 and the declaration of President Buchanan that the United States was satisfied with that adjustment.

The full reply of the British government to Mr. Blaine's arguments was given in two dispatches dated respectively January 7 and 14, 1882. Lord Granville took exception to certain conclusions which Mr. Blaine had sought to establish by analogy with the conduct of Great Britain in regard to the Suez canal. His lordship fully concurred in what Mr. Blaine had said as to the unexampled development of the United States on the Pacific coast, but reminded him that the development of her majesty's possessions to the north of the United States, while less rapid, had been, nevertheless, on a scale that bore some relation even to that of the Pacific states. In the view of her majesty's government, the changes desired by the United States would not improve the situation as regarded the canal, while the declaration that the United States would always treat the waterway connecting the two oceans " as part of her coast-line " threatened the independence of the territory lying between that waterway and the United States.

Her majesty's government believed that the only way to relieve the situation was to extend the invitation to all maritime states to participate in an agreement based on the stipulations of the convention of 1850.[34]

The task of replying to Lord Granville's two dis-

[34] " Collected Correspondence," pp. 340-352.

patches fell upon Mr. Blaine's successor in the State
Department, Mr. Frelinghuysen. Mr. Frelinghuysen's voluminous dispatch of May 8, 1882, reiterated
in the main the arguments advanced by Mr. Blaine.
He adduced evidence at great length to try to show
that the Clayton-Bulwer treaty was a special contract
for the accomplishment of a specific object, which had
never been achieved, and was no longer binding; that
Great Britain had violated the treaty by converting
her *settlement* of British Honduras into a *possession*
without ever receiving the assent of the United States,
and that such act would entitle the United States to
renounce the treaty. The dispatch was further char-
acterized by a direct appeal to the Monroe Doctrine
in these words:

The President believes that the formation of a protectorate
by European nations over the isthmus transit would be in
conflict with a doctrine which has been for many years
asserted by the United States. This sentiment is properly
termed a doctrine, as it has no prescribed sanction and its
assertion is left to the exigency which may invoke it. It has
been repeatedly announced by the executive department of
this government, and through the utterances of distinguished
citizens; it is cherished by the American people, and has
been approved by the government of Great Britain.

After quoting a part of President Monroe's message
of December 2, 1823, and reviewing the circumstances
under which it was delivered, Mr. Frelinghuysen said:

Thus the doctrine of non-intervention by European powers
in American affairs arose from complications in South
America, and was announced by Mr. Monroe on the suggestion of the official representative of Great Britain.[88]

[88] " Collected Correspondence," pp. 160-161.

In his reply of December 30, 1882, Lord Granville proved conclusively that Article VIII. of the treaty was understood by the American government during the discussions of 1850-1860 as establishing a general principle applicable to all waterways connecting the two oceans. In answer to the second point, Lord Granville adduced the notes exchanged between Mr. Clayton and Sir Henry Bulwer in July, 1850, which made it perfectly clear that, in the understanding of both governments at that time, the claims of Great Britain to Belize or British Honduras were not affected one way or the other by the treaty.[36]

In a later dispatch, August 17, 1883, Lord Granville briefly touched upon Mr. Frelinghuysen's appeal to the Monroe Doctrine, reminding him very pertinently that neither the American administration which negotiated the treaty nor the Senate which ratified it considered that they were precluded by the utterances of President Monroe from entering into such a treaty with one or more of the European powers.[37]

The correspondence on the treaty closed with Mr. Frelinghuysen's dispatch of November 22, 1883, in which he reiterated with no small degree of bluntness and pertinacity the arguments of his earlier dispatches.

The Clayton-Bulwer treaty was designed at the time of its execution to establish a permanent principle of control over interoceanic communication in Central America. No provision was made, as in most treaties, for its abrogation, and the American government could not terminate it without the consent of Great Britain

---

[36] "Collected Correspondence," pp. 353-359.
[37] *Ibid.,* p. 364.

for fear that she would return to her position of vantage at the time the treaty was made. For this reason, while Mr. Frelinghuysen claimed that the treaty was voidable, he did not actually declare it void.

Mr. Blaine's efforts to secure a modification were the result of the development of a new policy by the United States and the arguments presented by Mr. Blaine and Mr. Frelinghuysen in support of this policy were disingenuous and flimsy. It may be safely said that no state papers have ever emanated from our government on so serious a question equally lacking in logical consistency and moral force.

The result was that Great Britain refused to consent to a modification of the treaty and the United States saw before her the alternative of abiding by the terms of the treaty or ultimately resorting to war with England.

In December, 1884, Mr. Frelinghuysen negotiated a treaty with Nicaragua providing for the construction of a canal by the United States to be under the joint ownership and protection of the United States and Nicaragua. The United States also guaranteed the integrity of the territory of Nicaragua. When Mr. Cleveland became president this treaty was still before the Senate for consideration. Mr. Cleveland withdrew the treaty, and in his first annual message, December 8, 1885, reverted to our traditional policy. He declared himself opposed to entangling alliances with foreign states and declared:

Whatever highway may be constructed across the barrier dividing the two greatest maritime areas of the world, must be for the world's benefit, a trust for mankind, to be removed from the chance of domination by any single power, nor become a point of invitation for hostilities or a prize for warlike ambition.[38]

No discussion as to the validity of the Clayton-Bulwer treaty took place between the two governments after the close of President Arthur's administration. Mr. Cleveland's message above quoted was accepted as a reaffirmation of the treaty on the part of the American government.

Upon two occasions subsequently questions arose between the two governments involving the stipulations of the treaty. In 1888, and again in 1894, the United States felt called upon to protest against British interference in the affairs of the Mosquito coast.[39] The ground of interposition on the part of Great Britain was alleged to be found in the treaty of Managua, signed between Great Britain and Nicaragua on the 28th of January, 1860. This convention, it will be remembered, was one of the three treaties entered into by Great Britain with Central American republics with a view to removing the causes of dispute in the construction of the Clayton-Bulwer treaty. The treaty of Managua assigned a district to the Mosquito Indians within the limits of the republic of Nicaragua. The sovereignty of Nicaragua over the district was recognized, but the Indians were secured in the possession and enjoyment of their own domestic customs and regulations. It was agreed, however, that nothing in the treaty should prevent the Mosquitos at any subsequent date from voluntarily agreeing to absolute incorporation with the republic of

[38] "Messages and Papers of the Presidents," Vol. VIII, p. 327.
[39] See Mr. Bayard to Mr. Phelps, Nov. 23, 1888. For. Rel., 1888, Pt. I, pp. 759-768.

Nicaragua. By the terms of the treaty the protectorate of Great Britain over the Mosquito coast was to cease three months after the exchange of ratifications.

In reply to the protest of 1888, Lord Salisbury said that her majesty's government had no intention to assert a protectorate in substance or in form over the Mosquito nation, but that according to the convention with Nicaragua of 1860, Great Britain undertook " to secure certain rights and privileges to the Mosquito Indians, and in the event, which has arisen, of the Mosquito Indians complaining that their rights are infringed by Nicaragua, by whom is remonstrance to be made to Nicaragua unless by Great Britain, with whom she has concluded the convention in question? " [40]

In the spring of 1894, yet more serious trouble arose. The Mosquito territory was invaded by the troops of Nicaragua and Bluefields was surrounded. The British consul at that point protested against this act as contrary to the treaty of Managua. The protest being unheeded, a force of troops was landed from the British ship *Cleopatra* and on March 9, the Nicaraguans were forced to retire. Mr. Bayard was instructed by telegraph " to ascertain and report fully by cable the occasion for this action." The British government disavowed all intention of violating the Clayton-Bulwer treaty, which it recognized " as extant and in full force."

In July, 1894, United States marines were landed at Bluefields to protect American interests and to restore order. Later the British government assured

[40] For. Rel., 1889, p. 468.

Mr. Bayard that its action had been wholly uncon-
nected with any political or conventional question
touching the Mosquito reservation, but simply to protect British interests.

By a convention signed November 20, 1894, the
Mosquito Indians surrendered their rights under the
treaty of 1860 and were incorporated with Nicaragua.
This voluntary incorporation took away all further
occasion for interposition on the part of Great Britain,
and Mr. Bayard reported that it was received with
" the most open expression of satisfaction at the foreign office." [41]

The attempts of Blaine and Frelinghuysen to bring
about a modification of the Clayton-Bulwer treaty
were, as we have seen, unsuccessful. In fact, their
only effect was to strengthen the British government
for the time being in the determination to hold us
more strictly to the terms of that convention. In 1896
Secretary Olney in a review of the situation declared:

Upon every principle which governs the relations to each
other, either of nations or of individuals, the United States is
completely estopped from denying that the treaty is in full
force and vigor. If changed conditions now make stipulations, which were once deemed advantageous, either inappli-
cable or injurious, the true remedy is not in ingenious attempts to deny the existence of the treaty or to explain away
its provisions, but in a direct and straightforward application
to Great Britain for a reconsideration of the whole matter.[42]

It was precisely in this spirit that Secretary Hay
undertook in 1899 to negotiate a new treaty with England. The original draft of the Hay-Pauncefote

---

[41] See Foreign Relations, 1894, App. 1. "Affairs at Bluefields," pp.
234-363.
[42] Senate Doc. No. 160, Fifty-sixth Cong., First Sess.

treaty, signed February 5, 1900, provided for a neutralized canal and drafted for its control rules substantially in accord with the Constantinople convention of 1888, providing for the regulation of the Suez canal. The most important provision of the new treaty was that authorizing the United States to construct and to assume the management of an isthmian canal, either directly or through a company. The United States Senate, however, amended the treaty in three important particulars: (1) by declaring that the Clayton-Bulwer treaty was thereby superseded; (2) by providing that the restrictions in the regulations governing the use of the canal should not apply to measures which the United States might adopt for its own defense and for the maintenance of public order along the canal; and (3) by cutting out entirely the article providing for the adherence of other powers. The British government refused to accept these amendments, and a year elapsed before an agreement was finally reached.[43] The revised treaty which was ratified by the Senate December 16, 1901, was a compromise between the original draft and the Senate amendments. The new treaty abrogated in express terms the Clayton-Bulwer convention, and provided that the United States might construct a canal under its direct auspices, to be under its exclusive management. The principle of neutralization was nominally retained, but under the sole guarantee of the United States, with power to police the canal, and the clause of the first draft forbidding fortifications was omitted.[44]

---

[43] Moore, " Digest of Int. Law," Vol. III, p. 211.
[44] Foreign Relations, 1901, p. 245.

This convention removed the principal diplomatic obstacles which stood in the way of constructing a canal through the isthmus. For several years the United States had been investigating the cost of constructing a canal through Nicaragua, that route being the one which had always been considered most feasible by the great majority of American engineers. Two commissions, one in 1895 and another in 1897, had reported favorably on the practicability of that route. A third commission, headed by Admiral John G. Walker, was appointed under act of March 3, 1899, which authorized an expenditure of $1,000,000 for the purpose of making a thorough investigation of all available routes. While the Walker commission was carrying on investigations in Nicaragua, at Panama, and along the Atrato river, the various financial interests concerned in the choice of routes were actively at work in Washington, each trying to influence Congress in favor of its particular project. The New Panama Canal Company had secured, at the time of the reorganization, an extension of its concession to October, 1904, and subsequently another concession to October, 1910, but the validity of the latter arrangement was in doubt. The company could not raise the necessary funds to continue the work at Panama and was therefore threatened with the forfeiture of its franchise and property. It concluded, therefore, that its only hope lay in transferring its concession and property to the American government. With this end in view, an active lobby was maintained at Washington for the purpose of influencing public opinion in favor of the Panama route.

But the Panama Company had a powerful rival

in the Maritime Canal Company, which held a charter from Congress and had secured a concession from Nicaragua. This company had started work at Greytown in 1890, but having been forced from lack of funds to stop work in 1893, was now urging Congress to make its enterprise a national one. It found a ready champion in Senator Morgan of Alabama, who had for years taken a lively interest in the canal question and who had strong convictions as to the superiority of the Nicaragua route. In 1900 Nicaragua declared the concession of the Maritime Canal Company null and void, and granted a new concession to a group of New York capitalists known as the Grace-Eyre-Cragin Syndicate. The Maritime Canal Company, however, refused to abandon its claims, and a contest between the two concerns was carried to the lobbies of Congress. The opposition of the transcontinental railroads to a canal at either point brought into play another set of powerful interests, usually arrayed against the plan which appeared for the time being most likely to succeed.[45]

On November 16, 1901, the Walker commission after a thorough investigation of the Nicaragua and Panama routes made its report. It estimated the cost of construction of the Nicaragua canal at $189,864,062, and the cost of completing the Panama canal at $144,-233,358. To this latter sum had to be added the cost of acquiring the rights and property of the French company, which had stated to the commission that it estimated its interests at $109,141,500, making the total cost of the Panama canal $253,374,858. The commission expressed the opinion that the interests of

[45] Johnson, " Four Centuries of the Panama Canal," Chap. VIII.

the French company were not worth over $40,000,000. In conclusion the report stated:

> After considering all the facts developed by the investigations made by the commission and the actual situation as it now stands, and having in view the terms offered by the New Panama Company, this commission is of the opinion that the most practicable and feasible route for an isthmian canal, to be under the control, management, and ownership of the United States, is that known as the Nicaragua route."

A bill was promptly introduced into the House of Representatives by Mr. Hepburn providing for the construction of the canal through Nicaragua, and on January 9, 1902, this bill passed the House by the almost unanimous vote of 308 to 2. The report of the commission had meanwhile created great consternation among the stockholders of the New Panama Canal Company, and on January 4, 1902, a definite offer to sell out to the United States at $40,000,000 was made to the commission by cable. On January 18, the commission filed a supplementary report which recommended the adoption of the Panama route instead of that through Nicaragua.

When the Hepburn bill came up for discussion in the Senate, the situation had thus been radically changed, and a long debate ensued as to the relative merits of the two routes. Senator Morgan continued to fight for Nicaragua as the traditional American route, declaring that the Panama Company could not give a valid transfer of its property and interests. But this objection was cleverly met by Senator Spooner, who offered an amendment, which was vir-

---

" Report of the Isthmian Canal Commission (Sen. Doc. No. 54, Fifty-seventh Cong., First Sess.).

tually a substitute, authorizing the President to acquire the rights and property of the French company at a cost not exceeding $40,000,000; to acquire from the Republic of Colombia, upon such terms as he might deem reasonable, perpetual control of a strip of land, not less than six miles in width, extending from the Caribbean Sea to the Pacific Ocean, with jurisdiction over said strip; and to proceed as soon as these rights were acquired, to construct a canal. But should the President be unable to obtain a satisfactory title to the property of the French company and the control of the necessary strip of land from the Republic of Colombia " within a reasonable time and upon reasonable terms," then he was instructed to secure control of the necessary strip through Nicaragua and to proceed to construct a canal there. The bill as amended passed the Senate June 19, 1902, by a vote of 67 to 6. The House at first refused to concur in the Spooner amendment, but after a conference it finally gave way and the measure was adopted by a vote of 260 to 8. The act was signed by President Roosevelt June 28.[47]

Attorney-General Knox was sent to Paris to make a thorough investigation of the affairs of the Panama Company. He reported that it could give a clear title. The next step was to secure a right of way through Colombia. After considerable delay Secretary Hay and Mr. Herran, the Colombian chargé d'affaires, signed, January 22, 1903, a canal convention, by the terms of which the United States agreed to pay Colombia $10,000,000 in cash and an annuity of $250,000 for the lease of a strip of land six miles wide across

[47] U. S. Statutes at Large, Vol. XXXII, Pt. I, p. 481.

the isthmus. Objection was raised to this treaty because it failed to secure for the United States full governmental control over the canal zone, but it was considered the best that could be gotten and it was ratified by the United States Senate March 17, 1903.

The Colombian Senate, however, did not regard the treaty with favor. They felt that Panama was their greatest national asset, and they knew perfectly well that in spite of threats to the contrary President Roosevelt was determined not to adopt the alternative of the Spooner amendment and go to Nicaragua. After discussing the treaty for nearly two months, they finally rejected it August 12 by the unanimous vote of all the senators present.[48] They probably thought that they could get better terms from the United States and particularly that they might reserve a fuller measure of sovereignty over the isthmus. President Roosevelt declared that the action of the Colombian Senate was due to an " anti-social spirit " and to the cupidity of the government leaders, who merely wished to wait until they could confiscate the $40,000,-000 worth of property belonging to the French company and then sell out to the United States. This view is not borne out by the dispatches of Mr. Beaupré, the American minister, who repeatedly warned Secretary Hay that there was a " tremendous tide of public opinion against the canal treaty," which even the Colombian government could not ignore. The charge of bad faith against Colombia does not come in good grace from a country whose constitution also requires the ratification of treaties by the Senate.

As soon as the Hay-Herran convention was rejected

---

[48] Senate Doc. No. 51, Fifty-eighth Cong., Second Sess., p. 56.

by the Colombian Senate, the advocates of the Nicaragua route began to take courage and to demand that as the " reasonable time " allowed in the Spooner act for the President to acquire the right of way through Panama had expired, it was now his duty to adopt the Nicaragua route. The directors of the French company were again in a state of consternation. If they could not sell to the United States they would have to sacrifice their property entirely, or sell to some other purchaser at a lower figure. It was rumored that Germany was willing to buy their interests. The directors of the company were so completely demoralized that William Nelson Cromwell, their American attorney, hastened to Paris to dissuade them from taking any rash step. The rejection of the Hay-Herran treaty was a great disappointment to the inhabitants of the isthmus, who considered this action a sacrifice of their interests, and some of the foremost citizens conferred with the American agent of the Panama Railroad Company as to the advisability of organizing a revolution. Before taking any step in this direction, it was considered advisable to send one of their number to the United States, and Dr. Amador was selected for this mission. He had conferences with William Nelson Cromwell and with Secretary Hay. The latter merely outlined what he considered the rights and duties of the United States under the treaty of 1846, but refused of course to commit the government to a definite support of the revolutionary project. Amador was somewhat discouraged at the result of his conference with Hay, but his hopes were revived by the sudden arrival of Philippe Bunau-Varilla, the former chief engineer of the French company, who entered with enthusiasm into the revolutionary scheme.[49]

The Colombian Congress adjourned October 30 without any reconsideration of the treaty, and President Roosevelt at once ordered the *Boston, Dixie, Atlanta,* and *Nashville* to proceed within easy reach of the isthmus. Their commanders received orders to keep the transit open and to " prevent the landing of any armed force with hostile intent, either government or insurgent, at any point within fifty miles of Panama." The *Nashville* arrived off Colon November 2. It can hardly be denied that these measures created a situation very favorable to revolution.[50]

The revolutionists had been greatly disappointed at Dr. Amador's failure to get a definite promise of support from the American government, but their spirits revived when they learned of the presence of American war vessels. Still they were slow in taking advantage of their opportunities and the government at Washington was growing impatient. At 3.40 P. M. November 3 the following dispatch was sent to the American consuls at Panama and Colon: " Uprising on isthmus reported. Keep Department promptly and fully informed. Loomis, Acting." At 8.15 a reply was received from the consul at Panama: " No uprising yet. Reported will be in the night. Situation is critical." At 9 P.M. a second dispatch was received from the same source: " Uprising occurred to-night, 6; no bloodshed. Army and navy officials taken prisoners. Government will be organized to-night." [51]

[49] Johnson, " Four Centuries of the Panama Canal," pp. 162-171.
[50] Senate Doc. No. 53, Fifty-eighth Cong., Second Sess.
[51] House Doc. No. 8, Fifty-eighth Cong., First Sess.

Before the *Nashville* received the order to prevent the landing of armed forces, 450 Colombian troops arrived at Colon. The principal officers were provided with a special train to take them across the isthmus to Panama. When they arrived they were seized by the revolutionary leaders and locked up for safe-keeping, while the railroad officials saw to it that there were no trains for their troops to use. The next day Commander Hubbard landed fifty marines from the *Nashville* at Colon, and a day later the officer in charge of the Colombian forces was persuaded by a generous bribe to reëmbark his troops and leave. Events continued to follow one another with startling rapidity. On the 6th the *de facto* government was recognized and a week later Bunau-Varilla was received by President Roosevelt as envoy extraordinary and minister plenipotentiary of the Republic of Panama. Such hasty recognition of a new government was of course without precedent in the annals of American diplomacy, and it naturally confirmed the rumor that the whole affair had been prearranged. On October 10 President Roosevelt had written a personal letter to Dr. Albert Shaw, editor of the *Review of Reviews,* who was a strong advocate of the Panama route, in which he said:

Privately, I freely say to you that I should be delighted if Panama were an independent state, or if it made itself so at this moment; but for me to say so publicly would amount to an instigation of a revolt, and therefore I cannot say it.[52]

This letter throws an interesting light on an article in the *Review of Reviews* for November of the same

---

[52] *Literary Digest,* October 29, 1904.

year in which Dr. Shaw discussed the question, "What if Panama should Revolt?" and outlined with remarkable prophetic insight the future course of events.

In his annual message of December 7, 1903, the President discussed the Panama revolution and undertook to justify his course under the treaty of 1846. This message failed to allay public criticism, and on January 4, 1904, he sent a special message to Congress in defense of his action. He held that Colombia was not entitled "to bar the transit of the world's traffic across the isthmus," and that the intervention of the United States was justified, (1) by our treaty rights, (2) by our international interests, and (3) by the interests of "collective civilization." The "legal" argument in this message, if we may dignify it by that name, is reported to have been prepared by Root and Knox, both at that time members of the Cabinet. Several years later, after Mr. Roosevelt had retired from the presidency, he expressed the real truth in a public speech when he said:

If I had followed traditional conservative methods I should have submitted a dignified state paper of probably two hundred pages to the Congress and the debate would be going on yet, but I took the Canal zone and let Congress debate, and while the debate goes on the canal does also.

The reason why the President did not wish the matter to go before Congress again was that he had decided upon the Panama route, and he knew that when Congress convened in December, the situation remaining unchanged, action would be taken to compel him to adopt the alternative of the Spooner amendment and go to the Nicaragua route. His object in the hasty recognition of the Panama revolution was therefore to make the Panama route an accomplished fact before Congress should meet. This was the attitude definitely assumed in the message of January 4, 1904, in the course of which he said:

> The only question now before us is that of the ratification of the treaty. For it is to be remembered that a failure to ratify the treaty will not undo what has been done, will not restore Panama to Colombia, and will not alter our obligation to keep the transit open across the Isthmus, and to prevent any outside power from menacing this transit.

The treaty referred to was the convention with Panama which had been signed November 18, 1903, and which was ratified by the Senate February 23, 1904, by a vote of 66 to 14. By the terms of this agreement the United States guaranteed the independence of the Panama Republic, and agreed to pay the Panama Republic a sum of $10,000,000 upon the exchange of ratifications and an annual rental of $250,-000 a year beginning nine years thereafter. Panama on her part granted to the United States in perpetuity a zone of land ten miles wide for the construction of a canal, the United States receiving as full power and authority over this strip and the waters adjacent as if it were the sovereign of the said territory.[53] The construction of the canal was at once undertaken and the work was carried through successfully by General Goethals and a corps of army engineers. It was opened to commerce August 15, 1914. though it was not completed at that time and traffic was subsequently interrupted by landslides.

---

[53] Foreign Relations, 1904, p. 543.

Colombia naturally felt aggrieved at the course pursued by President Roosevelt and refused to recognize the Republic of Panama. She objected to his interpretation of the convention of 1846. In this convention the United States pledged itself to keep the isthmian transit open and guaranteed Colombia's sovereignty over the same. This treaty established an obligation to Colombia alone, and it is difficult to accept the President's view that it established an obligation to the world at large against Colombia. Colombia demanded that the whole question be submitted to arbitration. As the United States had always held the ground that disputes arising out of the interpretation of treaties should be settled by arbitration, it was inconsistent for the United States to refuse to arbitrate. But President Roosevelt did refuse. The Panama episode created strained relations with Colombia and made a very bad impression throughout Latin America. The United States has since been eyed with suspicion by its weaker Southern neighbors. The Taft and Wilson administrations both tried to appease Colombia by a money payment, but this subject will be discussed in a subsequent chapter.

CHAPTER V

French Intervention in Mexico

THE attempt of Louis Napoleon to establish a European monarchy in Mexico under the tutelage of France was the most serious menace that republican institutions in the new world have had to face since the schemes of the Holy Alliance were checked by Monroe and Canning. The thwarting of that attempt may be accounted one of the greatest triumphs of American diplomacy. The internal disorders common to South and Central American republics have always been a fruitful source of embarrassment to the United States, on account of the liability to European intervention to which these governments continually subject themselves in such periods by their open and flagrant disregard of international obligations. Of no country is this statement truer than of Mexico, where the well-nigh interminable strife of parties gave rise between the years 1821 and 1857 to thirty-six different governments. In 1857 a favorable change occurred in the affairs of the republic. A constituent congress, elected by the people of the different states, framed and adopted a republican constitution which promised better things for the future. Under the provisions of this constitution an election was held in July (1857) and General Comonfort chosen president almost without opposition. His term of office was to begin December 1, 1857, and to continue four years. Within one brief month, however, President Comonfort was driven from the capital, and ultimately from the country, by an uprising headed by General Zuloaga. As soon as Comonfort abandoned the presidency, General Benito Juarez, the president of the Supreme Court of Justice, became according to the constitution, the president *de jure* of the republic for the remainder of the unexpired term, that is, until December 1, 1861. General Zuloaga had, however, assumed the name of president, with indefinite powers, and the entire diplomatic corps, including the minister of the United States, had recognized his government. But Zuloaga was speedily expelled, and the supreme power seized by General Miramon, the head of the church party, whom the diplomatic corps likewise recognized. Meanwhile Juarez, the constitutional president, had proceeded to Vera Cruz, where he put his administration into successful operation.

For several months, Mr. John Forsyth, the American minister, continued at the city of Mexico in the discharge of his duties. In June, 1858, however, he suspended his diplomatic connection with the Miramon government. Our relations, which had been bad under former governments, were now rendered almost intolerable under that of Miramon by outrages towards American citizens and personal indignities to Mr. Forsyth himself. His action was approved by President Buchanan, and he was directed to return to the United States. All diplomatic intercourse was thus terminated with the government of Miramon, but as yet none was established with the Juarez government. The ultimate success of the latter became, however, so probable that the following year the President sent a confidential agent to Mexico to inquire into and report upon the actual condition of the belligerents, and in consequence of his report, Mr. Robert M. McLane was dispatched to Mexico, March 8, 1859, " with discretionary authority to recognize the government of President Juarez, if on his arrival in Mexico he should find it entitled to such recognition according to the established practice of the United States." On the 7th of April, Mr. McLane presented his credentials to President Juarez, having no hesitation, he said, " in pronouncing the government of Juarez to be the only existing government of the republic." He was cordially received by the authorities at Vera Cruz, and during all the vicissitudes of the next eight years the United States government continued to extend its sympathy and moral support to the government of Juarez as the only one entitled to the allegiance of the people of Mexico.

Juarez thus came forward, in the rôle of reformer, as the champion of constitutionalism and the supremacy of the state against the overreaching power, influence, and wealth of the church party. He was a full-blooded Indian, without the slightest admixture of Spanish blood. In December, 1860, he finally succeeded in overthrowing the party of Miramon and driving the latter into exile. Immediately, on reoccupying the city of Mexico, the Constitutionalists proceeded to execute with severity the decree issued at Vera Cruz nationalizing or sequestrating the property of the church.

The most difficult question which the new government had to face was that of international obligations recklessly contracted by the various revolutionary leaders who had successively been recognized as constituting the government of Mexico. In consequence of debts contracted and outrages and enormities perpetrated, for the most part during the régime of Miramon and the church party, the governments of England, France, and Spain determined to intervene in Mexico.

The grievances of the British government were based on the following facts: non-settlement of claims of British bondholders; the murder of the British vice-consul at Tasco; the breaking into the British legation and the carrying off £152,000 in bonds belonging to British subjects, besides numerous other outrages committed on the persons and property of individuals.[1]

The claims of the British bondholders referred to had been recognized by the Pakenham convention of October 15, 1842, and formed into a consolidated fund of $250,000, which was to be paid off, principal and interest, by a percentage on import duties at the custom-houses of Vera Cruz and Tampico. This convention was not carried out by the Mexican government, and on December 4, 1851, Mr. Doyle signed on behalf of Great Britain a new convention, in which not only the claims under the Pakenham convention, but others, recognized by both governments, were likewise formed into a consolidated fund, on which the Mexican government bound itself to pay five per cent. as a sinking fund and three per cent. as interest until the debt should be paid off. This five and three per cent. were to be met by a percentage of customs receipts.

---

[1] Brit. and For. St. Pap., 1861-62, Vol. LII. Also House Exec. Doc. No. 100, Thirty-seventh Cong., Second Sess.

In 1857 the sinking fund was to be raised to six per cent. and the interest to four per cent.

Two days after the signing of this Doyle convention the Spanish minister in Mexico also signed a convention on behalf of some Philippine missionaries, known as the " Padre Moran " convention, on almost the same basis as the British. The consolidated fund in this case was $983,000, the sinking fund five per cent., and the interest three per cent.

The interest was paid on both funds in almost the whole amount, but the sinking fund was not kept up. Succeeding agreements were made in 1858, in 1859, and in 1860, by which the custom-house assignments to satisfy both conventions (British and Spanish) were raised from twelve per cent. in 1851, to twenty-nine per cent. in 1860.[2]

It will thus be seen that the British and Spanish claims were perfectly legitimate. The French claims, however, were of a somewhat different character. During Miramon's administration arrangements were made through the agency of Jecker, a Swiss banker, by which $750,000 were to be raised through an issue of $15,000,000 of bonds. These bonds fell into the hands of Jecker's French creditors and were pressed by the French government, which thus demanded the repayment of twenty times the original sum advanced. A claim was made also for $12,000,000 for torts on French subjects.[3]

When the Liberal party came into power again in 1860, they were unable to meet the situation and showed a disposition to question the obligatory force

[2] Brit. and For. St. Pap., Vol. LII, p. 359.
[3] Wharton's Digest, Sec. 58, Vol. I, p. 312.

of engagements entered into by their various revolutionary predecessors. The British government had undertaken to provide against this contingency upon the occasion of extending recognition to the Juarez administration. Under date of March 30, 1861, Lord John Russell wrote to Sir Charles Wyke, recently appointed minister to Mexico, as follows:

> The instructions addressed to Mr. Mathew, both before and since the final triumph of the Liberal party, made the recognition by Great Britain of the constitutional government contingent upon the acknowledgment by that government of the liability of Mexico for the claims of British subjects who, either in their persons or in their property, for a long series of years, can be proved to have suffered wrong at the hands of successive governments in Mexico.[4]

And further on in the same communication the attitude of the British government is expressed yet more strongly:

> Her majesty's government will not admit as an excuse for hesitation in this respect the plea that the robbery was committed by the late government. For, as regards this, as indeed all other claims, her majesty's government cannot admit that the party who committed the wrong is alone responsible. Great Britain does not recognize any party as constituting the republic in its dealing with foreign nations, but holds the entire republic, by whatever party the government of it may from time to time be administered, to be responsible for wrongs done to British subjects by any party or persons at any time administering the powers of government.

Mexico, however, was slow to admit this principle of international law. In a letter to Lord John Rus-

---

* Brit. and For. St. Pap., Vol. LII, p. 237.

sell, June 25, 1861, and in other communications, Sir Charles Wyke urged the necessity of a naval demonstration against Mexico. His plan was to take possession of the custom-houses of Vera Cruz, Tampico, and Matamoros on the Atlantic, and of one or two on the Pacific, lower the duties so as to attract the great bulk of trade from other ports, and pay themselves by the percentage to which they were entitled by treaty stipulation.

On the 17th of July, 1861, President Juarez brought matters to a crisis by the publication of a decree, the first article of which declared that " all payments are suspended for two years, including the assignments for the loan made in London and for the foreign conventions." [5]

On the 23rd, Sir Charles Wyke, the British minister, demanded the repeal of this law within forty-eight hours. On the 24th, the French minister demanded its repeal within twenty-four hours. These demands were not complied with and diplomatic relations were immediately broken off by the British and French representatives.

The Spanish government had acted somewhat in advance of the other governments and was already preparing to back its claims by an armed expedition against Mexico. The rupture with the British and French governments very naturally pointed to joint action with Spain as the best means of securing their interests. The United States government, which had just entered upon one of the greatest struggles of modern times and had its hands practically tied as far as Mexico was concerned, regarded the contem-

[5] Brit. and For. St. Pap., Vol. LII, p. 294.

plated intervention of European powers in Mexico with grave apprehension, not to say suspicion. So great was the uneasiness occasioned in the United States by the measures in contemplation and so strong was the desire to ward off the threatened danger to republican institutions on this continent, that Mr. Seward authorized (September 2, 1861) the negotiation of a treaty with Mexico for the assumption by the United States of the payment of the interest, at three per cent., upon the funded debt of Mexico (the principal of which was about $62,000,-000) for the term of five years from the date of the decree of the Mexican government suspending such payment, " provided that the government of Mexico will pledge to the United States its faith for the reimbursement of the money so to be paid, with six per cent. interest thereon, to be secured by a specific lien upon all the public lands and mineral rights in the several Mexican states of Lower California, Chihuahua, Sonora, and Sinaloa, the property so pledged to become absolute in the United States at the expiration of the term of six years from the time when the treaty shall go into effect, if such reimbursement shall not have been made before that time." [6] All this, of course, was subject to the confirmation of the Senate.

This step was communicated informally to the British and French governments, and the validity of the convention was to be conditioned upon those governments engaging not to take any measures against Mexico to enforce the payment of the interest of the loan until time should have been given to submit the

---

[6] Mr. Seward to Mr. Corwin, Sept. 2, 1861. House Exec. Doc. No. 100, p. 22, Thirty-seventh Cong., Second Sess.

convention to the ratification of the United States Senate at its approaching session. It was also to be a condition that, if the convention should be ratified, Great Britain and France should engage, on their part, not to make any demand upon Mexico for the interest, except upon its failing to be punctually paid by the United States.[7]

Grave objections to Mr. Seward's plan of paying the interest on the Mexican debt were entertained both in Paris and in London. The French minister of state, M. Thouvenel, said to the British minister at Paris:

It might not be possible to prevent the United States offering money to Mexico, or to prevent Mexico receiving money from the United States, but neither England nor France ought in any way to recognize the transaction.[8]

Lord Lyons declared to Mr. Seward:

That her majesty's government were as apprehensive as Mr. Seward himself could be, of an attempt to build upon a foundation of debts due, and injuries inflicted, by Mexico, a pretension to establish a new government in that country. Her majesty's government thought, however, that the most effectual mode of guarding against this danger would be for Great Britain, the United States, and France to join Spain in a course of action, the objects and limits of which should be distinctly defined beforehand. This certainly appeared more prudent than to allow Spain to act alone now, and afterwards to oppose the results of her operations, if she should go too far.[9]

---

[7] Brit. and For. St. Pap., Vol. LII, p. 325.
[8] Earl Cowley to Earl Russell, Sept. 24, 1861. Brit. and For. St. Pap., Vol. LII, p. 329.
[9] Earl Lyons to Earl Russell, Oct. 14, 1861. Brit. and For. St. Pap., Vol LII, p. 375.

The British government avoided beforehand the necessity of a point-blank refusal of the plan of Mr. Seward, in case the treaty should go through, by declaring that the interest on the funded debt was not the only cause of complaint, but that there remained over and above that the outrages perpetrated upon British subjects still unredressed.

Mr. Charles Francis Adams, the United States minister to England, did not approve the plan of guaranteeing the Mexican interest, and in his dispatch to Mr. Seward of November 1, 1861, he expressed his opinion rather more frankly than is usual for a minister to do in discussing an instruction from the state department.

You will permit me here, however, to make a single remark in this connection upon the importance of appearing to divest the United States of any personal and selfish interest in the action it may think proper to adopt. The view customarily taken in Europe is that their government is disposed to resist all foreign intervention in Mexico, not upon any principle, but simply because it is itself expecting, in due course of time, to absorb the whole country for its own benefit. Hence any proposal like that which I had the honor to receive, based upon the mortgage of portions of Mexican territory as security for engagements entered into by the United States, naturally becomes the ground of an outcry that this is but the preliminary to an entry for inevitable foreclosure. And then follows the argument that if this process be legitimate in one case, why not equally in all. As against Great Britain and France, it would be difficult to oppose to this the abstract principle contained in what has been denominated the Monroe Doctrine, however just in substance.[19]

While Mr. Corwin was still in negotiation with the

<hr/>

[19] Thirty-Seventh Cong., Second Sess., House Exec. Doc. No. 100, p. 201.

Mexican government in reference to some method of releasing Mexico from her complications with the allied governments of Europe, the United States Senate, in reply to two successive messages of the President, passed a resolution, February 25, 1862, declaring the opinion " that it is not advisable to negotiate a treaty that will require the United States to assume any portion of the principle or interest of the debt of Mexico, or that will require the concurrence of European powers." This effectually put an end to Mr. Seward's plan.

Meanwhile Sir Charles Wyke had reopened negotiations with the Mexican government and negotiated a treaty which might have satisfied British claims, but the treaty was thrown out by the Mexican congress by a large majority, and also disapproved by the British government in view of an agreement entered into with France and Spain unknown to Sir Charles Wyke.[11]

The agreement referred to was the convention signed at London, October 31, 1861, between Spain, France, and Great Britain, in reference to the situation of affairs in Mexico and looking to armed intervention for the purpose of securing their rights. The preamble of the convention recites that the three contracting parties " being placed by the arbitrary and vexatious conduct of the authorities of the republic of Mexico under the necessity of exacting from those authorities a more efficient protection for the persons and property of their subjects, as well as the performance of the obligations contracted toward them by the republic of Mexico, have arranged to conclude a con-

---

[11] Sir C. Wyke to Earl Russell, Nov. 25, 1861. Brit. and For. St. Pap., Vol. LII, p. 398.

vention between each other for the purpose of combining their common action." The most important article of the convention in view of its subsequent violation by the Emperor Napoleon, was the second, which declared that:

> The high contracting parties bind themselves not to seek for themselves, in the employment of coercive measures foreseen by the present convention, any acquisition of territory, or any peculiar advantage, and not to exercise in the subsequent affairs of Mexico any influence of a character to impair the right of the Mexican nation to choose and freely to constitute the form of its own government.

The fourth article, recognizing that the United States also had claims against Mexico, provided:

> that immediately after the signing of the present convention, a copy of it shall be communicated to the government of the United States, that that government shall be invited to accede to it. . . . But, as the high contracting parties would expose themselves, in making any delay in carrying into effect articles one and two of the present convention, to fail in the end which they wish to attain, they have agreed not to defer, with a view of obtaining the accession of the government of the United States, the commencement of the above-mentioned operations beyond the period at which their combined forces may be united in the vicinity of Vera Cruz.[12]

The advisability of inviting the coöperation of the United States had been the subject of considerable discussion and difference of opinion among the three European governments. England and France had urged the coöperation of the United States, while Spain had opposed it.

---

[12] Thirty-Seventh Cong., Second Sess., House Exec. Doc. No. 100, pp. 186-7.

FRENCH INTERVENTION IN MEXICO

In compliance with the fourth article the convention was submitted to the government of the United States by a note dated November 30, 1861, signed jointly by the representatives of Spain, France, and Great Britain at Washington.

Mr. Seward's reply conveying the declination of the United States to the invitation to coöperate with the three allied European powers in the demonstration against Mexico was dated December 4, 1861. After reviewing the substance of the convention, he said:

First. As the undersigned has heretofore had the honor to inform each of the plenipotentiaries now addressed, the President does not feel himself at liberty to question, and he does not question, that the sovereigns represented have undoubted right to decide for themselves the fact whether they have sustained grievances, and to resort to war against Mexico for the redress thereof, and have a right also to levy the war severally or jointly.

In the second place, Mr. Seward expressed the satisfaction of his government that the allied powers had clearly repudiated in the convention all idea of carrying on the war for their own ambitious ends and all intention of exercising in the subsequent affairs of Mexico any influence of a character to impair the right of the Mexican people to choose and freely to constitute the form of their own government.

It is true, as the high contracting parties assume, that the United States have, on their part, claims to urge against Mexico. Upon due consideration, however, the President is of opinion that it would be inexpedient to seek satisfaction of their claims at this time through an act of accession to the convention. Among the reasons for this decision which the undersigned is authorized to assign, are, first, that the United States, so far as it is practicable, prefer to adhere to a traditional policy recommended to them by the father of their country and confirmed by a happy experience, which forbids them from making alliances with foreign nations; second, Mexico being a neighbor of the United States on this continent, and possessing a system of government similar to our own in many of its important features, the United States habitually cherish a decided good-will toward that republic, and a lively interest in its security, prosperity, and welfare. Animated by these sentiments, the United States do not feel inclined to resort to forcible remedies for their claims at the present moment, when the government of Mexico is deeply disturbed by factions within, and exposed to war with foreign nations. And of course, the same sentiments render them still more disinclined to allied war against Mexico, than to war to be waged against her by themselves alone.

In conclusion, Mr. Seward referred to the fact that the United States government had authorized their representative in Mexico to enter into a treaty conceding to the Mexican government material aid, which might, he hoped, enable that government to satisfy the just claims and demands of the allied sovereigns and so to avert the war which they have agreed among each other to levy against Mexico.[13]

As already related, the efforts of the executive in this direction were not approved by the Senate and the negotiations in regard to guaranteeing the interest on the Mexican loan were broken off. The treaty negotiated by Mr. Corwin was in fact never submitted to the Senate, for by the time it was ready the French forces occupied a part of Mexican territory, and it was feared that a loan to Mexico under

[13] House Exec. Doc. No. 100, pp. 187-190, Thirty-seventh Cong., Second Sess. Brit. and For. St. Pap., Vol. LII, p. 394.

such conditions would be considered a breach of neutrality.

In pursuance of the London convention, Vera Cruz was occupied in the early part of 1862 by a Spanish force of 6,000 men under command of Marshal Prim; a French force of 2,500, which was largely reinforced soon afterward; and a force of 700 British marines.

The first intimation of the real purposes of the Emperor Louis Napoleon was given in the letter of instructions of M. Thouvenel to the admiral commanding the French expedition to Mexico, dated November 11, 1861. He said that in case of the withdrawal of the Mexican forces from the coast into the interior of the country, an advance upon the capital might become necessary. He reminded the admiral of the self-abnegatory character of the second article of the convention, but continued:

There are, however, certain hypotheses which present themselves to our foresight and which it was our duty to examine. It might happen that the pressure of the allied forces upon the soil of Mexico might induce the sane portion of the people, tired of anarchy, anxious for order and repose, to attempt an effort to constitute in the country a government presenting the guarantees of strength and stability which have been wanting to all those which have succeeded each other since the emancipation.

To such efforts the admiral was expressly told that he was not to refuse his encouragement.[14]

In view of this order, the British government at once instructed its agent, Sir Charles Wyke, that, while there was nothing to be said against the reasoning of the French government in reference to the prob-

---

[14] House Exec. Doc. No. 100, p. 174, Thirty-seventh Cong., Second Sess.

able necessity of marching against the city of Mexico, he was to decline to take part in the advance into the interior, and that the fact, that the whole available British force was only 700 marines, would be sufficient reason for declining.[15]

The seriousness of the situation was fully appreciated by the United States government. Shortly after the occupation of Vera Cruz by the Spanish forces and the announcement of the outfit of a French force to follow up the advantage, Mr. Charles Francis Adams wrote to his government from London:

It is no longer concealed that the intention is to advance to the capital, and to establish a firm government, *with the consent of the people,* at that place. But who are meant by that term does not appear. This issue is by no means palatable to the government here, though it is difficult to imagine that they could have been blind to it. Feeble murmurs of discontent are heard, but they will scarcely be likely to count for much in the face of the obligation under which the action of the emperor in the Trent case has placed them. The military occupation will go on, and will not cease with the limits now assigned to it. It is not difficult to understand the nature of the fulcrum thus obtained for operations in a new and a different quarter, should the occasion be made to use it. The expedition to the city of Mexico may not stop until it shows itself in the heart of the Louisiana purchase.[16]

About this time reports began to be circulated that the Archduke Ferdinand Maximilian of Austria would be invited by a large body of Mexicans to place himself on the throne of Mexico, and that the Mexican people would gladly hail such a change. To what-

---

[15] Brit. and For. St. Pap., Vol. LII, p. 381.
[16] Adams to Seward, January 24, 1862. House Ex. Doc. No. 100 p. 206, Thirty-seventh Cong., Second Sess.

ever extent such reports might be credited, the United States could not call into question the good faith of the parties to the London convention. The British government, as the issue showed, acted with perfect sincerity in the matter; and the Spanish government, whatever may have been its original intentions, followed the lead of Great Britain. When the reports in regard to Maximilian were first circulated, the British government declared to its agent, Sir Charles Wyke, that:

If the Mexican people, by a spontaneous movement, place the Austrian Archduke on the throne of Mexico, there is nothing in the convention to prevent it. On the other hand, we could be no parties to a forcible intervention for this purpose. The Mexicans must consult their own interests.[17]

At the time, however, the attitude of the British government was not at all understood. Mr. Adams wrote:

Great Britain occupies the post of holding the door, whilst her two associates, with her knowledge, go in, fully prepared, if they can, to perpetrate the act which she, at the outset, made them denounce, at the same time that she disavowed every idea of being made to participate in it.[18]

In the face of armed invasion, the Mexican government assumed a more reasonable attitude, and on the 19th day of February, 1862, the plenipotentiaries of Spain, Great Britain, and France signed, at Soledad, with the secretary of state of the Mexican government a preliminary agreement or convention, in which

---

[17] Brit. and For. St. Pap., Vol. LII, p. 418.
[18] H. Ex. Doc. No. 100, p. 209, Thirty-seventh Cong., Second Sess.

they recognized the constitutional government as then organized. Declaring that they had "no designs against the independence, sovereignty and integrity of the Mexican republic," they agreed to open negotiations for the settlement of all the demands which they had to make at Orizaba. During the negotiations the forces of the allies were to be allowed to leave the unhealthy locality of Vera Cruz and occupy the three towns of Cordova, Orizaba, and Tehuacan, with their natural approaches. In the event of negotiations being broken off, the allies agreed to abandon the towns above named before reopening hostilities.[19]

The convention of Soledad proved, however, of short duration. On the 9th of April, 1862, the representatives of the allies announced in a formal note to the Mexican government, "that not having been able to agree about the interpretation which ought to be given in the present circumstances to the convention of the 31st of October, 1861 (the convention of London), they have resolved to adopt for the future an entirely separate and independent line of action. In consequence, the commander of the Spanish forces will immediately take the necessary measures to reimbark his troops. The French army will concentrate in Paso Aucho as soon as the Spanish troops have passed from this position, that is to say, probably about the 20th of April, thereupon beginning their operations."[20] According to instructions already alluded to, the British force, which was limited to 700 marines, had declined to advance into the interior, and hence was not present when the breach occurred.

---

[19] H. Ex. Doc. No. 54, p. 46, Thirty-seventh Cong., Third Sess.
[20] *Ibid.*, p. 48.

FRENCH INTERVENTION IN MEXICO

In spite of all appearances to the contrary, the French government still persisted in disavowing to the United States government, in the most emphatic terms, all designs upon the independence of the Mexican republic. Even after the rupture at Orizaba, M. Thouvenel assured Mr. Dayton, the United States minister at Paris, that all that France wanted was that there should be a stable government in Mexico, not an anarchy with which other nations could have no relations.

That if the people of that country chose to establish a republic it was all well; France would make no objection. If they chose to establish a monarchy, as that was the form of government here, it would be charming (charmant), but they did not mean to do anything to induce such a course of action. That all the rumors that France intended to establish the Archduke Maximilian on the throne of Mexico were utterly without foundation.[21]

M. Thouvenel's disclaimer to the British government was equally emphatic.[22]

To return to the situation of affairs at Orizaba, the disagreement between the allies requires some explanation. The immediate cause of the rupture and of the withdrawal from the convention of London was the protection extended by the French agents to General Almonte, Padre Miranda, and other leading men of the reactionary or church party who had been banished from the country and who now from the French camp maintained an active correspondence with Marquez, Cobos, and other notorious chiefs of the armed bands

---

[21] Dayton to Seward, April 22, 1862.
[22] Earl Cowley to Earl Russell, May 15, 1862, H. Ex. Doc. No. 54, p. 746, Thirty-seventh Cong., Third Sess.

then in open rebellion against the constituted government of the country. Almonte and his associates openly favored the scheme of placing Maximilian on the throne.

The Mexican government demanded the removal of General Almonte and his associates from the camp of the allies, and in this demand the British and Spanish representatives concurred. A somewhat stormy conference was held between the commissioners of the allied powers at Orizaba, April 2, 1862, at which the French agents virtually said that they did not regard the convention of London or the preliminaries of Soledad as binding upon them. Specifically then the two causes of the rupture were (1) the persistency of the French commissioners in opposing the removal of the Mexican exiles, and (2) their refusal to take part in the conferences which had been arranged by the convention of Soledad to be held with the Juarez government at Orizaba, April 15, 1862. The British government heartily approved of the action of its agent, Sir Charles Wyke, in breaking up the conference and putting an end to the joint action of the three powers.[23] The policy of Spain was completely in accord with that of England.

The French government was not satisfied with the convention of Soledad, but did not dispute its validity, and declared that if the negotiations should be broken off, its provisions in regard to the withdrawal of the troops from their vantage ground must be observed. The French government further assumed that, when negotiations with the Mexican government should be broken off, the allied forces would proceed to act

[23] Earl Russell to Sir C. Wyke, May 22, 1862.

jointly under the convention of London.[24] The British and Spanish governments, however, having become convinced of the duplicity of the French government in the matter, terminated the London convention without further discussion and ordered the immediate withdrawal of their forces and agents from Mexican territory.

The government of Louis Napoleon, thus left to its own devices by the withdrawal of Great Britain and Spain, and by the helpless condition, for the time being, to which the war of secession had reduced the government of the United States, greatly reinforced its Mexican expedition and placed General Forey in command. Soon after the withdrawal of the British and Spanish contingents, General Almonte instituted a government in the territory occupied by the French and assumed the title of " Supreme Chief of the Nation," but it soon became evident, as Mr. Dayton expressed it, that instead of the emperor having availed himself of the services of General Almonte, Almonte had availed himself of the services of the emperor. Accordingly, shortly after General Forey assumed command, he issued an order dissolving the ministry of Almonte, depriving him of his title and limiting him thereafter " in the most exact manner to the instructions of the emperor, which are to proceed as far as possible, with other Mexican generals placed under the protection of our flag, to the organization of the Mexican army."

The misfortunes which had overtaken Mexico and the dangers that threatened the permanence of her re-

---

[24] Earl Cowley to Earl Russell, April 25, 1862, H. Ex. Doc. No. 54, p. 694, Thirty-seventh Cong., Third Sess.

publican institutions, had now thoroughly alarmed her sister republics of Central and South America, and a correspondence began between them relative to organizing an international American conference to oppose European aggression.

During the remarkable series of events that took place in Mexico in the spring of 1862, Mr. Seward consistently held to the opinion well expressed in a dispatch to Mr. Dayton, June 21, 1862:

> France has a right to make war against Mexico, and to determine for herself the cause. We have a right and interest to insist that France shall not improve the war she makes to raise up in Mexico an anti-republican and anti-American government, or to maintain such a government there. France has disclaimed such designs, and we, besides reposing faith in the assurances given in a frank, honorable manner, would, in any case, be bound to wait for, and not anticipate a violation of them.[25]

For some months the French troops gradually extended their military operations and occupied a greater extent of territory without, however, any material change in the situation. The Juarez government still held the capital. In the spring of 1863, however, military operations were pushed forward with greater activity, and in June, General Forey organized a junta of government composed of thirty-five Mexican citizens designated by decree of the French emperor's minister. The members of this supreme junta were to associate with them two hundred and fifteen citizens of Mexico to form an assembly of two hundred and fifty notables. This assembly was to occupy itself with

---

[25] H. Ex. Doc. No. 54, p. 530, Thirty-seventh Cong., Third Sess.

the form of the permanent government of Mexico. The junta appointed an executive body of three, of whom General Almonte was the head.

On the 10th of July, 1863, the capital of Mexico was occupied by the French army, and on the following day the Assembly of Notables declared:

1. The Mexican nation adopts as its form of government a limited hereditary monarchy, with a Catholic prince.

2. The sovereign shall take the title of Emperor of Mexico.

3. The imperial crown of Mexico is offered to his imperial and royal highness the Prince Ferdinand Maximilian, Archduke of Austria, for himself and his descendants.

4. If, under circumstances which cannot be foreseen, the Archduke of Austria, Ferdinand Maximilian, should not take possession of the throne which is offered to him, the Mexican nation relies on the good will of his majesty, Napoleon III, Emperor of the French, to indicate for it another Catholic prince.[26]

The crown of Mexico was formally offered to Maximilian by a deputation of Mexicans headed by Señor Estrada, October 3, 1863; but Maximilian replied that he could not accept the proffered throne until the whole nation should " confirm by a free manifestation of its will the wishes of the capital." This was a wise decision, had it been given in good faith and had it been wisely adhered to, but the sequel shows that the archduke was either not sincere in his protestations or else was woefully deceived by representations subsequently made to him. Six months later he accepted the crown without the question having been submitted

---

[26] Sen. Ex. Doc. No. 11, pp. 254-268, Thirty-eighth Cong., First Sess.

to the wishes of any but a very small portion of the Mexican people.

In spite of the declaration of the Mexican Assembly, which showed so unmistakably the hand of Napoleon, the French government continued to repudiate the designs imputed to it against the independence of Mexico, and Mr. Seward continued to express, officially at least, the satisfaction of the American government at the explanations vouchsafed by France. September 11, 1863, he stated the case as follows:

When France made war against Mexico, we asked of France explanations of her objects and purposes. She answered, that it was a war for the redress of grievances; that she did not intend to permanently occupy or dominate in Mexico, and that she should leave to the people of Mexico a free choice of institutions of government. Under these circumstances the United States adopted, and they have since maintained entire neutrality between the belligerents, in harmony with the traditional policy in regard to foreign wars. The war has continued longer than was anticipated. At different stages of it France has, in her intercourse with us, renewed the explanations before mentioned. The French army has now captured Pueblo and the capital, while the Mexican government, with its principal forces, is understood to have retired to San Luis Potosi, and a provisional government has been instituted under French auspices in the city of Mexico, which being supported by arms, divides the actual dominion of the country with the Mexican government, also maintained by armed power. That provisional government has neither made nor sought to make any communication to the government of the United States, nor has it been in any way recognized by this government. France has made no communication to the United States concerning the provisional government which has been established in Mexico, nor has she announced any actual or intended departure from the policy in regard to that country which her before-mentioned explanations have authorized us to expect her to pursue.[27]

The probable acceptance of the crown by Maximilian was, however, the subject of frequent communications between the governments of France and the United States. In the course of a somewhat familiar conversation with M. Drouyn de Lhuys, the French minister of state, in August, 1863, Mr. Dayton expressed the fear that in quitting Mexico France might leave a *puppet* behind her. De Lhuys replied: "No; the strings would be too long to work."

The chances of Maximilian's success in Mexico had been from the first deliberately calculated on the basis of the probable success of the Southern Confederacy; and, therefore, the cause of the Juarez government and the cause of the Union were considered the same. The active sympathy of the Unionists with the Mexican republic made it difficult for the administration to maintain neutrality. This difficulty was further enhanced by the doubt entertained in the United States as to the intentions of France. In this connection Mr. Seward wrote to Mr. Dayton, September 21, 1863, as follows:

The President thinks it desirable that you should seek an opportunity to mention these facts to Mr. Drouyn de Lhuys, and to suggest to him that the interests of the United States, and, as it seems to us, the interests of France herself, require that a solution of the present complications in Mexico be made, as early as may be convenient, upon the basis of the unity and independence of Mexico.[28]

---

[27] Seward to Motley, Sept. 11, 1863, Dipl. Corr., 1863; Sen. Ex. Doc. No. 11, p. 479, Thirty-eighth Cong., First Sess.
[28] Sen. Ex. Doc. No. 11, p. 464, Thirty-eighth Cong., First Sess.

In reply, the French minister declared that the question of the establishment of Maximilian on the Mexican throne was to be decided by a majority vote of the entire nation; that the dangers of the government of the archduke would come principally from the United States, and the sooner the United States showed itself satisfied, and manifested a willingness to enter into peaceful relations with that government, the sooner would France be ready to leave Mexico and the new government to take care of itself, which France would, in any event, do as soon as she with propriety could; but that she would not lead or tempt the archduke into difficulty, and then desert him before his government was settled. He said that the early acknowledgment of that government by the United States would tend to shorten, or perhaps to end, all the troublesome complications of France in that country; that they would thereupon quit Mexico.[29]

To this communication, Mr. Seward replied that the French government had not been left uninformed of the opinion of the United States that the permanent establishment of a foreign and monarchical government in Mexico would be found neither easy nor desirable; that the United States could not anticipate the action of the Mexican people; and that the United States still regarded Mexico as the scene of a war which had not yet ended in the subversion of the government long existing there, with which the United States remained in the relation of peace and friendship.[30]

---

[29] Dayton to Seward, Oct. 9, 1863, Sen. Ex. Doc. No. 11, p. 471, Thirty-eighth Cong., First Sess.

[30] Seward to Dayton, Oct. 23, 1863. *Ibid.*

FRENCH INTERVENTION IN MEXICO

Before formally accepting the crown, the archduke visited England with a view to securing a promise of recognition for his new position. He was, of course, to pass through Paris, and in view of his approaching visit, Mr. Dayton asked for instructions as to his conduct on the occasion. Mr. Seward replied, February 27, 1864:

I have taken the President's direction upon the question. If the Archduke Maximilian appears in Paris only in his character as an imperial prince of the house of Hapsburg, you will be expected to be neither demonstrative nor reserved in your deportment toward him. If he appears there with any assumption of political authority or title in Mexico, you will entirely refrain from intercourse with him. Should your proceeding be a subject of inquiry or remark, you will be at liberty, in the exercise of your own discretion, to say that this government, in view of its rights and duties in the present conjuncture of its affairs, has prescribed fixed rules to be observed, not only by this department, but by its representatives in foreign countries. We acknowledge revolutions only by direction of the President, upon full and mature consideration.[1]

The archduke visited London in company with his father-in-law, Leopold of Belgium. The British government declined to act on the subject at that juncture, " but gave them reason to hope that, so soon as the action in Mexico would appear to justify it, they would acknowledge him." [2] Spain and Belgium were ready to follow in the wake of France.

About the time of this visit of Maximilian to England, Mr. McDougall, of California, introduced in the Senate a resolution declaring " that the movements

[1] Dip. Corr., 1864.
[2] Adams to Seward, March 24, 1864.

of the government of France, and the threatened movement of an emperor, improvised by the Emperor of France, demand by this republic, if insisted upon, war." This resolution was not carried, but some days later, on the 4th of April, 1864, the House of Representatives passed by a unanimous vote a resolution declaring its opposition to the recognition of a monarchy in Mexico. Mr. Seward, fearing a rupture with France on this account, took pains to inform the government of that country, through Mr. Dayton, that this action of the House was in no way binding on the executive, even if concurred in by the Senate.

The formal acceptance of the crown of Mexico by Maximilian took place April 10, 1864, at Miramar, the palace he had built near Trieste, in the presence of the Mexican deputation. The next day the Emperor and Empress of Mexico, as they styled themselves, set out for their new dominions by way of Rome, where they received the blessing of the Pope. Before leaving Europe Maximilian signed with the Emperor of the French a convention in the following terms:

The French troops in Mexico were to be reduced as soon as possible to 25,000 men.

The French troops were to evacuate Mexico in proportion as the Emperor of Mexico could organize troops to replace them.

The " foreign legion," composed of 8,000 men, was to remain in Mexico six years after all the other French troops should have been recalled.

The expenses of the French expedition to Mexico, to be paid by the Mexican government, were fixed at the sum of two hundred and seventy million francs for the whole duration of the expedition down to

July 1, 1864. From July 1st all expenses of the Mexican army were to be met by Mexico.[33]

The resolution of the House referred to above came very near producing the rupture that Mr. Seward was striving to avert, or at least to postpone, during the continuance of the war of secession. When Mr. Dayton visited M. Drouyn de Lhuys just after the resolution reached Europe, the remark which greeted Mr. Dayton when he entered the room was: "Do you bring us peace, or bring us war?" Mr. Dayton replied that he did not think France had a right to think that the United States was about to make war against her on account of anything contained in that resolution; that it embodied nothing more than the principles which the United States had constantly held out to France from the beginning.

The Confederate agents were taking advantage of the resolution to stir up trouble between the United States and France. In fact they had long caused reports to be spread in Europe, and had succeeded in gaining credence for them, to the effect that the United States government was only awaiting the termination of domestic troubles to drive the French from Mexico. The French naturally concluded that if they were to have trouble with the United States, it was safest for them to choose their own time.[34] Napoleon was all the while coquetting with the Confederate government, and holding above Mr. Seward's head a veiled threat of recognition of Confederate independence. The Confederate government quickly caught at the suggestion of an alliance between Maxi-

---

[33] Dipl. Corr., 1865, Part III, pp. 356-849.
[34] Dipl. Corr., 1864; also Sen. Ex. Doc. No. 11, Thirty-eighth Cong., First Sess.

milian and the South with the power of France to back them. A Confederate agent was actually accredited to the government of Maximilian, but did not reach his destination. Although Napoleon's calculations were based on the overthrow of the Union, and although he had assumed at the outset, with England and Spain, an attitude decidedly unfriendly to the Federal government, nevertheless he was not willing to go the full length of recognizing the Confederacy as an independent power while the issue of the conflict was still in doubt.

In speaking of Slidell's movements in Europe and the encouragement given him in France, Mr. Bigelow wrote to Mr. Seward, February 14, 1865:

I am strongly impressed with the conviction that, but for the Mexican entanglement, the insurgents would receive very little further countenance from the imperial government, and that a reconciliation of the national policies of the two countries on that question would speedily dispose of all other sources of dissatisfaction.

As the war of secession seemed nearing its end, the French papers became uneasy in view of possible intervention in Mexico by the United States on the ground of the Monroe Doctrine. This principle of American diplomacy, which was likened to the sword of Damocles suspended over the head of Maximilian, was discussed in all its bearings on the present case by the journals of Europe.[35]

Throughout all this period of turmoil, the United States recognized no authority in Mexico but that of the Juarez government. In April, 1864, the French

---

[35] Dipl. Corr., 1865, Part III, pp. 380-385.

minister at Washington complained that serious complications with France were likely to arise out of grants of land made by "ex-President Juarez" in Sonora to emigrants from California. The French government regarded these grants as illegal and proposed to send forces there to prevent the parties from taking " illicit possession."

In May, 1864, the French government sought explanations in regard to a club formed in New Orleans, called the " D. M. D.," Defenders of the Monroe Doctrine. Mr. Seward replied that the object of the club, so far as the government had been able to ascertain, was to bring moral influences to bear upon the government of the United States in favor of a maintenance of the Monroe Doctrine, but not to act in violation of the law, or of the well-understood governmental policy of neutrality in the war which existed between France and Mexico. Members of the association did, however, actually start on an expedition to Brownsville, but the steamer was taken possession of by United States officials. During the year 1864 constant complaint was made by the French government of shipments of arms to the Juarez government from California and from various points along the Rio Grande, particularly Brownsville, in violation of American neutrality.

Shortly after the surrender of General Lee, several Confederate officers of high position and influence went to Mexico and identified themselves with the government of Maximilian. Dr. Wm. M. Gwin, a former United States Senator from California, organized a plan for colonizing the states of northern Mexico with ex-Confederates. This scheme was the subject of several representations to the French government on the part of Mr. Seward. He reminded them that the sympathies of the American people were already considerably excited in favor of the republic of Mexico; that they were disposed to regard with impatience the continued intervention of France in that country; and that any favor shown to the proceedings of Dr. Gwin by the titular Emperor of Mexico or by the imperial government of France would tend greatly to increase the popular impatience. He further requested an assurance that the pretenses of Dr. Gwin and his associates were destitute of any sanction from the Emperor of France.

Among the most prominent Confederates connected with this scheme were Matthew F. Maury, the distinguished geographer and naval officer, who became a naturalized Mexican citizen and was appointed Imperial Commissioner of Immigration and an honorary councillor of state; and General John B. Magruder, who was charged with the supervision of the survey of lands for colonization. It was hoped that the prominence of these men and the high rank they had held under the Confederate government would, in the general uncertainty that prevailed as to the treatment of the South by the victorious Union party, induce many persons to emigrate to Mexico. Maximilian issued a special decree, September 5, 1865, regarding colonization with a view to inducing Southern planters to emigrate to Mexico with their slaves—the latter to be reduced to a state of *peonage,* regular slavery being prohibited by the laws of the empire. This scheme was altogether impracticable.

In July, 1865, Maximilian finally made an effort to

secure recognition of his government by the United States. On the 17th of July, the Marquis de Montholon, the French minister at Washington, called at the department of state and informed Mr. Seward that a special agent had arrived at Washington, bearing a letter signed by Maximilian and addressed to the President of the United States, a copy of which the marquis presented to the secretary of state. On the 18th, Mr. Seward delivered back the copy of the letter to the Marquis de Montholon, and said that, as the United States were on friendly relations with the republican government of Mexico, the President declined to receive the letter or to hold any intercourse with the agent who brought it. The French government expressed to its representative at Washington its annoyance and embarrassment at this step, and said that Maximilian should have taken measures to learn the disposition of the United States before sending the agent.[36]

Mr. Tucker, in his book on the Monroe Doctrine, makes the statement that Mr. Bigelow, who succeeded Mr. Dayton as minister to France, announced to the French government that the United States would recognize the empire of Maximilian upon the immediate withdrawal of the French troops from the territory of Mexico, but that this statement, made upon the envoy's own authority, was disavowed by the President. This is hardly a correct version of the case. It seems that Mr. Bigelow, in the course of a conversation with M. Drouyn de Lhuys, asked him, " in his own name, and without prejudicing the opinion of his government, if he did not think that the recognition of Maximilian by

[36] Dipl. Corr. 1865, Part III.

the United States would facilitate and hasten the re-call of the French troops." [37]

On the 3rd of October, 1865, Maximilian issued a decree at the city of Mexico, the first article of which declared:

All persons belonging to armed bands or corps, not legally authorized, whether they proclaim or not any political princi-ples, and whatever be the number of those who compose the said bands, their organization, character and denomination shall be tried militarily by the courts-martial; and if found guilty even of the only fact of belonging to the band, they shall be condemned to capital punishment, within the twenty-four hours following the sentence. [38]

The United States, through Mr. Bigelow, protested to France against this decree, as repugnant to the sentiments of modern civilization and the instincts of humanity. M. Drouyn de Lhuys replied with a touch of sarcasm:

Why do you not go to President Juarez? We are not the government of Mexico and you do us too much honor to treat us as such. We had to go to Mexico with an army to secure certain important interests, but we are not responsible for Maximilian or his government. He is accountable to you, as to any other government, if he violated its rights, and you have the same remedies there that we had. [39]

The American government was now relieved from the burden of civil war, and for several months the correspondence of Mr. Seward had been assuming a more decided tone. On September 6, 1865, he re-minded the French government that the attention of

[37] Tucker, p. 104; Dipl. Corr., 1865, Part III.
[38] Sen. Ex. Doc. No. 5, p. 3, Thirty-ninth Cong., First Sess.
[39] Mr. Bigelow to Mr. Seward, Nov. 30, 1865, Sen. Ex. Doc. No. 5, Thirty-ninth Cong., First Sess.

the country was now no longer occupied by the civil war, and that henceforth both the Congress and the people of the United States might be expected to give a very large share of their attention to questions of foreign policy, chief among which was likely to be that of their relations with France in regard to Mexico. About this time Major General Schofield was sent to Paris on a mission, the precise object of which was long a matter of mystery. It appears from John Bigelow's memoirs that Grant, Schofield, and a number of other army officers were bringing great pressure to bear upon the government to intervene by force and drive Maximilian from Mexico. Seward, with his usual political sagacity, concluded that the best method of holding Grant and his followers in check was to send Schofield to Paris on an informal mission. According to the latter, Seward said to him: " I want you to get your legs under Napoleon's mahogany and tell him he must get out of Mexico." Seward knew perfectly well that Schofield would not be as belligerent in the presence of the Emperor as he was in Washington, and above all he had confidence in Bigelow's tact and ability to handle Schofield when he arrived in Paris. The plan worked beautifully. Neither Bigelow nor Schofield reported just what took place at the interview with the Emperor, but we may be sure that Schofield did not say in Paris what he had intended to say when he left Washington. After Bigelow returned from Paris in 1867, he had a conversation with Seward in which the latter said:

I sent General Schofield to Paris to parry a letter brought to us from Grant insisting that the French be driven head over heels and at once out of Mexico. It answered my purpose. It gave Schofield something to do, and converted him to the policy of the Department by convincing him that the French were going as fast as they could. That pacified Grant and made everything easy.[40]

On November 6 Seward wrote:

The presence and operations of a French army in Mexico, and its maintenance of an authority there, resting upon force and not the free will of the people of Mexico, is a cause of serious concern to the people of the United States. . . . They still regard the effort to establish permanently a foreign and imperial government in Mexico as disallowable and impracticable. For these reasons they could not now agree to compromise the position they have hitherto assumed. They are not prepared to recognize any political institutions in Mexico which are in opposition to the republican government with which we have so long and so constantly maintained relations of amity and friendship.

Finally, on December 16, 1865, Seward addressed what was practically an ultimatum to France. He pointed out the likelihood that Congress, then in session, would direct by law the action of the executive on this important subject, and stated that:

It has been the President's purpose that France should be respectfully informed upon two points, namely: First, that the United States earnestly desire to continue and to cultivate sincere friendship with France. Second, that this policy would be brought into imminent jeopardy, unless France could deem it consistent with her interest and honor to desist from the prosecution of armed intervention in Mexico, to overthrow the domestic republican government existing there, and to establish upon its ruins the foreign monarchy which

---

[40] Bigelow, "Retrospections of an Active Life," Vol. IV, p. 42; Bancroft, "Life of Seward," Vol. II, p. 435.

has been attempted to be inaugurated in the capital of that country.

In conclusion he added:

It remains now only to make known to M. Drouyn de Lhuys my profound regret that he has thought it his duty to leave the subject, in his conversation with you, in a condition that does not authorize an expectation on our part that a satisfactory adjustment of the case can be effected on any basis that thus far has been discussed.

As late as November 29, 1865, the French government, through the Marquis de Montholon, still insisted on recognition of Maximilian by the United States as the only basis for an arrangement for the recall of the French troops.[41]

The formal reply to Mr. Seward's note of December 16 was received through the Marquis de Montholon, January 29, 1866. M. Drouyn de Lhuys still insisted that the French expedition had in it nothing hostile to the institutions of the new world, and assuredly still less to those of the United States. He called attention to the fact that the United States had acknowledged the right of France to make war on Mexico, and continued: "On the other part, we admit, as they do, the principle of non-intervention; this double postulate includes, as it seems to me, the elements of an agreement." He also contended that the right to make war implied the right to secure the results of war; that they had to demand guarantees, and these guarantees they could not look for from a government whose bad faith they had proven on so many occa-

---

[41] Sen. Ex. Doc. No. 6, p. 98, Thirty-ninth Cong., First Sess.

229

sions; that they found themselves engaged in the establishment of a regular government, which showed itself disposed to keep its engagements; that the Mexican people had spoken, and that the Emperor Maximilian had been called to the throne by the will of the people of the country.[42]

Mr. Seward's counter-reply was dated February 12, 1866. He declared that the proceedings in Mexico were regarded in the United States as having been taken without the authority, and prosecuted against the will and opinions of the Mexican people; that the United States had not seen any satisfactory evidence that the people of Mexico had spoken and called into being or accepted the so-called empire, and that the withdrawal of the French troops was deemed necessary to allow such a proceeding to be taken. He added, however, that:

France need not for a moment delay her proposed withdrawal of military forces from Mexico, and her putting the principle of non-intervention into full and complete practice in regard to Mexico through any apprehension that the United States will prove unfaithful to the principles and policy in that respect which, on their behalf, it has been my duty to maintain in this now very lengthened correspondence.[43]

He concluded with a virtual ultimatum:

We shall be gratified when the Emperor shall give to us . . . definite information of the time when French military operations may be expected to cease in Mexico.

---

[42] House Ex. Doc. No. 93, Thirty-ninth Cong., First Sess.
[43] Dipl. Corr., 1865, Part III; also H. Ex. Doc. No. 93, Thirty-ninth Cong., First Sess.

Napoleon finally decided that, in view of the European situation, he could not risk a war with the United States, and in the issue of April 5, 1866, the *Moniteur* announced that the Emperor had decided that the French troops should evacuate Mexico in three detachments: the first to leave in November, 1866; the second in March, 1867; and the third in November, 1867. In the course of a conversation with Mr. Bigelow the day following M. Drouyn de Lhuys acknowledged that this statement was official.[44] The decision of the emperor was officially made known to the United States in a note of April 21, 1866. Seward had very fortunately left a loophole in his dispatch of February 12, in the statement that the United States would continue to pursue its policy of neutrality after the French evacuation. De Lhuys said:

We receive this assurance with entire confidence and we find therein a sufficient guarantee not any longer to delay the adoption of measures intended to prepare for the return of our army.[45]

American historians have usually attributed Napoleon's backdown to Seward's diplomacy supported by the military power of the United States, which was, of course, greater then than at any other time in our history. All this undoubtedly had its effect on Napoleon's mind, but it appears that conditions in Europe just at that particular moment had an even greater influence in causing him to abandon his Mexican scheme. Within a few days of the receipt of Seward's ultimatum Napoleon was informed of Bismarck's de-

[44] H. Ex. Doc. No. 93, p. 42, Thirty-ninth Cong., First Sess.
[45] *Ibid.*

termination to force a war with Austria over the Schleswig-Holstein controversy. Napoleon realized that the territorial aggrandizement of Prussia, without any corresponding gains by France, would be a serious blow to his prestige and in fact endanger his throne. He at once entered upon a long and hazardous diplomatic game in which Bismarck outplayed him and eventually forced him into war. In order to have a free hand to meet the European situation he decided to yield to the American demands.

About the time that the French government announced its intention of withdrawing its forces from Mexico, it was found that troops were being enlisted in Austria for the Mexican " foreign legion." The United States government at once took measures to prevent the French troops from being replaced by Austrians by declaring to the Austrian government through Mr. Motley, " that in the event of hostilities being carried on hereafter in Mexico by Austrian subjects, under the command or with the sanction of the government of Vienna, the United States will feel themselves at liberty to regard those hostilities as constituting a state of war by Austria against the republic of Mexico; and in regard to such war, waged at this time and under existing circumstances, the United States could not engage to remain as silent and neutral spectators." [46]

Mr. Motley seems to have been somewhat surprised and puzzled at the sudden and emphatic change of tone in the instructions of his government, and failed to carry them out in the spirit intended by Mr. Seward. This brought forth a sharp reprimand. Mr.

[46] Wharton's Digest, Sec. 58, Vol. I, p. 328.

Seward expressed his strong disapproval of the position taken by Mr. Motley in his communication of the instructions of the department to the Austrian government, and directed him to carry out his instructions according to the strict letter, adding:

I refrain from discussing the question you have raised, " Whether the recent instructions of this department harmonize entirely with the policy which it pursued at an earlier period of the European intervention in Mexico."

Mr. Motley was instructed to withdraw from Vienna in case troops were sent from Austria to Mexico. The embarkation of troops for this purpose was stopped. Austria was in a great state of excitement over the approaching war with Prussia, and, besides needing all her available troops at home, did not care to antagonize the United States.

It was now a question of great interest in this country and in Europe, whether Maximilian would withdraw from Mexico with the French troops or attempt to maintain himself there without foreign support. Napoleon sent one of his aides to Mexico to make known his intentions to Maximilian. This fact was communicated to the United States government, October 16, 1866:

Mr. de Castelnau has for his mission to make it well understood that the limit of our sacrifices is reached and that if the Emperor Maximilian, thinking to find in the country itself a point of sufficient support, may wish to endeavor to maintain himself there, he cannot for the future count on any succor on the part of France. But it may happen that, deeming it impossible to triumph through his own resources over the difficulties which surround him, this sovereign may determine to abdicate. We will do nothing to dissuade him from this, and we think that on this hypothesis there would be ground to proceed, by way of election, in the establishment of a new government.[47]

When the time came for the withdrawal of the first contingent of French troops, no action to that end was taken by the French government, and the United States had once more to seek an explanation. The Emperor assured the American government, however, that he had decided from military considerations to withdraw all his troops in the spring in a body, as the recent successes of the insurgents would render any large reduction of his forces perilous to those who remained. He further stated that he had counselled Maximilian to abdicate.[48] To the surprise of everyone, however, Maximilian seemed to think that honor demanded that he should remain in Mexico and share the fate of his supporters.

After the withdrawal of Mr. Corwin, owing to the unsettled state of affairs in Mexico, the United States had no one accredited to that government until May, 1866, when Mr. Lewis D. Campbell, of Ohio, was appointed. He left New York for his post in November, 1866, accompanied by Lieutenant General William T. Sherman of the army. They proceeded in the U. S. S. *Susquehanna* by way of Havana, but as they found the principal Mexican ports on the Atlantic still occupied by the French, they proceeded to New Orleans, from which point Mr. Campbell tried to establish regular communication with President Juarez. The President had first decided to dispatch General Grant with Mr.

[47] Dipl. Corr., 1866, Part I, p. 387.
[48] H. Ex. Doc. No. 30, Fortieth Cong., First Sess.

Campbell, in the hope " that some disposition might be made of the land and naval forces of the United States without interfering within the jurisdiction of Mexico, or violating the laws of neutrality, which would be useful in favoring the restoration of law, order and republican government in that country." This demonstration was intended to insure the withdrawal of the French army according to the promises of the Emperor. A hitch occurred through some question raised by General Grant and General Sherman was substituted.[49]

The French army was withdrawn in the spring of 1867, and it very soon became evident that Maximilian's cause would speedily collapse. In view of the almost inevitable capture of Maximilian, Mr. Seward telegraphed to Mr. Campbell at New Orleans, April 6, 1867:

> You will communicate to President Juarez, promptly and by effectual means, the desire of this government, that in case of capture, the prince and his supporters may receive the humane treatment accorded by civilized nations to prisoners of war.

Some of the prisoners already taken had been summarily executed.

Mr. Campbell at once dispatched a special messenger, who succeeded in getting through to the headquarters of Juarez, and who returned with an answer from the Mexican government, dated April 22, 1867. This answer not only undertook to defend the execution of prisoners above referred to, but also intimated that similar severity would be practiced on Maximilian

[49] Dipl. Corr., 1866, Part III.

and his leading associates, if captured, on the ground that, by his harsh decrees, he had placed himself beyond the pale of the law of nations.[50]

Maximilian and his chief supporters were taken prisoners, May 15, 1867. This information was received in the United States toward the last of the month, and along with it a report, not well authenticated and which afterward proved to be false, that they had been executed on the 16th. As soon as these rumors reached Washington, Mr. Seward telegraphed to Mr. Campbell, then at New Orleans, June 1, 1867, directing him to proceed at once to the residence of the President of Mexico and enter on his mission, and if necessary to urge clemency to Maximilian and the other prisoners of war. Mr. Campbell failed to act under these instructions. He requested first that a public vessel of the United States should be detailed to carry him to Mexico. When it was found that no ship was available for this purpose, he was ordered to proceed to Havana and thence by the British or French line of steamers to Vera Cruz. He replied that under the circumstances he did not think it becoming the dignity of the representative of the United States to return to Mexico under the flag of a nation which had shown such hostility to that country. He thus remained at New Orleans from the first to the fifteenth of June. He was then ordered peremptorily to proceed at once according to instructions. He replied that he was ill and was afraid to go by way of Havana, where yellow fever was raging; that he would resign, if desired. The same day Mr. Seward telegraphed him that his resignation would be accepted.

[50] Dipl. Corr., 1866, Part III.

Mr. Seward then informed Mr. Romero, the Mexican minister at Washington, that Austria, France, and Great Britain had appealed to the United States to use its good offices to avert the execution of Prince Maximilian. He strongly recommended clemency to President Juarez, as good policy, and requested Mr. Romero to make the same known to his government at once. This was June 15, the same day that Mr. Campbell's resignation was accepted. On the 21st, Mr. Seward requested Mr. Romero to inform President Juarez that the Emperor of Austria would restore Maximilian to all his rights of succession upon his release and renouncing forever all projects in Mexico.[51]

Meanwhile Maximilian of Hapsburg, Miguel Miramon, and Tomas Mejia had been tried by court-martial and sentenced to death, June 14. The sentence was confirmed by the government on the 15th, and the execution fixed for the 16th, but at the request of Maximilian's counsel, it was suspended by order of President Juarez until the 19th, in order to allow the prince to arrange certain business affairs of a private character. At seven o'clock on the morning of June 19 the prisoners were shot.

[51] Sen. Ex. Doc. No. 20, Fortieth Cong., First Sess.

CHAPTER VI

THE TWO VENEZUELAN EPISODES

As a result of Blaine's unsuccessful attempt to force Great Britain to relinquish her rights under the Clayton-Bulwer treaty the Monroe Doctrine had fallen somewhat into disrepute when in 1895 it was suddenly revived in a striking and sensational way by President Cleveland's intervention in the Venezuelan boundary controversy. The dispute between Great Britain and Venezuela in regard to the boundary line between the latter and British Guiana was of long standing. In 1814, by treaty with the Netherlands, Great Britain acquired "the establishments of Demerara, Essequibo, and Berbice," now known as British Guiana. From that time on the boundary line between British Guiana and Venezuela was a matter of dispute. Venezuela always claimed the line of the Essequibo river.

In 1840, Sir Robert Schomburgk, acting under the instructions of the British government, established a line some distance to the west of the Essequibo river and marked it by monuments on the face of the country. Venezuela at once protested. The British government explained that the line was only tentative and the monuments set up by Schomburgk were removed.

Various other lines were from time to time claimed by Great Britain, each one extending the frontier of British Guiana farther and farther to the west. The

British Colonial Office List, a government publication, in the issue for 1885, put the area of British Guiana at about 76,000 square miles. In the issue of the same list for 1886 the same statement occurs in reference to British Guiana with the change of area to "about 109,000 square miles." Here was a gain of 33,000 square miles without any statement whatever in explanation of how this additional territory had been acquired.

After the failure of repeated efforts on the part of Venezuela to secure an adjustment with England, she finally came to the conclusion in 1882 that the only course open to her was arbitration of the controversy. She persistently urged arbitration, but Great Britain refused to submit to arbitration any but a comparatively small part of the territory in dispute. In 1887 Venezuela suspended diplomatic relations with Great Britain, protesting "before her British majesty's government, before all civilized nations, and before the world in general, against the acts of spoliation committed to her detriment by the government of Great Britain, which she at no time and on no account will recognize as capable of altering in the least the rights which she has inherited from Spain and respecting which she will ever be willing to submit to the decision of a third power."

After repeated efforts to promote the reëstablishment of diplomatic relations between Venezuela and Great Britain and after repeated offers of its good offices for the purpose of bringing about an adjustment of the controversy, President Cleveland finally determined to intervene in a more positive manner with a view to forcing, if need be, a settlement of the controversy. This resolution on the part of the American executive, with a full statement of its views on the general principles involved in the dispute, was forwarded to Mr. Bayard for transmission to the British government in Mr. Olney's dispatch of July 20, 1895.[1] After reviewing the history of the controversy Mr. Olney stated in the following concise form what he considered the important features of the situation as it then existed:

1. The title to territory of indefinite but confessedly very large extent is in dispute between Great Britain on the one hand and the South American republic of Venezuela on the other.

2. The disparity in the strength of the claimants is such that Venezuela can hope to establish her claim only through peaceful methods—through an agreement with her adversary either upon the subject itself or upon an arbitration.

3. The controversy, with varying claims on the part of Great Britain, has existed for more than half a century, during which period many earnest and persistent efforts of Venezuela to establish a boundary by agreement have proved unsuccessful.

4. The futility of the endeavor to obtain a conventional line being recognized, Venezuela for a quarter of a century has asked and striven for arbitration.

5. Great Britain, however, has always and continuously refused to arbitrate, except upon the condition of a renunciation of a large part of the Venezuelan claim and of a concession to herself of a large share of the territory in controversy.

6. By the frequent interposition of its good offices at the instance of Venezuela, by constantly urging and promoting the restoration of diplomatic relations between the two countries, by pressing for arbitration of the disputed boundary, by offering to act as arbitrator, by expressing its

---

[1] For. Rel., 1895-96, Part I, p. 552.

grave concern whenever new alleged instances of British aggression upon Venezuelan territory have been brought to its notice, the government of the United States has made it clear to Great Britain and to the world that the controversy is one in which both its honor and its interests are involved and the continuance of which it cannot regard with indifference.

The greater part of the dispatch was taken up with a discussion of the bearing of the Monroe Doctrine upon the case and the most striking feature of it was that the Monroe Doctrine was appealed to by name. Mr. Olney's statement of the Monroe Doctrine is worthy of the most careful consideration as it was the fullest and most definite official construction of its meaning and scope that had been given to the world. He said:

That America is in no part open to colonization, though the proposition was not universally admitted at the time of its first enunciation, has long been universally conceded. We are now concerned, therefore, only with that other practical application of the Monroe Doctrine the disregard of which by an European power is to be deemed an act of unfriendliness towards the United States. The precise scope and limitations of this rule cannot be too clearly apprehended. It does not establish any general protectorate by the United States over other American states. It does not relieve any American state from its obligations as fixed by international law, nor prevent any European power directly interested from enforcing such obligations or from inflicting merited punishment for the breach of them. It does not contemplate any interference in the internal affairs of any American state or in the relations between it and other American states. It does not justify any attempt on our part to change the established form of government of any American state or to prevent the people of such state from altering that form according to their own will and pleasure. The rule in question has but a single purpose and object. It is that no European power or combination of European powers shall forcibly deprive an American state of the right and power of self-government and of shaping for itself its own political fortunes and destinies.

Lord Salisbury's reply to Mr. Olney was given in two dispatches of the same date, November 26, 1895, the one devoted to a discussion of the Monroe Doctrine, the other to a discussion of the rights of the controversy as between Great Britain and Venezuela. In the first dispatch Lord Salisbury argued that Mr. Olney's views went far beyond the scope of the Monroe Doctrine, that no attempt at colonization was being made, and that no political system was being imposed upon any state of South America. He also denied that the Monroe Doctrine was a part of international law, since it had not received the consent of other nations, and he utterly repudiated Mr. Olney's principle that " American questions are for American discussion."

In the second dispatch of the same date Lord Salisbury enters fully into the rights of the controversy between Great Britain and Venezuela, controverting the arguments of the earlier part of Mr. Olney's dispatch, which he characterizes as *ex parte*.

In view of the very positive character of Mr. Olney's dispatch and of the assertion that the honor and interests of the United States were concerned, the refusal of Great Britain to arbitrate placed the relations of the two countries in a very critical position. The American executive, however, had intervened for the purpose of settling the controversy, peaceably if possible, forcibly if need be, and President Cleveland did not now shrink from the logic of events. In a message to Congress, December 17, 1895,[2] he laid before that body Mr. Olney's dispatch of July 20, together with Lord Salisbury's reply. He not only reaffirmed the soundness of the Monroe Doctrine and its application to the case in question, but claimed for that principle of American diplomacy a place in the code of international law.

In regard to the applicability of the Monroe Doctrine to the Venezuelan boundary dispute Mr. Cleveland declared:

If a European power by an extension of its boundaries takes possession of the territory of one of our neighboring republics against its will and in derogation of its rights, it is difficult to see why to that extent such European power does not thereby attempt to extend its system of government to that portion of this continent which is thus taken. This is the precise action which President Monroe declared to be "dangerous to our peace and safety," and it can make no difference whether the European system is extended by an advance of frontier or otherwise.

In regard to the right of the United States to demand the observance of this principle by other nations, Mr. Cleveland said:

Practically the principle for which we contend has peculiar, if not exclusive, relation to the United States. It may not have been admitted in so many words to the code of international law, but since in international councils every nation is entitled to the rights belonging to it, if the enforcement of the Monroe Doctrine is something we may justly claim, it has its place in the code of international law as

---

[2] "Messages and Papers of the Presidents," Vol. IX, p. 655.

certainly and as securely as if it were specifically mentioned; and when the United States is a suitor before the high tribunal that administers international law the question to be determined is whether or not we present claims which the justice of that code of law can find to be right and valid. The Monroe Doctrine finds its recognition in those principles of international law which are based upon the theory that every nation shall have its rights protected and its just claims enforced.

Mr. Cleveland concluded that the dispute had reached such a stage as to make it incumbent upon the United States to take measures to determine with sufficient certainty for its justification what was the true divisional line between the republic of Venezuela and British Guiana. He therefore recommended that Congress make an appropriation for the expenses of a commission, to be appointed by the executive, which should make the necessary investigations and report upon the matter with the least possible delay. "When such report is made and accepted," he continued, "it will, in my opinion, be the duty of the United States to resist by every means in its power, as a willful aggression upon its rights and interests, the appropriation by Great Britain of any lands or the exercise of governmental jurisdiction over any territory which after investigation we have determined of right belongs to Venezuela." "In making these recommendations," he added, "I am fully alive to the responsibility incurred and keenly realize all the consequences that may follow."

The publication of this message and the accompanying dispatches created the greatest excitement both in the United States and in England, and called forth the severest criticism of the President's course.

The main grounds of this criticism were the contentions:

(1) That the Monroe Doctrine was not a part of international law and therefore its observance as such could not be urged upon other nations.

(2) That it was not even an established principle of American diplomacy, since the original declaration was merely a protest against apprehended aggression on the part of a combination of European powers which had long since ceased to threaten this continent.

(3) That even granting that the Monroe Doctrine was a declaration of American policy, it was merely a policy and imposed no obligation on the government to enforce it except where our interests were directly concerned.

(4) That the occupation of a few thousand acres of uninhabited territory by Great Britain, even if it did rightfully belong to Venezuela, was not a matter that affected the interests of the United States one way or the other or that threatened the permanence or stability of American institutions.

(5) That granting the wisdom and correctness of the President's position, the language of his message and of Mr. Olney's dispatch was indiscreet at best and unnecessarily offensive to British pride.

It may be well to consider these objections in detail. In regard to the first point it may be said that neither President Cleveland nor Mr. Olney asserted or maintained that the Monroe Doctrine was a part of international law by virtue of its assertion by President Monroe and succeeding presidents. The position they took was that the Monroe Doctrine was an American statement of a well recognized principle of inter-

245

national law, viz., the right of a state to intervene in a controversy between other states, when it deems its own interests threatened. Mr. Cleveland declared: " The Monroe Doctrine finds its recognition in those principles of international law which are based upon the theory that every nation shall have its rights protected and its just claims enforced." Mr. Olney's analysis of the doctrine was clearer and more specific. He said: " That there are circumstances under which a nation may justly intervene in a controversy to which two or more other nations are the direct and immediate parties is an admitted canon of international law." After discussing the general principle of intervention, he adds: " We are concerned at this time, however, not so much with the general rule as with a form of it which is peculiarly and distinctively American." [3]

In answer to the second objection it is only necessary to refer to accepted works on public law and to the official correspondence of the state department to show that the Monroe Doctrine had for three-quarters of a century been the cardinal principle of American diplomacy.[4]

The third point, namely as to the expediency of enforcing the Monroe Doctrine in all cases of European aggression on this continent, raises an important question. If, however, the Monroe Doctrine is a wise principle and one which it is our interest to maintain, it is right that it should be asserted on every occasion of its violation. The force of precedent is so great

---

[3] Olney to Bayard, July 20, 1895.
[4] Moore's " Digest of Int. Law," Vol. VI, pp. 368-604, especially Mr. Fish's Report on Relations with the Spanish-American Republics of July 14, 1870, pp. 429-431.

that in the present state of international law, it would be dangerous to do otherwise.

In the fourth place while it was perfectly true that the occupation of the disputed territory by Great Britain could not in itself conceivably endanger the peace and integrity of the United States, yet as the open violation of a principle upon which we had laid so much stress we could not in honor and dignity have overlooked it.

As to the tone of Mr. Olney's dispatch and of Mr. Cleveland's message, it must be acknowledged that while the positions assumed were in the main correct, the language was in some cases unfortunate, either from vagueness or generalization. Thus Mr. Olney's statement, that "3,000 miles of intervening ocean make any permanent political union between a European and an American state unnatural and inexpedient,"—whatever he may have meant by it—appears in view of Great Britain's connection with Canada, to have been both untrue and calculated to give offense. Likewise Mr. Cleveland's reference to "the high tribunal that administers international law" was too rhetorical a figure for a state paper.

It has, indeed, been suggested that President Cleveland and Mr. Olney deliberately undertook to play a bluff game in order to browbeat the British government. In any case, it should be remembered that the test of a diplomatic move is its success, and judged from this standpoint Mr. Cleveland's Venezuelan policy was vindicated by the results. The British government at once adopted the most friendly attitude and placed valuable information in its archives at the disposal of the commissioners appointed by President

247

Cleveland to determine the true boundary line. On November 12, 1896, before the final report of this commission was made, a complete accord was reached between Great Britain and the United States by which the terms of a treaty to be ratified by Great Britain and Venezuela were agreed on, the provisions of which embraced a full arbitration of the whole controversy. Lord Salisbury's sudden change of front has been the subject of much interesting speculation. How far he was influenced by the South African situation has never been revealed, but it undoubtedly had its effect. President Cleveland's message was sent to Congress December 17. Before the end of the month came Dr. Jameson's raid into the Transvaal, and on the 3rd of January the German Kaiser sent his famous telegram to Paul Kruger. The attention of England was thus diverted from America to Germany, and Lord Salisbury doubtless thought it prudent to avoid a rupture with the United States in order to be free to deal with the situation in South Africa.

The Anglo-Venezuelan treaty provided that an arbitral tribunal should be immediately appointed to determine the true boundary line between Venezuela and British Guiana. This tribunal was to consist of two members nominated by the judges of the Supreme Court of the United States and two members nominated by the British Supreme Court of Justice and of a fifth selected by the four persons so nominated, or in the event of their failure to agree within three months of their appointment, selected by the king of Sweden and Norway. The person so selected was to be president of the tribunal, and it was expressly stipulated that the persons nominated by the Supreme

Court of the United States and England respectively might be members of said courts. Certain general rules were also laid down for the guidance of the tribunal.[5]

A treaty embodying substantially these proposals was signed by the British and Venezuelan representatives at Washington, February 2, 1897. The decision of the tribunal which met in Paris gave a large part of the disputed area to Great Britain and this occasioned further criticism of President Cleveland's action in bringing the United States and England to the verge of war on what was termed an academic issue. The award was a matter of secondary importance. The principle for which the United States contended was vindicated when Great Britain agreed to arbitrate. It was a great triumph of American diplomacy to force Great Britain just at this time to recognize in fact, if not in words, the Monroe Doctrine, for it was not long before Germany showed a disposition to question that principle of American policy, and the fact that we had upheld it against England made it easier to deal with Germany.

The attention of Europe and America was drawn to Venezuela a second time in 1902 when Germany made a carefully planned and determined effort to test out the Monroe Doctrine and see whether we would fight for it. In that year Germany, England, and Italy made a naval demonstration against Venezuela for the purpose of forcing her to recognize the validity of certain claims of their subjects which she had persistently refused to settle. How England was led into the trap is still a mystery, but the Kaiser thought

[5] Foreign Relations, 1896, p. 254.

that he had her thoroughly committed and that if she once started in with him she could not turn against him. But he had evidently not profited by the experience of Napoleon III in Mexico forty years earlier under very similar circumstances.

In the case of Germany, though the facts were somewhat obscured, the real purpose of the intervention was to collect claims which originated in contract between German subjects and the government of Venezuela. One claim was for the recovery of interest seven years in arrears on five per cent. bonds, for which Venezuelan customs were pledged as security. Another was for seven per cent. dividends guaranteed by the Venezuelan government on the capital stock of a railroad built by German subjects at a cost of nearly $20,000,000. There were still other claims amounting to about $400,000 for forced loans and military requisitions.[6]

These claims were brought to the attention of the United States government by the German ambassador on December 11, 1901. Their dubious character, regarded from the standpoint of international law, led Germany to make what purported to be a frank avowal of her intentions to the United States, and to secure for her action the acquiescence of that government. Her ambassador declared that the German government had " no purpose or intention to make even the smallest acquisition of territory on the South American continent or the islands adjacent." This precaution was taken in order to prevent a subsequent assertion of the Monroe Doctrine. In conclusion the German ambassador stated that his government had de-

---

[6] Foreign Relations, 1901, p. 193; 1903, p. 429.

cided to "ask the Venezuelan government to make a declaration immediately, that it recognizes in principle the correctness of these demands, and is willing to accept the decision of a mixed commission, with the object of having them determined and assured in all their details." At the same time the British government demanded a settlement of claims for the destruction of property and for the ill-treatment and imprisonment of British subjects in the recent civil wars, as well as a settlement of the foreign debt.

On December 16, 1901, Mr. Hay replied to the German note, thanking the German government for its voluntary and frank declaration, and stating that he did not consider it necessary to discuss the claims in question; but he called attention to the following reference to the Monroe Doctrine in President Roosevelt's message of December 3, 1901:

This doctrine has nothing to do with the commercial relations of any American power, save that it in truth allows each of them to form such as it desires. In other words, it is really a guarantee of the commercial independence of the Americas. We do not ask under this doctrine for any exclusive commercial dealings with any other American state. We do not guarantee any state against punishment if it misconducts itself, provided that punishment does not take the form of the acquisition of territory by any non-American power.

A year later, after fruitless negotiations, the German government announced to the United States that it proposed, in conjunction with Great Britain and Italy, to establish a pacific blockade of Venezuelan harbors. The United States replied that it did not recognize a pacific blockade which adversely affected the rights of third parties as a valid proceeding. The powers then proposed to establish a " warlike blockade," but " without any declaration of war." This device was resorted to at the suggestion of the German government, in order to avoid a formal declaration of war, which could not be made without the consent of the Bundesrath. Meanwhile, Venezuela's gunboats had been seized and her ports blockaded, acts which Mr. Balfour admitted on the floor of the House of Commons constituted a state of war; and on December 20 a formal blockade was announced in accordance with the law of nations, which created a status of belligerency.[7]

The hostilities thus commenced were brought to a close by the diplomatic intervention of the United States. Acting under instructions from Washington, the American minister Herbert W. Bowen succeeded in persuading Venezuela to recognize in principle the claims of the foreign powers and to refer them to mixed commissions for the purpose of determining the amounts.[8] Great Britain and Italy agreed to this arrangement, but the German Kaiser remained for a time obdurate. What followed Germany's refusal to arbitrate is described in Thayer's " Life and Letters of John Hay " in the following words:

One day, when the crisis was at its height, [President Roosevelt] summoned to the White House Dr. Holleben, the German Ambassador, and told him that unless Germany consented to arbitrate, the American squadron under Admiral Dewey would be given orders, by noon ten days later, to proceed to the Venezuelan coast and prevent any taking

---

[7] Foreign Relations, 1903, pp. 419, 454; Moore, "Digest of Int. Law," Vol. VII, p. 140.
[8] Moore, " Digest of Int. Law," Vol. VI, p. 590.

possession of Venezuelan territory. Dr. Holleben began to protest that his Imperial master, having once refused to arbitrate, could not change his mind. The President said that he was not arguing the question, because arguments had already been gone over until no useful purpose would be served by repeating them; he was simply giving information which the Ambassador might think it important to transmit to Berlin. A week passed in silence. Then Dr. Holleben again called on the President, but said nothing of the Venezuelan matter. When he rose to go, the President asked him about it, and when he stated that he had received nothing from his government, the President informed him in substance that, in view of this fact, Admiral Dewey would be instructed to sail a day earlier than the day he, the President, had originally mentioned. Much perturbed, the Ambassador protested; the President informed him that not a stroke of a pen had been put on paper; that if the Emperor would agree to arbitrate, he, the President, would heartily praise him for such action, and would treat it as taken on German initiative; but that within forty-eight hours there must be an offer to arbitrate or Dewey would sail with the orders indicated. Within thirty-six hours Dr. Holleben returned to the White House and announced to President Roosevelt that a dispatch had just come from Berlin, saying that the Kaiser would arbitrate. Neither Admiral Dewey (who with an American fleet was then manœuvering in the West Indies) nor any one else knew of the step that was to be taken; the naval authorities were merely required to be in readiness, but were not told what for.

On the announcement that Germany had consented to arbitrate, the President publicly complimented the Kaiser on being so stanch an advocate of arbitration. The humor of this was probably relished more in the White House than in the Palace at Berlin.[9]

The Holleben incident, as narrated for the first time by Thayer, was immediately called in question.

---

[9] Thayer, " Life and Letters of John Hay," Vol. II, pp. 286-288.

It will be noted that Thayer does not in any way quote Hay in the matter, and in the three volumes of "Diaries and Letters" of John Hay, privately printed by Mrs. Hay in 1908, there is no reference of any kind to the incident. It is evident that Thayer got his report of the interview directly from Roosevelt himself. It is said on good authority that while Colonel Roosevelt had no documentary evidence to support his statements at the time that he gave them to Thayer, such evidence came to hand in an interesting way shortly after the appearance of the book. Two German-Americans who had been intimate friends of Holleben promptly wrote to Colonel Roosevelt protesting, not against the facts as stated, but against the use that was made of them. Both correspondents stated that they had been told of the interview at the time by Holleben. Admiral Dewey confirmed the statement as to the preparedness of the fleet in a letter dated May 23, 1916, which was published four days later in the New York *Times*. In it he said:

I was at Culebra, Porto Rico, at the time in command of a fleet consisting of over fifty ships, including every battleship and every torpedo-boat we had, with orders from Washington to hold the fleet in hand and be ready to move at a moment's notice. Fortunately, however, the whole matter was amicably adjusted and there was no need for action.

In a speech delivered to several thousand Republican "Pilgrims" at Oyster Bay, May 27, Colonel Roosevelt made the following interesting comments on Dewey's letter:

Just today I was very glad to see published in the papers the letter of Admiral Dewey describing an incident that took place while I was President. When we were menaced with trouble I acted up to my theory that the proper way of handling international relations was by speaking softly and carrying a big stick. And in that particular case Dewey and the American fleet represented the big stick. I asked, on behalf of the nation, the things to which we were entitled. I was as courteous as possible. I not only acted with justice, but with courtesy toward them. I put every battleship and every torpedo-boat on the sea under the American flag and Dewey, with instructions to hold himself ready in entire preparedness to sail at a moment's notice. That didn't mean that we were to have war. Dewey was the greatest possible provocative of peace.[10]

After the agreement to arbitrate had been made, the situation was further complicated by the demands of the blockading powers that the sums ascertained by the mixed commissions to be due them should be paid in full before anything was paid upon the claims of the peace powers. Venezuela insisted that all her creditors should be treated alike. The Kaiser, from what motives it is not quite clear, suggested that this question should be referred to President Roosevelt, but as the United States was an interested party, Secretary Hay did not think it would be proper for the President to act, and it was finally agreed that the demands for preferential treatment should be submitted to the Hague Court.

During the summer of 1903 ten mixed commissions sat at Caracas to adjudicate upon the claims of as many nations against Venezuela. These commissions simply determined the amount of the claims in each case. The awards of these commissions are very instructive, as they show the injustice of resorting to

---

[10] Washington *Post*, May 28, 1916.

measures of coercion for the collection of pecuniary claims which have not been submitted to arbitration. Belgian claimants demanded 14,921,805 bolivars and were awarded 10,898,643; British claimants demanded 14,743,572 and were awarded 9,401,267; German claimants demanded 7,376,685 and were awarded 2,-091,908; Italian claimants demanded 39,844,258 and were awarded 2,975,906; Spanish claimants demanded 5,307,626 and were awarded 1,974,818; United States claimants demanded 81,410,952 and were awarded 2,313,711.[11]

The decision of the Hague Court, which was rendered February 22, 1904, held that the three allied powers were entitled to preferential treatment; that Venezuela had recognized in principle the justice of their claims while she had not recognized in principle the justice of the claims of the pacific powers; that the neutral powers had profited to some extent by the operations of the allies, and that their rights remained for the future absolutely intact.[12] This decision, emanating from a peace court, and indorsing the principle of armed coercion, was received with no small degree of criticism.

During the discussions on the Venezuelan situation that took place in Parliament in December, 1902, the members of the government repeatedly repudiated the charge of the opposition that they were engaged in a debt-collecting expedition, and tried to make it appear that they were protecting the lives and liberties of British subjects. Lord Cranborne declared:

---

[11] Venezuelan Arbitrations of 1903 (Sen. Doc. No. 316, Fifty-eighth Cong., Second Sess.); Foreign Relations, 1904, p. 871.
[12] Foreign Relations, 1904, p. 506. For a full report of the case see Sen. Doc. No. 119, Fifty-eighth Cong., Third Sess.

THE TWO VENEZUELAN EPISODES

I can frankly tell the House that it is not the claims of the bondholders that bulk largest in the estimation of the government. I do not believe the government would ever have taken the strong measures to which they have been driven if it had not been for the attacks by Venezuela upon the lives, the liberty, and the property of British subjects.

During the same discussion, Mr. Norman said:

This idea of the British fleet being employed to collect the debts of foreign bondholders is assuredly a mistaken one. It was said by Wellington once that the British army did not exist for the purpose of collecting certain debts. It is still more true of the British fleet that it does not exist for the purpose of collecting debts of bondholders. People who lend money to South American republics know what the security is and what they are likely to get in return, and they ought not to have the British fleet at their backs.

To this Mr. Balfour, the prime minister, replied:

I do not deny—in fact, I freely admit—that bondholders may occupy an international position which may require international action; but I look upon such international action with the gravest doubt and suspicion, and I doubt whether we have in the past ever gone to war for the bondholders, for those of our countrymen who have lent money to a foreign government; and I confess that I should be very sorry to see that made a practice in this country.

Against President Roosevelt's contention that the coercion of an American state was not contrary to the Monroe Doctrine, provided that it did " not take the form of acquisition of territory by any non-American power," Signor Drago, Minister of Foreign Relations of the Argentine Republic, vigorously protested in a note dated December 29, 1902.[13] This note contained

[13] Foreign Relations, 1903, p. 1.

a restatement of the "Calvo doctrine," which takes its name from a celebrated Argentine publicist. In his well-known book on international law, Calvo contends that a state has no right to resort to armed intervention for the purpose of collecting the private claims of its citizens against another state. This doctrine, which has received the indorsement of most of the Latin-American states, was applied to public bonds in the note above referred to and is now usually known as the "Drago doctrine." Signor Drago held, first, "that the capitalist who lends his money to a foreign state always takes into account the resources of the country and the probability, greater or less, that the obligations contracted will be fulfilled without delay. All governments thus enjoy different credit according to their degree of civilization and culture, and their conduct in business transactions," and these conditions are measured before making loans. Second, a fundamental principle of international law is the entity and equality of all states. Both the acknowledgment of the debt and the payment must be left to the nation concerned "without diminution of its inherent rights as a sovereign entity."

He said further:

As these are the sentiments of justice, loyalty, and honor which animate the Argentine people and have always inspired its policy, your excellency will understand that it has felt alarm at the knowledge that the failure of Venezuela to meet the payment of its public debt is given as one of the determining causes of the capture of its fleet, the bombardment of one of its ports and the establishment of a rigorous blockade along its shores. If such proceedings were to be definitely adopted they would establish a precedent dangerous to the security and the peace of the nations of this part of

America. The collection of loans by military means implies territorial occupation to make them effective, and territorial occupation signifies a suppression or subordination of the governments of the countries on which it is imposed.

The doctrine so ably expounded by Dr. Drago attracted much attention during the next few years and was given a place on the program of the Third Pan American Conference held at Rio de Janeiro in July, 1906. Dr. Drago had made his proposal as " a statement of policy " for the states of the American continents to adopt. After full discussion the Rio Conference decided to recommend to the governments represented " that they consider the point of inviting the Second Peace Conference at The Hague to consider the question of the compulsory collection of public debts; and, in general, means tending to diminish between nations conflicts having an exclusively pecuniary origin." [14]

As a result of this action the United States modified the regular program prepared by Russia for the Second Hague Conference by reserving the right to introduce the question of an " agreement to observe certain limitations in the use of force in collecting public debts accruing from contracts." General Horace Porter presented to The Hague Conference a resolution providing that the use of force for the collection of contract debts should not be permitted until the justice of the claim and the amount of the debt should have been determined by arbitration. A large number of reservations were introduced, but the following resolutions were finally adopted by the votes

---

[14] *Am. Journal of Int. Law*, Vol. II, p. 78.

of thirty-nine states, with five states abstaining from voting:

> The contracting powers agree not to have recourse to armed force for the recovery of contract debts claimed from the government of one country by the government of another country as being due to its nationals.
>
> This undertaking is, however, not applicable when the debtor state refuses or neglects to reply to an offer of arbitration, or, after accepting the offer, prevents any " compromis " from being agreed on, or, after the arbitration, fails to submit to the award.[15]

---

[15] *Am. Journal of Int. Law,* Vol. II, Supplement, p. 82.

CHAPTER VII

The Advance of the United States in the Caribbean

At the beginning of the nineteenth century Spain was still in possession of all the shores of the Caribbean Sea and the Gulf of Mexico, but the downfall of her vast colonial empire was rapidly approaching. By the secret treaty of San Ildefonso she agreed to cede Louisiana back to France, and in 1803 Napoleon sold the entire province to the United States. This was our first acquisition of territory on the Gulf of Mexico, and it insured a free outlet for the vast region of the Mississippi valley. The boundaries of the province were indefinite, and there ensued a long controversy with Spain as to whether Louisiana included West Florida on the one hand and Texas on the other. These questions were finally adjusted by the Florida treaty of 1819, which ceded both East and West Florida to the United States and fixed the western boundary of Louisiana on the Gulf at the Sabine river. By this treaty the United States gained undisputed possession of the region extending from Mobile bay to the Mississippi, but abandoned the claim to Texas.

It was not many years before American settlers began pouring into Texas and came into conflict with the government of Mexico, which had by this time become independent of Spain. There followed the war of independence and the establishment of the Republic of Texas in 1836. Texas promptly applied for admission to the United States, but mainly through the opposition of the Abolitionists she was kept waiting for nine years. The new republic was recognized by the United States and by the principal powers of Europe, but Mexico refused to concede independence. Texas was thus in constant danger of attack from Mexico and unable to secure admission to the American Union. In April, 1844, a treaty providing for the annexation of Texas was submitted to the Senate by President Tyler, but it was rejected by that body. Under these circumstances the public men of Texas lent a ready ear to British and French intrigues. Great Britain wished to encourage the development of Texas as a cotton-growing country from which she could draw a large enough supply to make her independent of the United States. If Texas should thus devote herself to the production of cotton as her chief export crop, she would naturally adopt a free trade policy and thus create a considerable market for British goods. Great Britain, therefore, consistently opposed the annexation of Texas by the United States and entered into negotiations with France, Mexico, and the Republic of Texas for the express purpose of preventing it. Lord Aberdeen proposed that the four powers just mentioned should sign a diplomatic act, or perpetual treaty, securing to Texas recognition from Mexico and peace, but preventing her from ever acquiring territory beyond the Rio Grande or joining the American Union. While the United States would be invited to unite in this act, it was not expected that the government of that country would agree to

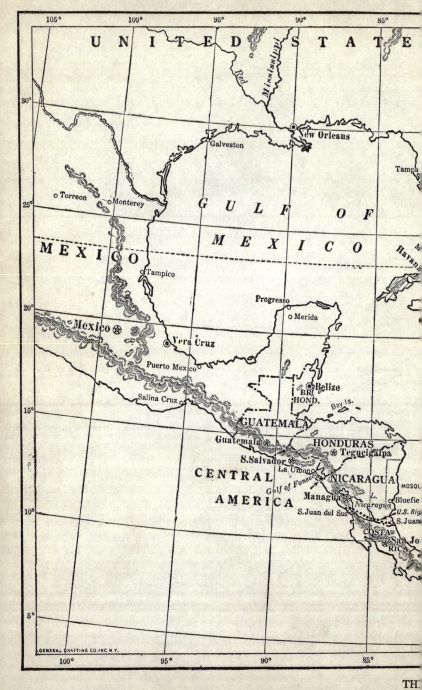

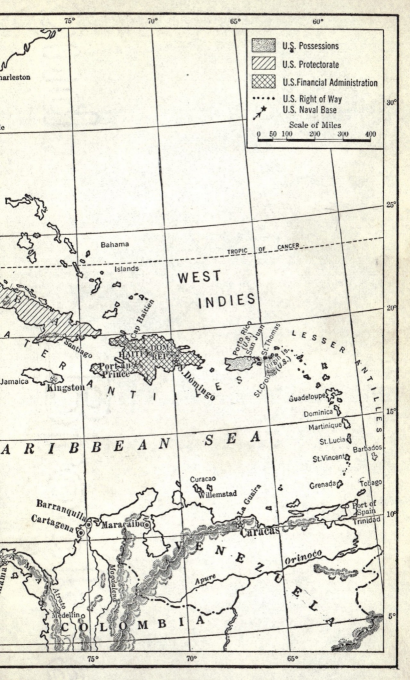

it. Despairing of being received into the American Union, Texas was apparently ready to accept the British proposal, but Lord Aberdeen's plan was defeated by the refusal of Mexico to recognize under any conditions the independence of Texas. Aberdeen was willing to coerce Mexico and, if need be, to fight the United States, but Louis Philippe was not willing to go that far. Meanwhile the Texas question had become the leading political issue in the United States. The Democratic platform of 1844 demanded "the re-annexation of Texas at the earliest practicable period," and on this platform Polk was elected President. Tyler, however, did not wait for his successor to carry out this mandate of the American people, but in the last days of his administration pushed through Congress a joint resolution providing for the admission of Texas.[1]

Mexico promptly severed diplomatic relations with the United States. As Mexico had never recognized the independence of Texas, she had of course never agreed upon any boundary with the new republic. This was a matter which had to be adjusted and there were also a number of private claims of American citizens against the government of Mexico which that government refused to settle. President Polk took up both questions with characteristic vigor, and on the refusal of Mexico to receive a special minister sent by him for the purpose of discussing these questions, he ordered General Taylor to occupy the disputed area between the Nueces river and the Rio

---

[1] E. D. Adams, "British Interests and Activities in Texas, 1838-1845" (1910); Justin H. Smith, "The Annexation of Texas" (1911) and "The War with Mexico," 2 vols. (1919); Diplomatic Correspondence of the Republic of Texas, edited by G. P. Garrison (Annual Reports, Am. Hist. Ass'n, 1907, 1908).

Grande. Thus began the Mexican War, which established the boundary of the United States on the Rio Grande and added the vast region of New Mexico and California to the Union. Here the tide of American expansion to the South was stayed for a full half century.

With the decline of the Spanish power Great Britain had succeeded to naval supremacy in the Caribbean. As has been related in previous chapters, the United States and Great Britain long regarded Cuba with jealous eyes and had a controversy lasting for half a century over the control of the proposed Isthmian canal. Secretary Seward at the close of the civil war sought to strengthen the position of the United States in the Caribbean by the acquisition of Santo Domingo and the Danish West Indies. In 1867 a treaty was concluded with Denmark providing for the cession of the islands of St. Thomas and St. John for $7,500,000, on condition that the inhabitants should by popular vote give their consent. In undertaking these negotiations the United States was influenced on the one hand by the desire to acquire a naval base, and on the other by the fear that these islands might fall into the hands of one of the greater European powers. The plebiscite in St. John and St. Thomas was overwhelmingly in favor of the cession, and the treaty was promptly ratified by the Danish Rigsdag, but the Senate of the United States took no action until March, 1870, when Senator Sumner presented an adverse report from the Committee on Foreign Relations and the treaty was rejected.

In 1867 Admiral Porter and Mr. F. W. Seward, the assistant secretary of state, were sent to Santo

Domingo for the purpose of securing the lease of Samana bay as a naval station. Their mission was not successful, but the following year the president of the Dominican Republic sent an agent to Washington proposing annexation and requesting the United States to occupy Samana bay at once. In his annual message of December 8, 1868, President Johnson advocated the annexation of Santo Domingo and a joint resolution to that effect was introduced into the House, but it was tabled without debate by an overwhelming vote. President Grant became much interested in this scheme, and soon after entering the White House he sent one of his private secretaries, Colonel Babcock, to the island to report on the condition of affairs. Babcock negotiated a treaty for the annexation of the Dominican Republic, and another for the lease of Samana bay. As Colonel Babcock was without diplomatic authority of any kind, the Cabinet received the treaties in silent amazement, and Hamilton Fish, who was secretary of state, spoke of resigning, but Grant persuaded him to remain in office. The annexation treaty was submitted to the Senate in January, 1870, but encountered violent opposition, especially from Sumner, Chairman of the Committee on Foreign Relations. It was finally rejected June 30 by vote of 28 to 28.

The advance of the United States into the Caribbean was thus delayed until the Spanish War. As a result of that conflict the United States acquired Porto Rico and a protectorate over Cuba. The real turning-point in the recent history of the West Indies was the Hay-Pauncefote treaty of 1901, under the terms of which Great Britain relinquished her claim to an equal voice with the United States in the control of an Isthmian canal on which she had insisted for half a century. While the Hay-Pauncefote treaty was limited in terms to the canal question, it was in reality of much wider significance. It amounted in effect to the transference of naval supremacy in the West Indies to the United States, for since its signature Great Britain has withdrawn her squadron from this important strategic area. So marked was Great Britain's change of attitude toward the United States at this time that some writers have concluded that a secret treaty of alliance was made between the two countries in 1897. The absurdity of such a statement was pointed out by Senator Lodge several years ago. England's change of attitude is not difficult to understand. For one hundred years after the battle of Trafalgar England had pursued the policy of maintaining a navy large enough to meet all comers. With the rapid growth of the navies of Russia, Japan, and Germany during the closing years of the nineteenth century, England realized that she could no longer pursue a policy of isolation. Our acquisition of the Philippines, the Hawaiian Islands, and Porto Rico and our determination to build an Isthmian canal made a large American navy inevitable. Great Britain realized, therefore, that she would have to cast about for future allies. It was on considerations of this kind that she signed the Hay-Pauncefote treaty with the United States in 1901, and the defensive alliance with Japan in 1902. In view of the fact that the United States was bent on carrying out the long deferred canal scheme, Great Britain realized that a further insistence on her rights under the Clayton-Bulwer treaty would lead to friction and possible conflict. She wisely decided, therefore, to recede from the position which she had held for half a century and to give us a free hand in the acquisition and control of the canal at whatever point we might choose to build it. In signing the Hay-Pauncefote treaty she gracefully recognized the fact that the United States had paramount interests in the Caribbean which it was unwise for her to contest. Since the signature of that treaty American supremacy in this area has not been seriously questioned.

The determination to build a canal not only rendered inevitable the adoption of a policy of naval supremacy in the Caribbean sea, but led to the formulation of new political policies to be applied in the zone of the Caribbean—what Admiral Chester calls the larger Panama Canal Zone—that is, the West Indies, Mexico and Central America, Colombia and Venezuela. The policies referred to included the establishment of protectorates, the supervision of finances, the control of all naval routes, the acquisition of naval stations, and the policing and administration of disorderly countries.

The advance of the United States in the Caribbean since the Spanish War has been rapid. The acquisition of Porto Rico and the establishment of a protectorate over Cuba were the natural outcome of that struggle. In 1903 we acquired the canal zone under circumstances already described. The following year President Roosevelt established financial supervision over the Dominican Republic. In 1915 the United States landed marines in Haiti and a treaty was soon drafted under which we assumed financial supervision and administrative control over the affairs of that country. In 1916 we acquired by treaty from Nicaragua an exclusive right of way for a canal through her territory and the lease of a naval station on Fonseca bay, and in 1917 we acquired by treaty from Denmark her holdings in the West Indies known as the Virgin Islands. These successive steps will be considered in detail.

The methods employed by President Roosevelt in the acquisition of the Panama Canal Zone described in a previous chapter caused indignation and alarm throughout Latin America and created strained relations with Colombia. The Colombian government refused to recognize the independence of the Republic of Panama and demanded that her claim to Panama as well as her interests in the canal should be submitted to arbitration. Colombia claimed that President Roosevelt had misinterpreted the treaty of 1846, which established mutual obligations between the United States and Colombia with reference to the isthmus, by construing its provisions as obligations to the world at large against Colombia. As the United States had always advocated the submission to arbitration of questions involving the construction of treaties, the demand of Colombia proved embarrassing, but both Secretary Hay and his successor, Secretary Root, rejected the demand for arbitration on the ground that the questions involved were of a political nature.[2]

In January, 1909, shortly before the close of the Roosevelt administration, Secretary Root undertook

---

[2] House Doc. No. 1444, Sixty-second Cong., Third Sess., pp. 2, 3; Sen. Ex. Doc. No. 1, Sixty-fifth Cong., Special Sess., pp. 47, 48.

to reëstablish friendly relations with Colombia through the negotiation in the city of Washington of three treaties, one between the United States and the Republic of Colombia, one between the United States and the Republic of Panama, and one between Colombia and Panama. In the treaty between Colombia and Panama the Republic of Colombia recognized fully the independence of Panama, and the Republic of Panama made an assignment to Colombia of the first ten installments of $250,000, the amount due annually to the Republic of Panama from the United States as rental for the canal. According to the treaty between the United States and the Republic of Panama, concluded November 18, 1903, the payment of this annual sum was to begin nine years from date. It was now agreed that the first annual payment should be regarded as due four years from the exchange of ratifications of the said treaty, so that of the $2,500,000 to be paid to Colombia, half would be paid by the United States and half by Panama. In the new treaty between the United States and Panama the necessary modification of the treaty of 1903 was made so as to permit of this assignment of the first ten installments to Colombia. In the treaty between the United States and Colombia the most important provision was as follows:

The Republic of Colombia shall have liberty at all times to convey through the ship canal now in course of construction by the United States across the Isthmus of Panama the troops, materials for war, and ships of war of the Republic of Colombia, without paying any duty to the United States; even in the case of an international war between Colombia and another country.

It was further provided that the products of the soil and industry of Colombia should be admitted to the canal zone subject only to such duty as would be payable on similar products of the United States under similar conditions, and Colombian mails were to have free passage through the canal zone on payment of such duties or charges as were laid on the mails of the United States.[3]

These tripartite treaties were of course to stand or fall together. The United States and Panama promptly ratified the agreements to which they were parties, but Colombia rejected the arrangement with indignation. In fact, when the terms of the settlement were made public, the Colombian adminstration that urged their acceptance was overthrown, and the Colombian envoy who participated in the negotiation of the treaties was forced to flee from the country with an indignant mob at his heels. Colombia was not to be appeased by the paltry sum of $2,500,000.

The Taft administration made repeated efforts to placate Colombia, but without success. On September 30, 1912, Mr. Du Bois, the American minister to Colombia, submitted to Secretary Knox an interesting review of the whole question in the course of which, after referring to the friendly relations that had so long subsisted between the two countries, he said:

Nine years ago this was changed suddenly and unexpectedly when President Roosevelt denied to Colombia the right to land her troops upon her own soil to supress a threatened revolt and maintain a sovereignty guaranteed by treaty stipulations. The breach came and it has been

[3] Sen. Ex. Doc. No. 1, Sixty-fifth Cong., Special Sess., pp. 24-34.

growing wider since that hour. By refusing to allow Colombia to uphold her sovereign rights over a territory where she had held dominion for eighty years, the friendship of nearly a century disappeared, the indignation of every Colombian, and millions of other Latin-Americans, was aroused and is still most intensely alive. The confidence and trust in the justice and fairness of the United States, so long manifested, has completely vanished, and the maleficent influence of this condition is permeating public opinion in all Latin-American countries, a condition which, if remedial measures are not invoked, will work inestimable harm throughout the Western Hemisphere.[4]

Mr. Du Bois reported that on inquiry of prominent Colombians of the causes of the rejection of the Root proposals he received replies to the following effect:

Five years after President Roosevelt had taken Panama from us with rank injustice, your government, still under his chief magistracy, offered us a paltry $2,500,000 if Colombia would recognize the independence of her revolted province, fix our frontier at a further loss of territory, open all our ports free to the refuge of vessels employed in the canal enterprise, and exempt them from anchorage or tonnage dues, renounce our rights to all of our contracts and concessions relating to the construction and operation of the canal or railroad across the isthmus, release Panama from obligation for the payment of any part of our external debt, much of which was incurred in the interest of Panama, and enter into negotiations for the revision of the treaty of 1846, which five years before had been openly violated by the United States in their failure to help maintain the sovereignty over the rebellious province which they had solemnly guaranteed. The reply was to this, banishment of our minister who negotiated the treaty, and all South America applauded our attitude.[5]

[4] Sen. Ex. Doc. No. 1, Sixty-fifth Cong., Special Sess., p. 35.
[5] Ibid., p. 41.

Mr. Du Bois then proceeded to state at length Colombia's claims which he summarized as follows: " Panama Railroad annuities, $16,000,000; value of railroad, $16,446,942; Panama Canal rights, $17,500,-000; cost of Costa Rican boundary arbitration, $200,-000; total, $50,446,942. [The total should be $50,-146,942.] Besides this sum, Colombia has lost the Province of Panama, whose value cannot be readily estimated." [6]

In conclusion he urged the importance of a speedy adjustment of the differences with Colombia in the following words:

South America is advancing along commercial lines with giant strides. The character of the future relations of the United States with that country will be of signal importance. Friendly intercourse with all Latin America should be carefully developed and maintained, and especially is this important with Colombia, which borders the isthmus, has fine ports on both oceans, and is destined to become an influential factor in the political and commercial life of South America, especially in all countries bordering on the Caribbean sea. To approach Colombia in a conciliatory spirit and seek a renewal of her ancient friendship would not only be a wise and just move on the part of the United States, but as Colombia and all South and Central America firmly believe that the government of the United States was unjust in the Panama incident, from which has come infinite distress to Colombia, it would be a benevolent and fraternal act, and the time to move is the present, before the canal opens and while the public sentiment of both countries is in harmony with the movement.[7]

At the time that the above report on relations with Colombia was prepared by Mr. Du Bois he was in

---

[6] Sen. Ex. Doc. No. 1, Sixty-fifth Cong., Special Sess., p. 44.
[7] Ibid.

this country, having come home to confer with the Department of State as to the program to be followed in the settlement of the differences with Colombia. On his return to Bogota, Mr. Du Bois submitted the following proposals to the Colombian government: (1) ratification of the Root treaties, involving the payment to Colombia of the first ten installments of the annual rental of the canal zone amounting to $2,500,000; (2) the payment of $10,000,000 by the United States to Colombia for the right to build an interoceanic canal by the Atrato route and for the lease of the islands of Old Providence and St. Andrews as coaling stations; (3) the good offices of the United States on behalf of Colombia in bringing about an adjustment of the boundary line between Colombia and Panama; (4) the submission to arbitration of the claims of Colombia to reversionary rights in the Panama Railroad assumed by the United States under Article XXII of the treaty of 1903 between the United States and Panama, estimated by Mr. Taft's secretary of war at over $16,000,000; and (5) the granting of preferential rights to Colombia in the use of the Panama Canal.

The Colombian government promptly rejected these proposals and in reply demanded " arbitration of the whole question of Panama or a direct proposition on the part of the United States to give Colombia compensation for all the moral, physical, and financial losses which she sustained as a result of the separation of Panama." The Colombian minister declared:

Should Colombia grant any territorial privileges to the United States after the wrong that country has inflicted upon this republic, it would result in intense agitation and possible

revolution. It seems as though your people have never
fully realized the enormity of the wrong the United States
has perpetrated against the Colombian people.

Mr. Du Bois then asked whether Colombia would
accept $10,000,000, the good offices of the United
States in settling the differences with Panama, arbitration of the reversionary rights in the Panama Railroad, and preferential rights in the canal, without
granting to the United States any privileges or concessions whatever. Receiving a negative reply to this
proposal, Mr. Du Bois, acting on his own responsibility, then inquired informally whether $25,000,000
without options of any kind would satisfy Colombia.
The answer was that Colombia would accept nothing
but the arbitration of the whole Panama question.
Mr. Du Bois was instructed February 20, 1913, to stop
negotiations. In reporting the matter to the President,
Secretary Knox said that Colombia seemed determined
to treat with the incoming Democratic administration.[8]

When the Wilson administration came in, Secretary Bryan took up the negotiations with Colombia
where Knox dropped them, and concluded a treaty
according to the terms of which the United States
was to express " sincere regret that anything should
have occurred to interrupt or to mar the relations of
cordial friendship that had so long subsisted between
the two nations," and to pay Colombia $25,000,000.
The treaty further granted Colombia the same preferential rights in the use of the canal which the Taft
administration had proposed, and in return Colombia
agreed to recognize the independence of Panama and
to accept a boundary line laid down in the treaty.

[8] Sen. Ex. Doc. No. 1, Sixty-fifth Cong., Special Sess., pp. 53-79.

This treaty was submitted to the Senate June 16, 1914. As soon as its terms were made public ex-President Roosevelt denounced it as blackmail, and wrote a letter to the chairman of the Senate Committee on Foreign Affairs requesting to be heard before any action was taken on the treaty. During the first session of the Sixty-sixth Congress in 1919 the Colombian treaty was reported from the Committee on Foreign Relations with important amendments. Article I, containing expressions of regret on the part of the United States for the events that had taken place on the isthmus, was entirely stricken out. The clause giving Colombia the right to transport through the canal its troops, materials of war, and ships of war, " even in case of war between Colombia and another country," was amended by the elimination of the words in quotations. The sum of $25,000,000, instead of being paid in cash, was to be paid in five annual installments. The Senate refused, however, to give its consent to the ratification of the treaty even in this form, and it is understood that it was proposed to cut the payment to Colombia down to $15,000,000.

A great nation like the United States, which has always professed to be guided in international questions by high standards of justice and morality, cannot afford to delay indefinitely the settlement of a dispute of this kind with a weak nation like Colombia. President Roosevelt's action in the Panama matter made a bad impression throughout Latin America and caused our policy in the Caribbean to be regarded with grave suspicion. As to Colombia's rights in the matter, Secretary Bryan made the following statement in his argument before the Senate Committee on Foreign Relations in support of the treaty:

It is contended by some that the action taken by the United States was based upon the necessities of the case, and those necessities, as stated by those who take this position are, that Colombia was not able to build the canal herself and was not willing to sell to the United States upon reasonable terms the right to build the canal. Those who take this position put the United States in the attitude of exercising the right of eminent domain in the interest of the world's commerce; but the exercise of the right of eminent domain does not relieve those who exercise it of liability for actual damages suffered. Take, for illustration, the condemning of a block of ground for a public building. Suppose that every lot owner excepting one is willing to sell his land to the government at its market value, but that one of the lot owners, whose lot is necessary to the erection of the building, asks more than the land is worth. The government proceeds to condemn the property, but it does not attempt to escape from paying what the land is actually worth, and the actual value of the property is not reduced one dollar by any effort that the owner may make to obtain for it more than it is worth. If it is contended that the price offered by the United States prior to Panama's separation was a reasonable one, and that Colombia ought to have accepted it, that valuation cannot be reduced merely because Colombia was not willing to accept the offer. This illustration is based upon the theory adopted by those who say that Colombia was entirely in the wrong in refusing to accept the offer made by the United States, but this theory, it will be remembered, is disputed by the people of Colombia, who defend the position their government then took and, as has been said before, they have ever since asked that the controversy be arbitrated by some impartial tribunal.[9]

In 1904 President Roosevelt made a radical departure from the traditional policy of the United

---

[9] Sen. Ex. Doc. No. 1, Sixty-fifth Cong., Special Sess., pp. 87-88.

States in proposing that we should assume the financial administration of the Dominican Republic in order to prevent certain European powers from resorting to the forcible collection of debts due their subjects. On September 12, 1904, Minister Dawson reported to the State Department that the debt of Santo Domingo was $32,280,000, the estimated revenues from customs receipts $1,850,000, and the proposed budget for current expenses $1,300,000, leaving only $550,000 with which to meet payments of interest, then accruing and in arrears, amounting to $2,600,000. About $22,000,000 of this debt was due to European creditors. Most of this indebtedness had been incurred by revolutionary leaders who had at various times taken forcible possession of the government and hastened to raise all the money they could by the sale of bonds, leaving the responsibility with their successors. The European creditors of Santo Domingo were pressing for the recognition of their claims. Germany seemed especially determined to force a settlement of her demands, and it was well known that Germany had for years regarded the Monroe Doctrine as the main hindrance in the way of her acquiring a foothold in Latin America. The only effective method of collecting the interest on the foreign debt appeared to be the seizure and administration of the Dominican custom-houses by some foreign power or group of foreign powers. President Roosevelt foresaw that such an occupation of the custom-houses would, in view of the large debt, constitute the occupation of American territory by European powers for an indefinite period of time, and would therefore be a violation of the Monroe Doc-

trine. He had before him also the results of a somewhat similar financial administration of Egypt undertaken jointly by England and France in 1878, and
after Arabi's revolt continued by England alone, with
the result that Egypt soon became a possession of the
British Crown to almost as great a degree as if it
had been formally annexed. President Roosevelt concluded, therefore, that where it was necessary to place
a bankrupt American republic in the hands of a receiver, the United States must undertake to act as
receiver and take over the administration of its
finances.

The policy that he was about to adopt was stated
as follows in his annual message of December 6,
1904:

Any country whose people conduct themselves well can
count upon our hearty friendship. If a nation shows that
it knows how to act with reasonable efficiency and decency
in social and political matters, if it keeps order and pays its
obligations, it need fear no interference from the United
States. Chronic wrongdoing, or an impotence which results
in a general loosening of the ties of civilized society, may
in America, as elsewhere, ultimately require intervention
by some civilized nation, and in the Western Hemisphere, the
adherence of the United States to the Monroe Doctrine
may force the United States, however reluctantly, in flagrant
cases of such wrongdoing or impotence, to the exercise of an
international police power.

About the same time Minister Dawson was directed
by Secretary Hay to suggest to the Dominican government that it request the United States to take charge
of its customs. As the Dominican government saw
no other way out of its difficulties, it responded to

this suggestion, and on February 4, 1905, a protocol was signed by Mr. Dawson and the Dominican foreign minister which provided that the United States should guarantee the territorial integrity of the Dominican Republic, take charge of its custom-houses, administer its finances, and settle its obligations, foreign as well as domestic. In calling the new agreement a " protocol " instead of a " treaty," the President had probably not intended to submit it to the Senate, but the proposal to depart so radically from our past policy created so much criticism that the Senate was finally asked to ratify the protocol in regular form. This they failed to do, but the President did not propose to be thwarted in this way. As the Senate would not sanction his appointment of a receiver of customs for Santo Domingo, he drafted a *modus vivendi,* under the terms of which the President of the Dominican Republic appointed a receiver of customs named unofficially by President Roosevelt, who proceeded to administer the affairs of the republic under the protection of the United States navy, whose ships the President could as commander-in-chief order wherever he pleased. The President's course met with determined opposition both in and out of Congress, but as he was bent on having his way and continued to carry out his policy without the sanction of the Senate, that body finally decided that it would be best to give the arrangement a definite legal status. On February 25, 1907, the Senate agreed to the ratification of a revised treaty which omitted the territorial-guarantee clause, but provided that the President of the United States should appoint a general receiver of Dominican customs and such assistants as he might deem necessary; that the government of the United States should afford them such protection as might be necessary for the performance of their duties; and that until the bonded debt should be paid in full, the Dominican government would not increase its debt except with the consent of the United States. In the meantime, under the *interim* arrangement, conditions in Santo Domingo had greatly improved, the customs receipts had nearly doubled, and the creditors had agreed to compromise their claims, so that the total debt at the time the above treaty was ratified amounted to not more than $17,000,000.[10]

In spite of the criticism that President Roosevelt's policy encountered, the Taft administration not only continued it in Santo Domingo, but tried to extend it to Nicaragua and Honduras. The five republics of Central America had been for years in a state of political and economic disorder as the result of wars and revolutions. In 1906 there was a war between Guatemala and Salvador, in which Honduras became involved as the ally of Salvador. President Roosevelt invited President Diaz of Mexico to unite with him in an offer of mediation, which resulted in a peace conference held aboard the U. S. S. *Marblehead*. At this conference the belligerents agreed to suspend hostilities and to attend another conference for the purpose of drafting a general treaty of peace. The second conference was held at San José, Costa Rica, but President Zelaya of Nicaragua declined to send a representative because he was unwilling to recognize the right of the United States to intervene

---

[10] Foreign Relations, 1905, p. 298; Moore, " Digest of Int. Law," Vol. VI, pp. 518-529; *Am. Journal of Int. Law,* Vol. I, p. 287, and Documentary Supplement, p. 231.

in Central American affairs. At this time Zelaya was systematically interfering in the internal affairs of the other Central American states, and exercised such complete control over the government of Honduras that Guatemala and Salvador were endeavoring to stir up revolutions against him in that state and in Nicaragua. War was about to break out in the summer of 1907 when President Roosevelt and President Diaz again intervened diplomatically and persuaded the Central American governments to suspend warlike preparations and to attend a conference in the city of Washington. In November the delegates of the five Central American states met in the Bureau of American Republics and were addressed by Secretary Root and the Mexican ambassador. The delegates adopted a general treaty of peace, providing for the settlement of existing differences and for the establishment of a Central American court of justice composed of five judges, one to be elected by the legislature of each state. The five republics agreed to submit to this tribunal all controversies of whatever nature that might arise between them which could not be settled through ordinary diplomatic channels.

But President Zelaya of Nicaragua, who still controlled Honduras, continued his interference in the affairs of the other republics by encouraging revolutionary movements and sending out filibustering expeditions. He was also hostile to the Central American court of justice, and it became evident that there was little chance of permanent peace as long as Zelaya remained in power. When, therefore, in October, 1909, members of the conservative party started a revolution at Bluefields against Zelaya's government, the movement was regarded with sympathy in the other Central American republics and in Washington. Conditions became so intolerable that many people in Nicaragua and Honduras appealed to the United States to intervene for the purpose of restoring order. President Diaz of Mexico was friendly to Zelaya and informed the United States that he did not care to take any further action. This brought to an end the coöperative efforts of the two governments and thereafter the United States had to act alone. Nothing was done, however, until two Americans were executed by Zelaya's order in November, 1909. As a result of these executions, which were without legal excuse and attended by barbarous cruelties, President Taft promptly severed diplomatic relations with Zelaya's government. In a dispatch to the Nicaraguan chargé, December 1, 1909, Secretary Knox said:

Since the Washington conventions of 1907, it is notorious that President Zelaya has almost continuously kept Central America in tension or turmoil; that he has repeatedly and flagrantly violated the provisions of the conventions, and, by a baleful influence upon Honduras, whose neutrality the conventions were to assure, has sought to discredit those sacred international obligations, to the great detriment of Costa Rica, El Salvador, and Guatemala, whose governments meanwhile appear to have been able patiently to strive for the loyal support of the engagements so solemnly undertaken at Washington under the auspices of the United States and Mexico.

He added that under the régime of President Zelaya republican institutions had ceased to exist in Nicaragua except in name, that public opinion and the press had been throttled, and that prison had been the reward of any tendency to real patriotism. The government of the United States was convinced, he said, " that the revolution represents the ideals and the will of a majority of the Nicaraguan people more faithfully than does the government of President Zelaya." [11]

This note caused the speedy downfall of Zelaya's government. He tried to perpetuate his party in power by resigning the presidency to Dr. Madriz, but President Taft refused to recognize the Madriz government, and a few months later it was overthrown and the revolutionary party came into power, first under the presidency of Estrada and then under that of Adolfo Diaz.

The revolution had paralyzed agriculture and commerce and thrown the country into financial chaos. In October, 1910, the United States government sent Thomas C. Dawson to Managua to investigate conditions and to straighten out the political and financial affairs of Nicaragua. While he was engaged in this task, Secretary Knox negotiated at Washington two treaties, one between the United States and Honduras, signed January 10, 1911, and a similar treaty between the United States and Nicaragua, signed June 6. These treaties were intended to place the two countries concerned under the financial supervision of the United States. They provided for the appointment in each case of a collector of customs approved by the President of the United States, and made the customs receipts responsible for loans to be advanced by American bankers. The collectorship of customs was immediately established in Nicaragua without waiting for the ratification of the treaty by the Senate, and

---

[11] Foreign Relations, 1909, p. 455.

through the efforts of the State Department American bankers made preliminary loans to the Nicaraguan government. When the Senate rejected the treaty, the bankers refused to make further loans, and the situation was almost as bad as ever. In October, 1911, General Mena, minister of war and head of a faction of his own, was elected by the Assembly president of the republic, but as this was contrary to an agreement which had been made with Dawson, it did not meet with the approval of the United States, and President Diaz removed Mena from office and forced him to flee from the capital. Shortly afterwards Mena was taken seriously ill, and the opposition to President Diaz fell again under the control of Zelaya's followers. As President Diaz was unable to guarantee protection to the life and property of foreigners, he asked the United States for assistance. In answer to this request American marines were landed at Corinto and assumed control of the national railway which connected that port with the capital and the principal cities. The American minister made a public announcement to the effect that the United States intended to keep open the routes of communication and to protect American life and property. This announcement was a great blow to the revolutionists. Some of their leaders surrendered voluntarily to the American marines, while others were attacked and forced to surrender positions along the railroad which they insisted upon holding. In these operations seven American marines lost their lives. Since 1912 a legation guard of one hundred marines has been maintained at the capital of Nicaragua and a warship has been stationed at Corinto.

After the revolutionary movement was thus overthrown, Secretary Knox negotiated a new treaty for the purpose of helping the Nicaraguan government out of the financial straits in which it found itself. Great Britain was threatening to force the payment of its claims and certain German interests, which were operating banana plantations in Costa Rica, were trying to secure from the Nicaraguan government a concession for the construction of a canal from the Great Lake to the Atlantic along the San Juan river. According to the terms of the Knox treaty the United States was to pay Nicaragua $3,000,000 in return for an exclusive right of way for a canal through her territory, a naval base on the Gulf of Fonseca, and the lease for ninety-nine years of the Great Corn and Little Corn Islands in the Caribbean. This treaty was submitted to the Senate February 26, 1913, but the close of the Taft administration was then at hand, and no action was taken.

The Wilson administration followed the same policy, however, and in July, 1913, Secretary Bryan submitted a third treaty with Nicaragua containing the provisions of the second Knox treaty and in addition certain provisions of the Platt Amendment which defines our protectorate over Cuba. This treaty aroused strong opposition in the other Central American States, and Costa Rica, Salvador, and Honduras filed formal protests with the United States government against its ratification on the ground that it would convert Nicaragua into a protectorate of the United States and thus defeat the long-cherished plan for a union of the Central American republics. They also claimed that the treaty infringed their own rights.

In 1858 Costa Rica had been granted perpetual rights of free navigation in the lower part of the San Juan river, and Nicaragua had agreed to consult her before granting any concessions for the construction of an interoceanic canal. Salvador and Honduras objected to the establishment of a naval base in the Gulf of Fonseca in close proximity to their coasts. They also asserted proprietary rights in the Gulf of Fonseca, claiming that Salvador, Honduras, and Nicaragua, as successors of the old Central American Federation, exercised joint ownership over the gulf. Efforts were made by the United States to arrive at a settlement with Costa Rica and Salvador on the basis of a money payment, but without success. Moreover, the Senate of the United States objected to the protectorate feature of the treaty and refused to ratify it, but the negotiations were renewed, and on August 5, 1914, a new treaty, which omits the provisions of the Platt Amendment, was signed at Washington. This treaty, which was finally ratified by the Senate, February 18, 1916, grants to the United States in perpetuity the exclusive right to construct a canal by way of the San Juan river and Lake Nicaragua, and leases to the United States for ninety-nine years a naval base on the Gulf of Fonseca, and also the Great Corn and Little Corn Islands as coaling stations. The consideration for these favors was the sum of $3,000,000 to be expended, with the approval of the Secretary of State of the United States, in paying the public debt of Nicaragua, and for other purposes to be agreed on by the two contracting parties.

In consenting to the ratification of the treaty the Senate, in order to meet the objections raised by Costa

Rica, Salvador, and Honduras, attached to their resolution of ratification the proviso " that nothing in said convention is intended to affect any existing right of any of the said states." This reservation did not satisfy Costa Rica and Salvador, who took their cases to the Central American Court of Justice, requesting that Nicaragua be enjoined from carrying out the provisions of the treaty. Nicaragua refused to be a party to the action, but the court nevertheless assumed jurisdiction. Its decision in the case of Costa Rica was announced September 30, 1916. It declared that Nicaragua had violated Costa Rica's rights, but, as the court had no jurisdiction over the United States, it declined to declare the treaty void. A similar decision in the case of Salvador was handed down on March 2, 1917.[12]

Neither Nicaragua nor the United States has paid any attention to the decision of the Central American Court of Justice, which was set up under such favorable auspices by the Washington conventions. As a matter of fact, the court had not fulfilled the expectations of those who had been interested in its establishment, but it was unfortunate that it should have received its *coup de grâce* from the United States. Furthermore, it has been charged that the State Department, under the Knox régime, exploited the situation in Central America for the benefit of American capitalists, and that the Wilson administration has for years maintained a minority party in power through the presence of a body of American marines at the capital and a warship at Corinto. On the other hand, it cannot be denied that as a result

[12] D. G. Munro, " The Five Republics of Central America," p. 257.

of American policy, Central America has been freer from wars and revolutions for a longer period than at any other time in its history. The better element of the population appears to be satisfied with the situation.[13]

The treaty with the negro republic of Haiti, ratified by the Senate February 28, 1916, carries the new Caribbean policies of the United States to the farthest limits short of actual annexation. Shortly before the outbreak of the European war, Haitian finances were in such bad shape as the result of internal disorders that there was grave danger of European intervention, and the United States was considering the question of acquiring supervision over the finances of the republic. In June, 1915, a crisis in the internal affairs of Haiti seemed imminent and, at the request of the State Department, Read-Admiral Caperton was ordered to Haitian waters. Towards the latter part of July the government of President Guillaume was overthrown, and he and members of his cabinet took refuge in the French and Dominican legations. These buildings were entered by a mob, President Guillaume was slain at the gate of the French legation, his body cut in pieces, and dragged about the town. Admiral Caperton at once landed a force of marines at Port au Prince in order to protect the lives and property of foreigners. An additional force was brought from Guantanamo and the total number raised to two thousand and placed under the command of Colonel Waller. There was but slight resistance to the landing of the marines, but a few days later

---

[13] For recent and authoritative information on Central American affairs, see the volume by Dana G. Munro, "The Five Republics of Central America." (Carnegie Endowment for International Peace, 1918.)

a conflict occurred in which two Americans were killed.[14] On August 12 a new president was elected who coöperated with the American forces in their efforts to establish peace and order, and on September 16 a treaty with the United States was signed at Port au Prince. This treaty provides for the establishment of a receivership of Haitian customs under the control of the United States similar in most respects to that established over the Dominican Republic. It also provides for the appointment, on the nomination of the President of the United States, of a financial adviser, who shall assist in the settlement of the foreign debt and direct expenditures of the surplus for the development of the agricultural, mineral, and commercial resources of the republic. It provides further for a native constabulary under American officers appointed by the President of Haiti upon nomination of the President of the United States. And it extends to Haiti the main provisions of the Platt Amendment. By controlling the internal financial administration of the government the United States hopes to remove all incentives for those revolutions which have in the past had for their object a raid on the public treasury, and by controlling the customs and maintaining order the United States hopes to avoid all possibility of foreign intervention. The treaty is to remain in force for a period of ten years and for another period of ten years if either party presents specific reasons for continuing it on the ground that its purpose has not been fully accomplished.

The latest acquisition of the United States in the Caribbean is that of the Danish West Indies, or Virgin

---

[14] Secretary of the Navy, Annual Report 1915, pp. 15-17.

Islands.   Reference has already been made to the treaty negotiated by Secretary Seward in 1867 for the purchase of these islands, which was unfortunately rejected by the Senate.   Another attempt at purchase was made by President Roosevelt in 1902.   A treaty providing for the cession of the group to the United States was signed at Washington on January 24 of that year and approved by the Senate February 17, but this time the Danish Rigsdag refused to give its approval.   President Roosevelt was moved by the consideration that the Danish Islands were of great strategic importance in connection with the problem of guarding the approaches to the Panama canal.   The commercial value of the islands is also great.   Moreover, the United States was confronted by the possibility of their falling under the control of Germany or some other European power, which might use them as a naval base.   Had Germany been successful in the recent war, she might have forced Denmark to sell or cede the islands to her.   In view of this possibility, negotiations were taken up again with Denmark in 1916, and on August 4 Secretary Lansing concluded a treaty by which the United States acquired the islands of St. Thomas, St. John, and St. Croix, together with some adjacent small islands and rocks, for the sum of $25,000,000.   This treaty was duly ratified by the Senate and the ratifications were exchanged January 17, 1917.

The rapid advance of the United States in the Caribbean, described in the preceding pages, naturally aroused the fears of the smaller Latin-American states and lent color to the charge that the United States had converted the Monroe Doctrine from a policy of benevolent protection to one of imperialistic aggression. As a matter of fact, the Monroe Doctrine has never been regarded by the United States as in any sense a self-denying declaration. President Monroe said that we should consider any attempt on the part of the European powers "to extend their system to any portion of this hemisphere as dangerous to our peace and safety." The primary object of the policy outlined by President Monroe was, therefore, the peace and safety of the United States. The protection of Latin-American states against European intervention was merely a means of protecting ourselves. While the United States thus undertook to prevent the encroachment of European powers in Latin America, it has never admitted any limitation upon the possibility of its own expansion in this region. The silence of the Monroe Doctrine on this question has been remedied to some extent by President Wilson, who, at the outset of his administration, gave the assurance that "the United States will never again seek one additional foot of territory by conquest." This declaration, followed by his refusal to be forced into war with Mexico, has done much to remove the suspicion with which our recent policies in the Caribbean have been regarded by our Southern neighbors. His sincerity was further attested by his ready acceptance of the proffered mediation of the A B C powers in the Mexican embroglio and by the encouragement which he has given to the Pan American movement.

CHAPTER VIII

Pan Americanism

THE Pan American movement, which has for its object the promotion of closer social, economic, financial, and political relations between the independent republics of the Western Hemisphere, has attracted much attention in recent years. The Pan American ideal is an old one, dating back, in fact, to the Panama Congress of 1826. The object of this congress was not very definitely stated in the call which was issued by Simon Bolivar, but his purpose was to secure the independence and peace of the new Spanish-American republics either through a permanent confederation or through a series of diplomatic congresses. Henry Clay, who was secretary of state at the time, was enthusiastically in favor of accepting the invitation extended to the United States to participate in the congress. President Adams agreed, therefore, to the acceptance of the invitation, but the matter was debated at great length in both House and Senate. In the Senate the debate was particularly acrimonious. The policy of the administration was denounced as dangerous, and it was asserted that a participation in the congress at Panama could be of no benefit to the United States and might be the means of involving us in international complications. One of the topics proposed for discussion was " the manner in which all colonization of European powers on the American continent shall be restricted." The Senate Committee on Foreign Affairs objected strenuously to the United States in any way committing itself to guaranteeing the territory of any other American state. The slavery question also projected itself into the debate, mainly because the negro Republic of Haiti was to be represented and because most of the other states had proclaimed the emancipation of slaves. The Senate finally agreed to the nomination of Richard C. Anderson, of Kentucky, and John Sergeant, of Pennsylvania, as envoys extraordinary and ministers plenipotentiary to the assembly of American nations at Panama, and Congress made the necessary appropriation. The delay proved fatal to the plan, however, for the American delegates did not reach Panama until after the congress had adjourned.

In view of the opposition which the plan encountered in Congress, the instructions to the American delegates were very carefully drawn by Secretary Clay and their powers were strictly limited. They were cautioned against committing their government in any way to the establishment of " an amphictyonic council, invested with power finally to decide controversies between the American states or to regulate in any respect their conduct. Such a council might have been well enough adapted to a number of small contracted states, whose united territory would fall short of the extent of that of the smallest of the American powers. The complicated and various interests which appertain to the nations of this vast continent cannot be safely confided to the superintendence of one legislative authority. We should almost as soon expect to see an amphictyonic council to regulate the affairs of the

293

whole globe. But even if it were desirable to establish such a tribunal, it is beyond the competency of the government of the United States voluntarily to assent to it, without a previous change of their actual constitution."

The delegates were also instructed to oppose the formation of an offensive and defensive alliance between the American powers, for, as Mr. Clay pointed out, the Holy Alliance had abandoned all idea of assisting Spain in the conquest of her late colonies. Continuing, he said:

Other reasons concur to dissuade the United States from entering into such an alliance. From the first establishment of their present constitution, their illustrious statesmen have inculcated the avoidance of foreign alliances as a leading maxim of their foreign policy. It is true, that in its adoption, their attention was directed to Europe, which having a system of connections and of interests remote and different from ours, it was thought most advisable that we should not mix ourselves up with them. And it is also true, that long since the origin of the maxim, the new American powers have arisen, to which, if at all, it is less applicable. Without, therefore, asserting that an exigency may not occur in which an alliance of the most intimate kind between the United States and the other American republics would be highly proper and expedient, it may be safely said that the occasion which would warrant a departure from that established maxim ought to be one of great urgency, and that none such is believed now to exist. Among the objections to such alliances, those which at all times have great weight are, first, the difficulty of a just and equal arrangement of the contributions of force and of other means between the respective parties to the attainment of the common object; and secondly, that of providing beforehand, and determining with perfect precision, when the *casus foederis* arises, and thereby guarding against all controversies about it. There is less necessity for any such alliance at this juncture on the part of the United States, because no compact, by whatever solemnities it might be attended, or whatever name or character it might assume, could be more obligatory upon them than the irresistible motive of self-preservation, which would be instantly called into operation, and stimulate them to the utmost exertion in the supposed contingency of an European attack upon the liberties of America.[1]

The British government sent a special envoy to reside near the congress and to place himself in frank and friendly communication with the delegates. Canning's private instructions to this envoy declared that,

Any project for putting the U. S. of North America at the head of an American Confederacy, as against Europe, would be highly displeasing to your Government. It would be felt as an ill return for the service which has been rendered to those States, and the dangers which have been averted from them, by the countenance and friendship, and public declarations of Great Britain; and it would probably, at no distant period, endanger the peace both of America and of Europe.

The Panama Congress was without practical results, and it possesses merely an historical interest. As a matter of fact, only four republics, Colombia, Central America, Peru, and Mexico, were represented. Several treaties and conventions were drafted with the view mainly of combined defense against Spain, but ratification was withheld by all of the states except Colombia, which gave only a partial approval to what had been done. Before adjourning, the Congress of Panama decided to meet again at the town of Tacu-

---

[1] International American Conference, Vol. IV (Historical Appendix), p. 122. Washington: Government Printing Office, 1890.

baya, near the city of Mexico, and to continue its sessions at stated intervals. But as the result of the failure of the states represented at the congress to ratify the agreements arrived at, and as the result of internal disorders, the plan was not carried out, although Mexico issued invitations for another congress in 1831, 1838, 1839, and 1840.

In 1847 the republics of Bolivia, Chile, Ecuador, New Granada, and Peru held a so-called " American Congress " at Lima, which drafted a treaty of confederation, one of commerce and navigation, a consular convention, and a postal convention. These treaties were not ratified and, therefore, the congress was without practical results. The preamble of the proposed treaty of confederation referred to the nations assembled as being " bound to each other by the ties of a common origin, a common language, a common religion, common customs, and the common cause for which they have struggled, as well as by their geographical position, the similarity of their institutions, and their analogous ancestors and reciprocal interests." It is evident, therefore, that this particular congress was Spanish-American rather than Pan American.[2]

In 1856 the republics of Peru, Chile, and Ecuador signed at Santiago a treaty of confederation, known as " the Continental Treaty," for the purpose of " cementing upon substantial foundations the union which exists between them, as members of the great American family, which are bound together by the ties of a common origin, similar institutions, and many other

---

[2] International American Conference, Vol. IV (Historical Appendix), p. 202.

signs of fraternity." This treaty was not ratified. It seems to have been dictated by a spirit of hostility to the United States as the result of the filibustering enterprise of William Walker in Central America.

The question of a " continental " league was discussed between Costa Rica and Colombia in 1862. After stating that, " There are not always at the head of the Great Republic moderate, just, and upright men as those who form the administration of President Lincoln," Costa Rica continued:

If our Republics could have the guaranty that they have nothing to fear from the United States of North America, it is indubitable that no other nation could be more useful and favorable to us. Under the shelter of her powerful eagles, under the influence of her wise institutions, and under the spur of her astonishing progress our newly-born nationalities should receive the impulse which they now need, and would be permitted to march with firm step, without experiencing the troubles and difficulties with which they have had to struggle. . . . In view of the above considerations, the idea has occurred to my government that a new compact might be draughted by which the United States of North America should bind themselves solemnly to respect, and cause others to respect, the independence, sovereignty, and territorial integrity of the sister republics of this continent; not to annex to their territory, either by purchase or by any other means, any part of the territory of the said republics; not to allow filibustering expeditions to be fitted up against the said nations, or to permit the rights of the latter to be in any way abridged or ignored.[8]

In January, 1864, the government of Peru issued invitations to all the governments of the Spanish na-

---

[8] International American Conference, Vol. IV (Historical Appendix). p. 208,

tions of America to join in a congress to be held at Lima. The objects of the meeting as stated in the invitation were " to declare that the American nations represented in this congress form one single family," to improve postal facilities, to exchange statistical data, to provide for the settlement of all boundary disputes, and " to irrevocably abolish war, superseding it by arbitration, as the only means of compromising all misunderstandings and causes for disagreements between any of the South American republics." In accepting the invitation to the congress Colombia expressed the opinion that " the United States ought not to be invited, because their policy is adverse to all kind of alliances, and because the natural preponderance which a first-class power, as they are, has to exercise in the deliberations, might embarrass the action of the congress." So far as definite results were concerned, this congress at Lima was of no greater importance than its predecessors.

The French invasion of Mexico and the war between Spain and the republics on the west coast of South America in 1865-66 brought about a realization of their danger on the part of the Spanish-American republics and a fuller appreciation of the friendship of the United States. In the war between Spain on the one hand and the allied republics of Peru, Chile, Bolivia, and Ecuador on the other, the United States declared its neutrality as usual, but at an early period of the struggle Secretary Seward offered to mediate between the warring nations. Spain refused to accept this offer, and the war dragged on in a state of " technical continuance " merely. The offer of mediation was again renewed by Secretary Fish, with the result that a conference was held at the State Department in 1870 attended by the representatives of Spain, Peru, Chile, and Ecuador. While it was found impossible to conclude a formal peace, the delegates signed an armistice April 11, 1871, by which the de facto suspension of hostilities was converted into an armistice which was to continue indefinitely and could not be broken by any of the belligerents without three years' notice, given through the government of the United States, of intention to renew hostilities.[4]

Within ten years of the signature of this perpetual armistice, war broke out between Chile, on the one hand, and Peru and Bolivia, on the other (1879-83). The subject of dispute was the nitrate deposits of northern Chile. In 1880 Chile signed with Colombia an arbitration treaty which provided that in case the two parties should be unable in any given case to agree upon an arbitrator, the matter should be referred to the President of the United States. Article III of this treaty was as follows:

The United States of Colombia and the Republic of Chile will endeavor, at the earliest opportunity, to conclude with the other American nations conventions like unto the present, to the end that the settlement by arbitration of each and every international controversy shall become a principle of American public law.

A few weeks later, without waiting for the ratification of this treaty, Colombia issued invitations to the other Spanish-American republics to attend a conference at Panama for the purpose of securing their adherence to the treaty. The failure to in-

---

[4] Moore, " Digest of International Law," Vol. VII, pp. 9-10.

clude the United States in the invitation to the conference was explained by our minister to Colombia as being due "to the reason that the position assigned to the government of the United States by the proposed treaty is to maintain and exercise a friendly and judicial impartiality in the differences which may arise between the powers of Spanish America." [5] The continuance of the war between Chile and Peru led to the indefinite postponement of the conference.

On November 29, 1881, Secretary Blaine extended "to all the independent countries of North and South America an earnest invitation to participate in a general congress, to be held in the city of Washington on the 24th day of November, 1882, for the purpose of considering and discussing the methods of preventing war between the nations of America." He expressed the desire that the attention of the congress should be strictly confined to this one great object, and he expressed the hope that in setting a day for the assembling of the congress so far ahead, the war that was then in progress on the South Pacific coast would be ended, and the nations engaged would be able to take part in the proceedings. [6] In this expectation Mr. Blaine was disappointed. The war between Chile and Peru continued, and the invitations to the conference were withdrawn.

Toward the close of President Cleveland's first administration, the Congress of the United States passed an act authorizing the President to invite the republics

---

[5] International American Conference, Vol. IV (Historical Appendix), p. 217.
[6] *Ibid.*, p. 255.

of Mexico, Central and South America, Haiti, Santo Domingo, and the Empire of Brazil, to join the United States in a conference at Washington on October 2, 1889. Among the subjects proposed for discussion were the adoption of a customs union, the improvement of the means of communication between the various countries, uniform customs regulations, a uniform system of weights and measures, laws for the protection of patents and copyrights, extradition, the adoption of a common silver coin, and the formulation of a definite plan for the arbitration of international disputes of every character. When the conference assembled, Mr. Blaine was again secretary of state, and presided over its opening sessions. The conference formulated a plan for international arbitration and declared that this means of settling disputes was " a principle of American international law." Unfortunately this treaty was not ratified by the governments whose representatives adopted it. The most lasting achievement of the conference was the establishment of the Bureau of American Republics in Washington. While the conference was in session Brazil went through a bloodless revolution, which converted the empire into a republic. Thus disappeared the only independent monarchy of European origin which ever existed on American soil.

Scarcely had the Washington conference adjourned, when the United States and Chile got into an ugly wrangle and were brought to the verge of war over an attack on American sailors on shore leave at Valparaiso. During the civil war between President Balmaceda and the Congressional party, the American minister, Mr. Egan, admitted to the American legation certain adherents of the President. The people of Chile resented the action of the American minister, and were further aroused against the United States by the detention of the *Itata,* a vessel which left San Diego, California, with a cargo of arms for the Congressional party and was overhauled by an American warship. The United States cruiser *Baltimore* was lying in the harbor of Valparaiso when news of this incident was received. Members of her crew who happened to be on shore leave were attacked by the populace and several of them killed. As this attack upon American sailors appeared to be due to resentment against the official acts of their government, an apology was immediately demanded, but refused. After considerable delay, President Harrison had just laid the matter before Congress when a belated apology from Chile arrived, and war was fortunately averted. The charge that the United States had interfered in behalf of one of the parties in a civil strife created an unfavorable impression throughout Latin America and counteracted, to a considerable extent, the good effects of the Washington conference.

The Second International American Conference was held in the city of Mexico 1901-02. This conference arranged for all Latin-American States to become parties to the Hague Convention of 1899 for the pacific settlement of international disputes, and drafted a treaty for the compulsory arbitration of pecuniary claims, the first article of which was as follows:

The High Contracting Parties agree to submit to arbitration all claims for pecuniary loss or damage which may be presented by their respective citizens, and which cannot be amicably adjusted through diplomatic channels and when said claims are of sufficient importance to warrant the expenses of arbitration.

This treaty was signed by the delegates of seventeen states, including the United States of America.[7]

The Third International American Conference was held at Rio de Janeiro in 1906. Among other things it extended the pecuniary claims convention drafted by the previous conference for another period of five years, and recommended to the governments represented that they invite the Second Hague Conference, which had been called for 1907, " to examine the question of the compulsory collection of public debts, and, in general, means tending to diminish between nations conflicts having an exclusively pecuniary origin."[8] Added significance was given to the Rio conference by the presence of Secretary Root who, although not a delegate, made it the occasion of a special mission to South America. The series of notable addresses which he delivered on this mission gave a new impetus to the Pan American movement.

The Fourth International American Conference was held at Buenos Aires in 1910. It drafted treaties relating to patents, trade-marks, and copyrights. It extended the pecuniary claims convention for an indefinite period. And finally, it enlarged the scope of the Bureau of American Republics and changed its name to the Pan American Union.[9] A fifth conference was

---

[7] Second International American Conference, English text (Mexico, Government Printing Office, 1902), p. 309.
[8] Third International American Conference, Minutes, Resolutions, Documents (Rio de Janeiro, Imprensa Nacional, 1907), p. 605.
[9] Bulletin of the Pan American Union, Vol. 31, p. 796.

called to meet at Santiago, Chile, in 1914, but was postponed on account of the European war.

The conferences above described were political or diplomatic in character. Besides these there have been held two Pan American scientific congresses in which the United States participated, one at Santiago, Chile, in 1908, and one at Washington, December, 1915, to January, 1916. There have also been held two Pan American financial conferences in the city of Washington, the first in May, 1915, and the second in January, 1920. These conferences have accomplished a great deal in the way of promoting friendly feeling and the advancement of science and commerce among the republics of the Western Hemisphere. The First Financial Conference recommended the establishment of an International High Commission, to be composed of not more than nine members resident in each country appointed by the Minister of Finance of such country for the purpose of carrying on the work of the conference. This recommendation was adopted by the various countries, and the Congress of the United States, by act of February 7, 1916, authorized the establishment of a section in this country. The International High Commission carries on its labors largely through the various national sections. Its first general meeting was held at Buenos Aires in April, 1916.

The American Institute of International Law, organized at Washington in October, 1912, is a body which is likely to have great influence in promoting the peace and welfare of this hemisphere. The Institute is composed of five representatives from the national society of international law in each of the twenty-one American republics. At the suggestion of Secretary

PAN AMERICANISM

Lansing the Institute at a session held in the city of Washington, January 6, 1916, adopted a Declaration of the Rights and Duties of Nations, which was as follows:

I. Every nation has the right to exist and to protect and to conserve its existence; but this right neither implies the right nor justifies the act of the state to protect itself or to conserve its existence by the commission of unlawful acts against innocent and unoffending states.

II. Every nation has the right to independence in the sense that it has a right to the pursuit of happiness and is free to develop itself without interference or control from other states, provided that in so doing it does not interfere with or violate the rights of other states.

III. Every nation is in law and before law the equal of every other nation belonging to the society of nations, and all nations have the right to claim and, according to the Declaration of Independence of the United States, "to assume, among the powers of the earth, the separate and equal station to which the laws of nature and of nature's God entitle them."

IV. Every nation has the right to territory within defined boundaries, and to exercise exclusive jurisdiction over its territory, and all persons whether native or foreign found therein.

V. Every nation entitled to a right by the law of nations is entitled to have that right respected and protected by all other nations, for right and duty are correlative, and the right of one is the duty of all to observe.

VI. International law is at one and the same time both national and international; national in the sense that it is the law of the land and applicable as such to the decision of all questions involving its principles; international in the sense that it is the law of the society of nations and applicable as such to all questions between and among the members of the society of nations involving its principles.[10]

---

[10] *Am. Journal of International Law*, Vol. 10, p. 212.

This Declaration has been criticized as being too altruistic for a world in which diplomacy has been occupied with selfish aims.

On the same day that the above Declaration was made public, President Wilson delivered a notable address before the Second Pan American Scientific Conference then in session at Washington. In the course of this address he said:

The Monroe Doctrine was proclaimed by the United States on her own authority. It has always been maintained, and always will be maintained, upon her own responsibility. But the Monroe Doctrine demanded merely that European governments should not attempt to extend their political systems to this side of the Atlantic. It did not disclose the use which the United States intended to make of her power on this side of the Atlantic. It was a hand held up in warning, but there was no promise in it of what America was going to do with the implied and partial protectorate which she apparently was trying to set up on this side of the water, and I believe you will sustain me in the statement that it has been fears and suspicions on this score which have hitherto prevented the greater intimacy and confidence and trust between the Americas. The states of America have not been certain what the United States would do with her power. That doubt must be removed. And latterly there has been a very frank interchange of views between the authorities in Washington and those who represent the other states of this hemisphere, an interchange of views charming and hopeful, because based upon an increasingly sure appreciation of the spirit in which they were undertaken. These gentlemen have seen that, if America is to come into her own, into her legitimate own, in a world of peace and order, she must establish the foundations of amity, so that no one will hereafter doubt them. I hope and I believe that this can be accomplished. These conferences have enabled me to foresee how it will be accomplished. It will be accomplished, in the first place, by the states of America uniting in guaranteeing to each other absolute political independence and territorial integrity. In the second place, and as a necessary corollary to that, guaranteeing the agreement to settle all pending boundary disputes as soon as possible and by amicable process; by agreeing that all disputes among themselves, should they unhappily arise, will be handled by patient, impartial investigation and settled by arbitration; and the agreement necessary to the peace of the Americas, that no state of either continent will permit revolutionary expeditions against another state to be fitted out in its territory, and that they will prohibit the exportation of the munitions of war for the purpose of supplying revolutionists against neighboring governments.

President Wilson's Pan Americanism went further than some of the Latin-American states were willing to go. A treaty embodying the above proposals was actually drafted, but some of the states held back through the fear that, though equal in terms, it would in fact give the United States a plausible pretext for supervising the affairs of weaker states.[11]

President Wilson has not hesitated to depart from many of the fundamental ideas which have hitherto guided so-called practical statesmen. His handling of the Mexican situation, although denounced as weak and vacillating, has been in full accord with his new Latin-American policy. On February 18, 1913, Francisco Madero was seized and imprisoned as the result of a conspiracy formed by one of his generals, Victoriano Huerta, who forthwith proclaimed himself dictator. Four days later Madero was murdered while in the custody of Huerta's troops. Henry Lane Wilson, the American ambassador, promptly urged his

---

[11] John Bassett Moore, "Principles of American Diplomacy," pp. 407-408.

government to recognize Huerta, but President Taft, whose term was rapidly drawing to a close, took no action and left the question to his successor.

President Wilson thus had a very disagreeable situation to face when he assumed control of affairs at Washington. He refused to recognize Huerta whose authority was contested by insurrectionary chiefs in various parts of the country. It was claimed by the critics of the administration that the refusal to recognize Huerta was a direct violation of the well known American policy of recognizing *de facto* governments without undertaking to pass upon the rights involved. It is perfectly true that the United States has consistently followed the policy of recognizing *de facto* governments as soon as it is evident in each case that the new government rests on popular approval and is likely to be permanent. This doctrine of recognition is distinctively an American doctrine. It was first laid down by Thomas Jefferson when he was secretary of state as an offset to the European doctrine of divine right, and it was the natural outgrowth of that other Jeffersonian doctrine that all governments derive their just powers from the consent of the governed. Huerta could lay no claim to authority derived from a majority or anything like a majority of the Mexican people. He was a self-constituted dictator, whose authority rested solely on military force. President Wilson and Secretary Bryan were fully justified in refusing to recognize his usurpation of power, though they probably made a mistake in announcing that they would never recognize him and in demanding his elimination from the presidential contest. This announcement made him deaf to advice from Washington and utterly indifferent to the destruction of American life and property.

The next step in the President's course with reference to Mexico was the occupation of Vera Cruz. On April 20, 1914, the President asked Congress for authority to employ the armed forces of the United States in demanding redress for the arbitrary arrest of American marines at Vera Cruz, and the next day Admiral Fletcher was ordered to seize the custom house at that port. This he did after a sharp fight with Huerta's troops in which nineteen Americans were killed and seventy wounded. The American chargé d'affaires, Nelson O'Shaughnessy, was at once handed his passports, and all diplomatic relations between the United States and Mexico were severed.

A few days later the representatives of the so-called A B C powers, Argentina, Brazil, and Chile, tendered their good offices for a peaceful settlement of the conflict and President Wilson promptly accepted their mediation. The resulting conference at Niagara, May 20, was not successful in its immediate object, but it resulted in the elimination of Huerta who resigned July 15, 1914. On August 20, General Venustiano Carranza, head of one of the revolutionary factions, assumed control of affairs at the capital, but his authority was disputed by General Francisco Villa, another insurrectionary chief. On Carranza's promise to respect the lives and property of American citizens the United States forces were withdrawn from Vera Cruz in November, 1914.

In August, 1915, at the request of President Wilson the six ranking representatives of Latin America at Washington made an unsuccessful effort to reconcile the contending factions of Mexico. On their advice, however, President Wilson decided in October to recognize the government of Carranza, who now controlled three-fourths of the territory of Mexico. As a result of this action Villa began a series of attacks on American citizens and raids across the border, which in March, 1916, compelled the President to send a punitive expedition into Mexico and later to dispatch most of the regular army and large bodies of militia to the border.[12]

The raids of Villa created a very awkward situation. Carranza not only made no real effort to suppress Villa, but he vigorously opposed the steps taken by the United States to protect its own citizens along the border, and even assumed a threatening attitude. There was a loud and persistent demand in the United States for war against Mexico. American investments in land, mines, rubber plantations, and other enterprises were very large, and these financial interests were particularly outraged at the President's policy of " watchful waiting." The President remained deaf to this clamor. No country had been so shamelessly exploited by foreign capital as Mexico. Furthermore it was suspected and very generally believed that the recent revolutions had been financed by American capital. President Wilson was determined to give the Mexican people an opportunity to reorganize their national life on a better basis and to lend them every assistance in the task. War with Mexico would have been a very serious undertaking and even a successful war would

---

[12] " Affairs in Mexico," Sixty-fourth Cong., First Sess., Sen. Doc. No. 324. The World Peace Foundation has issued two pamphlets containing documents on Mexico under the title of " The New Pan Americanism," Parts I and II (February and April, 1916).

have meant the military occupation of Mexico for an indefinite period. President Wilson's refusal to become involved in war with Mexico convinced the world of his sincerity and gave him a hearing during the Great War such as no political leader of any nation ever before commanded.

It has been charged that there was a lack of consistency between the President's Mexican policy and his Haitian policy. The difference between the two cases, however, was that the Haitian situation, if taken in time, could be handled without bloodshed, while the same method applied to Mexico would have led to a long and bloody conflict. It would be easy enough to go into Mexico, but exceedingly difficult to get out. The most novel feature of the President's Mexican policy was his acceptance of the mediation of the A B C powers and his subsequent consultation with the leading representatives of Latin America. This action has brought the Pan American ideal to the point of realization. It has been received with enthusiasm and it has placed our relations with Latin America on a better footing than they have been for years.

It has been suggested by more than one critic of American foreign policy that if we are to undertake to set the world right, we must come before the bar of public opinion with clean hands, that before we denounce the imperialistic policies of Europe, we must abandon imperialistic policies at home. The main features of President Wilson's Latin-American policy, if we may draw a general conclusion, have been to pledge the weaker American republics not to do anything which would invite European intervention, and to secure by treaty the right of the United States to intervene for the protection of life, liberty, and property, and for the establishment of self-government. The test of such a policy is the degree of unselfishness with which it is carried out.

The loyalty of the Latin-American states to the principles of Pan Americanism was put to a severe test when the United States entered the Great War. When President Wilson announced to Congress the severance of relations with Germany and declared his intention of protecting our commerce on the high seas, he expressed the confident hope that all neutral governments would pursue the same course. He probably had especially in mind our Latin-American neighbors, but if so, his expectation was not fully realized. Only eight of the twenty Latin-American republics eventually entered the war: Brazil, Costa Rica, Cuba, Guatemala, Haiti, Honduras, Nicaragua, and Panama. Five others broke off relations with Germany: Bolivia, Peru, the Dominican Republic, Ecuador, and Uruguay. Seven remained neutral: Argentina, Chile, Colombia, Mexico, Salvador, Venezuela, and Paraguay.[13]

Only two Latin-American states, Brazil and Cuba, took an active part in the war. At the request of the British government in December, 1917, Brazil sent two cruisers and four destroyers to European waters to coöperate with the British navy, and a few months later a group of Brazilian aviators took their place on the Western front. A number of physicians and several Red Cross units from Brazil also coöperated with the Allies. Cuba turned over to the United States several German steamships interned in her waters. A

[13] Percy A. Martin, "Latin America and the War" (issued by the World Peace Foundation, August, 1919).

compulsory military service law was passed and a number of training camps established. In October, 1918, the Cuban government announced that it had 25,000 troops ready to send to France, but the armistice was signed before arrangements could be made for their transportation. The only active service rendered by Cubans was in the field of aviation, where several individuals won high distinction.

Of the A B C powers Argentina and Chile remained neutral. So also did Mexico. Brazil was thus the only one of the larger states that actually entered the war. The relations between Brazil and the United States have almost always been peculiarly close and friendly. From the outbreak of the European war strong sympathy for the allied cause was manifested in Brazil, and a league for aiding the Allies through the agency of the Red Cross was organized under the presidency of Ruy Barbosa, the most distinguished statesman of Brazil and one of the most brilliant orators of Latin America. Brazil's experience during the period of neutrality was very similar to that of the United States. Her commerce was interfered with and her ships were sunk by German submarines. A few weeks after the United States entered the war, Brazil severed relations with Germany and seized the forty-six German ships interned in Brazilian harbors. In a circular note of June 2 the Brazilian government declared to the world that it had taken this step because the Republic of Brazil was bound to the United States " by a traditional friendship and by a similarity of political opinion in the defense of the vital interests of America and the principles accepted by international law," and because it wished to give to its foreign policy, in this critical moment of the world's history, "a practical form of continental solidarity—a policy indeed which was that of the old régime on every occasion on which any of the other friendly sister nations of the American continent were in jeopardy." President Wilson's reply to this note expressed the deep appreciation of the United States and the hope that the act of the Brazilian Congress was "the forerunner of the attitude to be assumed by the rest of the American states." On October 26, 1917, on the receipt of the news of the torpedoing of another Brazilian ship by a German submarine, a resolution recognizing "the state of war initiated by the German Empire against Brazil" was adopted by the unanimous vote of the Brazilian Senate and by a vote of 149 to 1 in the Chamber of Deputies.[14] Brazil's enthusiastic support of the United States and of the allied cause has been recognized by those powers in giving her representation on the Council of the League of Nations. In fact at the first meeting of the Council in London in February, 1920, Brazil was the sole American power represented.

Argentina, the largest and most important of the states of Spanish origin, remained neutral throughout the war, notwithstanding the fact that a large part of the population and some of the leading newspapers were strongly pro-Ally. When the United States declared war, Señor Drago, the former minister of foreign affairs and author of the doctrine that bears his name, issued a statement in which he said:

The war between Germany and America is a struggle of

---

[14] Martin, "Latin America and the War," pp. 13-15.

democracy *versus* absolutism, and no American nation can remain neutral without denying its past and compromising its future.

About the same time a note was sent through Ambassador Naón stating that " in view of the causes which have prompted the United States to declare war against the government of the German Empire," the Argentine government recognizes " the justice of that decision." But German propaganda, which had its headquarters in Buenos Aires, and the attitude of President Irrigoyen kept the country out of the war. Popular indignation was aroused by the Luxburg disclosures, which revealed the fact that the German representative, after coming to an understanding with the President, had advised his government that two Argentine ships then approaching the French coast " be spared if possible, or else sunk without a trace being left " (*spurlos versenkt*). The Senate and Chamber of Deputies passed by large majorities a resolution severing relations with Germany, but to the surprise of everybody President Irrigoyen expressed himself as satisfied with Germany's disavowal of Luxburg's conduct and continued his policy of neutrality.

Chile was so far removed from the scene of the war in Europe and had so few ships engaged in European trade that her government did not have the same provocation that others had. Furthermore, German propaganda had made great headway in Chile and the Chilean army, trained by German officers, was strongly pro-German. In the navy, on the other hand, sentiment was strongly in favor of the Allies. This was a matter of tradition, for since the days of Lord

Cochrane, whose exploits have been described in an earlier chapter of this book, the Chilean navy has followed English ideals. Under these circumstances Chile remained neutral, though before the end of the war public sentiment had shifted to the side of the Allies.[15]

Peru, Ecuador, Bolivia, and Uruguay in severing relations with Germany proclaimed their adherence to the principle of American solidarity. Paraguay's neutrality was due to her isolation. Colombia, still smarting under the loss of the Isthmus, was not disposed to take sides with the United States. In Venezuela most of the government officials were under German influence. Panama and four of the five Central American republics declared war on Germany, Salvador alone remaining neutral. Cuba and Haiti also declared war on Germany, while the Dominican Republic severed consular relations. Mexico proclaimed its neutrality, but permitted its soil to become a hot-bed of German intrigue and President Carranza exhibited at times a spirit of hostility to the United States which tended to increase the tension that already existed between the two countries.

In an article on " The European War and Pan Americanism " [16] Ambassador Naón of the Argentine Republic draws the following interesting conclusions, conclusions that are all the more interesting because his country was not one of those that took the course to which he gives his approval. He says: " The political action developed by the different governments of

---

[15] Enrique Rocuant, " The Neutrality of Chile and the Grounds that Prompted and Justified It," (Valparaiso, 1919).
[16] Reprinted in International Conciliation, Inter-American Division, Bulletin No. 20 (April, 1919).

the continent in the presence of the European conflict, especially since the breaking out of hostilities between the United States and Germany, has not been either the best advised or the most propitious for achieving the consolidation of Pan Americanism." The situation created by the European war, he continues, " affected the entire continent in the same manner and with the same political and economic intensity as the United States, and both self-interest and moral obligations ought to have counseled the consummating of solidarity, here and now, by making common cause and endorsing the attitude of the United States to the extreme limit, until the disturbing force should be overcome. The political action of America did not take this direction, however. Some of the most important governments of the continent, going counter to the political aspirations and doubtless to the political interests of their own countries, adhered to the policy of neutrality. In America this was equivalent to a policy of isolation, and thus the solidarity of the continent was broken, with consequent prejudice to Pan Americanism. Yet even if in those countries, the action of the governments could not be counted upon, nevertheless, the sentiment, expressed in eloquent manifestations of public opinion and in complete disagreement with that attitude of the governments, persisted throughout the crisis. Thus the *spirit* of Pan Americanism was saved, and we are justified in believing that there will come a reaction which will restore the disturbed equilibrium and save the mighty interests involved."

Ambassador Naón believes, however, that Pan Americanism has many obstacles in the way of its complete realization. Among them he mentions "the recognition of politico-intellectual inferiorities " by the peace conference at Paris in the classification of nations as great powers and small powers. The fundamental principle of Pan Americanism he believes to be the doctrine of equality. He further points out that as long as American states remain, whether as the result of their own shortcomings or not, in these conditions of inferiority in world politics, "there will continue to exist for the United States the causes that gave rise to the Monroe Doctrine and consequently all its objections will continue to exist." Finally he says that "the idea of solidarity is being weakened or thwarted by another idea, the unwholesome one of Latin Americanism, which is a Teutonic idea in its tendencies, and which is trying to replace it, basing itself upon supposed antagonisms of interests and ideals between the other countries of America and the United States. This purpose, which is anarchical, might cause American solidarity to fail if, in virtue of neglecting to foster this tendency, it should succeed, by pandering to paltry prejudices and flattering national vanities, in gaining a footing in the thought of the other governments of the continent to the extent of constituting itself a political force, capable of replacing the system of solidarity which Pan Americanism seeks, by a system of a continental equilibrium: a system which has just failed in the European conflict."

This summary of the views of the distinguished Argentine statesman is sufficient to show that his analysis of the situation is correct. The weakness and backwardness of certain states, specifically those in the zone of the Caribbean, lies at the heart of the difficulty. As long as they remain in their present condition the United States must continue to protect them against European intervention and, when occasion arises, supervise their affairs in order to prevent them from provoking such intervention. As long as it is necessary to pursue this course the United States will have to rest under the suspicion of having imperialistic designs on its weaker neighbors, and it is this suspicion which perpetuates the spirit of Latin Americanism which in turn must be overcome before we can fully realize the ideal of Pan Americanism.

CHAPTER IX

The Monroe Doctrine

In the foregoing chapters we have discussed the origin and the more important applications of the Monroe Doctrine. There remain, however, certain general aspects of the subject which require special consideration. In any discussion of the Monroe Doctrine it is important to bear in mind that it was in its origin and has always remained purely an executive policy. Neither house of Congress has ever expressly sanctioned the language of President Monroe or attempted to formulate a new definition of the policy. On January 20, 1824, a few weeks after Monroe's famous message, Henry Clay made an effort to get Congress to endorse the policy announced by the executive, but his resolution was tabled.[1] In 1856 Senator Clayton, who as secretary of state had negotiated the Clayton-Bulwer treaty, declared that he would be willing to vote to assert the Monroe Doctrine and maintain it, but that he would " not expect to be sustained in such a vote by both branches of Congress. Whenever the attempt has been made to assert the Monroe Doctrine in either branch of Congress, it has failed." And he added, " You cannot prevail on a majority, and I will venture to say that you cannot prevail on one-third, of either house of Congress to sustain it." [2] In fact, the Monroe Doc-

---

[1] Moore, " Digest of International Law," Vol. VI, p. 404.
[2] *Ibid.*, p. 427.

trine never received anything approaching legislative sanction until 1895, when, in response to President Cleveland's message on the Venezuelan boundary dispute, Congress appropriated $100,000 to pay the expenses of the commission which he proposed to appoint.

For nearly a hundred years we have successfully upheld the Monroe Doctrine without resort to force. The policy has never been favorably regarded by the powers of continental Europe. Bismarck described it as " an international impertinence." In recent years it has stirred up rather intense opposition in certain parts of Latin America. Until recently no American writers appear to have considered the real nature of the sanction on which the doctrine rested. How is it that without an army and until recent years without a navy of any size we have been able to uphold a policy which has been described as an impertinence to Latin America and a standing defiance to Europe? Americans generally seem to think that the Monroe Doctrine has in it an inherent sanctity which prevents other nations from violating it. In view of the general disregard of sanctities, inherent or acquired, during the past few years, this explanation will not hold good and some other must be sought. Americans have been so little concerned with international affairs that they have failed to see any connection between the Monroe Doctrine and the balance of power in Europe. The existence of a European balance of power is the only explanation of our having been able to uphold the Monroe Doctrine for so long a time without a resort to force. Some one or more of the European powers would long ago have stepped in and called our bluff, that is, forced us to repudiate the Monroe Doctrine or fight for it, had it not been for the well-grounded fear that as soon as they became engaged with us some other European power would attack them in the rear. What other satisfactory explanation is there for Louis Napoleon's withdrawal from Mexico, for Great Britain's backdown in the Venezuelan boundary dispute, and for the withdrawal of the German fleet from Venezuela in 1902?

While England has from time to time objected to some of the corollaries deduced from the Monroe Doctrine, she has on the whole been not unfavorably disposed toward the essential features of that policy. The reason for this is that the Monroe Doctrine has been an open-door policy, and has thus been in general accord with the British policy of free trade. The United States has not used the Monroe Doctrine for the establishment of exclusive trade relations with our Southern neighbors. In fact, we have largely neglected the South American countries as a field for the development of American commerce. The failure to cultivate this field has not been due wholly to neglect, however, but to the fact that we have had employment for all our capital at home and consequently have not been in a position to aid in the industrial development of the Latin-American states, and to the further fact that our exports have been so largely the same and hence the trade of North and South America has been mainly with Europe. There has, therefore, been little rivalry between the United States and the powers of Europe in the field of South American commerce. Our interest has been political rather than commercial. We have prevented the establishment of spheres of influence and preserved the open door. This situation has been in full accord with British policy. Had Great Britain adopted a high tariff policy and been compelled to demand commercial concessions from Latin America by force, the Monroe Doctrine would long since have gone by the board and been forgotten. Americans should not forget the fact, moreover, that at any time during the past twenty years Great Britain could have settled all her outstanding difficulties with Germany by agreeing to sacrifice the Monroe Doctrine and give her rival a free hand in South America. In the face of such a combination our navy would have been of little avail.

Contrary to a widely prevailing opinion the Monroe Doctrine has undergone very little change since the original declaration, and the official statements of the doctrine have on the whole been very consistent. The only important extension was made less than two years after the original declaration, when, in October, 1825, Secretary Clay, acting under the direction of President John Quincy Adams, who assisted in formulating the doctrine, notified the French government that we could not consent to the occupation of Cuba and Porto Rico " by any other European power than Spain under any contingency whatever." Similar declarations were made to the other European powers, the occasion being the fear that Spain would transfer her sovereignty over these islands to some other government. President Monroe had declared that the American continents were closed to colonization from Europe, meaning by colonization very probably, as Professor John Bassett

Moore says, " the acquisition of title to territory by original occupation and settlement."[3] He had made no declaration against the transfer of sovereignty in America from one European power to another. In fact he positively renounced any such idea, when he said: " With the existing colonies or dependencies of any European power we have not interfered, and shall not interfere." Here, then, within two years we have a distinct advance upon the position taken by President Monroe. Yet this advanced ground was held by succeeding administrations, until President Grant could say in the case of the same islands in his first annual message:

These dependencies are no longer regarded as subject to transfer from one European power to another. When the present relation of colonies ceases, they are to become independent powers, exercising the right of choice and of self-control in the determination of their future condition and relations with other powers.[4]

And Secretary Hamilton Fish said a few months later that the President had but followed " the teachings of all our history " when he made this statement.[5]

The failure of Blaine and Frelinghuysen to oust Great Britain from her interests in the canal under the Clayton-Bulwer treaty by an appeal to the Monroe Doctrine and the successful enforcement of the doctrine by President Cleveland and Secretary Olney in 1895 have been discussed at sufficient length in previous chapters. While the policy of Cleveland and

---

[3] *Political Science Quarterly*, Vol. XI, p. 3.
[4] " Messages and Papers of the Presidents," Vol. VII, p. 32.
[5] Foreign Relations, 1870, pp. 254-260; Moore, " Digest of International Law," Vol. VI, p. 431.

Olney was vehemently denounced at the time, it is now generally approved by American writers of authority on international law and diplomacy.

When President McKinley decided to demand from Spain the cession of the Philippine Islands, the opposition that the step encountered was based to some extent on the fear that it would amount to a repudiation of the Monroe Doctrine, that if we invaded the Eastern Hemisphere we could not expect to keep Europe out of the Western. The use of the term hemispheres in connection with the Monroe Doctrine has, of course, been merely a figure of speech. The Monroe Doctrine dealt with the relations between Europe and America, and Eastern Asia never came within its purview. As a matter of fact, the Monroe Doctrine has been more fully and more frequently asserted since the acquisition of the Philippines than ever before. The participation of the United States in the First Peace Conference at The Hague was taken by many Americans to mark the end of the old order and the introduction of a new era in American diplomacy, but, contrary to their expectations, this meeting was made the occasion for an emphatic and effective declaration before the assembled body of European nations of our adherence to the Monroe Doctrine. Before the Convention for the Pacific Settlements of International Disputes was adopted, the following declaration was read before the conference and the treaty was signed by the American delegates under this reservation:

Nothing contained in this convention shall be so construed as to require the United States of America to depart from its traditional policy of not intruding upon, interfering

with, or entangling itself in the political questions or policy
or internal administration of any foreign state; nor shall
anything contained in the said convention be construed to
imply a relinquishment by the United States of America of
its traditional attitude toward purely American questions.[6]

Prior to the Roosevelt administration the Monroe
Doctrine was regarded by the Latin-American states
as solely a protective policy. The United States did
not undertake to control the financial administration
or the foreign policy of any of these republics. It
was only after their misconduct had gotten them into
difficulty and some foreign power, or group of foreign powers, was on the point of demanding reparation by force that the United States stepped in and
undertook to see to it that foreign intervention did
not take the form of occupation of territory or interference in internal politics. The Monroe Doctrine has
always been in principle a policy of American intervention for the purpose of preventing European intervention, but American intervention always awaited
the threat of immediate action on the part of some
European power. President Roosevelt concluded that
it would be wiser to restrain the reckless conduct of
the smaller American republics before disorders or
public debts should reach a point which gave European powers an excuse for intervening. He held that
since we could not permit European powers to restrain or punish American states in cases of wrongdoing, we must ourselves undertake that task. As
long as the Monroe Doctrine was merely a policy of
benevolent protection, which Latin-American states
could invoke after their unwise or evil conduct had

[6] " Treaties and Conventions of the United States " (Compiled by W.
M. Malloy), vol. II, p. 2032.

brought European powers to the point of demanding just retribution, it was regarded with favor and no objection was raised to it; but the Roosevelt declaration, that if we were to continue to protect Latin-American states against European intervention, we had a right to demand that they should refrain from conduct which was likely to provoke such intervention, was quite a different thing, and raised a storm of criticism and opposition.

The Roosevelt interpretation of the Monroe Doctrine was undoubtedly a perfectly logical step. It was endorsed by the Taft administration and has been extended by the Wilson administration and made one of our most important policies in the zone of the Caribbean. President Roosevelt was right in drawing the conclusion that we had arrived at a point where we had either to abandon the Monroe Doctrine or to extend its application so as to cover the constantly increasing number of disputes arising from the reckless creation of public debts and loose financial administration. It was absurd for us to stand quietly by and witness the utterly irresponsible creation of financial obligations that would inevitably lead to European intervention and then undertake to fix the bounds and limits of that intervention. It is interesting to note that President Wilson has not hesitated to carry the new policy to its logical conclusion, and he has gone so far as to warn Latin-American countries against granting to foreign corporations concessions which, on account of their extended character, would be certain to give rise to foreign claims which would, in turn, give an excuse for European intervention. In discussing our Latin-American policy

shortly after the beginning of his administration,
President Wilson said:

> You hear of concessions to foreign capitalists in Latin
> America. You do not hear of concessions to foreign capital-
> ists in the United States. They are not granted concessions.
> They are invited to make investments. The work is ours,
> though they are welcome to invest in it. We do not ask them
> to supply the capital and do the work. It is an invitation, not
> a privilege, and the states that are obliged because their terri-
> tory does not lie within the main field of modern enterprise
> and action, to grant concessions are in this condition, that
> foreign interests are apt to dominate their domestic affairs—a
> condition of affairs always dangerous and apt to become in-
> tolerable. . . . What these states are going to seek, there-
> fore, is an emancipation from the subordination which has
> been inevitable to foreign enterprise and an assertion of the
> splendid character which, in spite of these difficulties, they
> have again and again been able to demonstrate.

These remarks probably had reference to the oil
concession which Pearson & Son of London had arranged with the president of Colombia. This concession is said to have covered extensive oil interests
in Colombia, and carried with it the right to improve
harbors and dig canals in the country. However, before the meeting of the Colombian Congress in November, 1913, which was expected to confirm the concession, Lord Cowdray, the president of Pearson & Son,
withdrew the contract, alleging as his reason the opposition of the United States.

Prior to the Great War, which has upset all calculations, it seemed highly probable that the Platt Amendment would in time be extended to all the weaker states
within the zone of the Caribbean. If the United States
is to exercise a protectorate over such states, the right

to intervene and the conditions of intervention should be clearly defined and publicly proclaimed. Hitherto whatever action we have taken in Latin America has been taken under the Monroe Doctrine,—a policy of doubtful legal sanction,—which an international court might not recognize. Action under a treaty would have the advantage of legality. In other words, the recent treaties with Caribbean states have converted American policy into law.

The imperialistic tendencies of our Caribbean policy, whether they be regarded as logical deductions from the Monroe Doctrine or not, have undoubtedly aroused the jealousies and fears of our Southern neighbors. One of the results has been the formation of the so-called A B C Alliance, based on treaties between Argentina, Brazil, and Chile, the exact provisions of which have not been made public. This alliance doubtless serves a useful purpose in promoting friendly relations between the three great states of South America, and since the acceptance of the mediation of these powers in Mexico by President Wilson there is no reason to regard it as in any sense hostile to the United States. While the United States may very properly accept the mediation of other American states in disputes like that arising out of the Mexican situation, the United States would not feel under any obligation to consult other American states or accept their advice on any question involving the enforcement of the Monroe Doctrine. The United States has always maintained the Monroe Doctrine as a principle of self-defense, and, consequently, on its own authority. In 1825 the Brazilian government proposed that the United States should enter into an alliance with it in order to maintain the independence of Brazil in case Portugal should be assisted by any foreign power in her efforts to reconquer Brazil. Secretary Clay replied that while President Adams adhered to the principles set forth by his predecessor, the prospect of peace between Portugal and Brazil rendered such an alliance unnecessary.[7]

In recent years the proposal has been more than once made that the Monroe Doctrine be Pan Americanized. This proposal was discussed by Mr. Root in his address before the American Society of International Law in 1914 in the course of which he said:

> Since the Monroe Doctrine is a declaration based upon this nation's right of self-protection, it cannot be transmuted into a joint or common declaration by American states or any number of them. If Chile or Argentina or Brazil were to contribute the weight of its influence toward a similar end, the right upon which that nation would rest its declaration would be its own safety, not the safety of the United States. Chile would declare what was necessary for the safety of Chile. Argentina would declare what was necessary for the safety of Argentina. Brazil, what was necessary for the safety of Brazil. Each nation would act for itself and in its own right and it would be impossible to go beyond that except by more or less offensive and defensive alliances. Of course such alliances are not to be considered.[8]

President Wilson in his address before the Second Pan American Scientific Congress in 1916 agreed in part with this when he said: " The Monroe Doctrine was proclaimed by the United States on her own authority. It has always been maintained, and always will be maintained, upon her own responsibility."

---

[7] Moore, " Digest of International Law," Vol. VI, p. 427.
[8] " Addresses on International Subjects," Elihu Root, p. 120.

THE MONROE DOCTRINE

The relation of the Monroe Doctrine to the Declaration of Rights and Duties of Nations, drafted by the American Institute of International Law, was discussed by Mr. Root in his address before the American Society of International Law in 1916. He said in part:

Whether the United States will soon have occasion or will long have the ability or the will to maintain the Monroe Doctrine lies in the uncertain future. Whether it will be necessary for her to act in defense of the doctrine or abandon it, may well be determined by the issue of the present war. Whether when the occasion comes she will prove to have the ability and the will to maintain the doctrine, depends upon the spirit of her people, their capacity for patriotic sacrifice, the foresight and character of those to whose initiative in foreign affairs the interests of the people are entrusted. Whether the broader doctrine affirmed by the American Institute of International Law is to be made effective for the protection of justice and liberty throughout the world depends upon whether the vision of the nations shall have been so clarified by the terrible lessons of these years that they can rise above small struggles for advantage in international affairs, and realize that correlative to each nation's individual right is that nation's duty to insist upon the observance of the principles of public right throughout the community of nations.[9]

It is not probable that our participation in the Great War will result in any weakening of the Monroe Doctrine. That principle has been fully justified by a century of experience. It has saved South America from the kind of exploitation to which the continents of Africa and Asia have, during the past generation, fallen a prey. It would be strange indeed if the

---

[9] "Addresses on International Subjects," by Elihu Root, p. 425.

United States, having insisted on the non-interference of European powers in America when it was itself a weak power from the military point of view, should now in the plenitude of its power relax what has been for so many years the cardinal principle of its foreign policy. The abandonment of our policy of neutrality and isolation does not by any means mean the abandonment of the Monroe Doctrine. President Wilson made this quite clear in his address to the Senate on January 22, 1917, when he said:

> I am proposing, as it were, that the nations should with one accord adopt the doctrine of President Monroe as the doctrine of the world; that no nation should seek to extend its polity over any other nation or people, but that every people should be left free to determine its own polity, its own way of development, unhindered, unthreatened, unafraid, the little along with the great and powerful. I am proposing that all nations henceforth avoid entangling alliances which would draw them into competitions of power, catch them in a net of intrigue and selfish rivalry, and disturb their own affairs with influences intruded from without. There is no entangling alliance in a concert of power.

The policy of isolation or the avoidance of entangling alliances, which so many Americans confuse with the Monroe Doctrine, is in principle quite distinct from it and is in fact utterly inconsistent with the position and importance of the United States as a world power. The difference in principle between the two policies can perhaps be best illustrated by the following supposition. If the United States were to sign a permanent treaty with England placing our navy at her disposal in the event of attack from some European power, on condition that England would unite with us in opposing the intervention of any European power in Latin America, such a treaty would not be a violation of the Monroe Doctrine, but a distinct recognition of that principle. Such a treaty would, however, be a departure from our traditional policy of isolation, originally announced by Washington and Jefferson.

The participation of the United States in the League of Nations would, if that League be considered an entangling alliance, be a departure from the policy of isolation but not a violation of the Monroe Doctrine. In order to allay the fears of Americans on this point, President Wilson caused to be inserted in the constitution of the League of Nations the following clause:

Nothing in this Covenant shall be deemed to affect the validity of international engagements, such as treaties of arbitration or regional understandings like the Monroe Doctrine, for securing the maintenance of peace.

This clause did not serve the purpose for which it was intended, and a heated controversy at once arose as to the meaning of the language employed. When the treaty came before the Senate this clause was the object of attack, and Senator Lodge included among the fourteen reservations which he proposed the following one on the Monroe Doctrine:

The United States will not submit to arbitration or to inquiry by the assembly or by the council of the League of Nations, provided for in said treaty of peace, any questions which in the judgment of the United States depend upon or relate to its long-established policy, commonly known as the Monroe Doctrine; said doctrine is to be interpreted by the United States alone and is hereby declared to be wholly outside the jurisdiction of said League of Nations and entirely unaffected by any provision contained in the said treaty of peace with Germany.

The recognition of the Monroe Doctrine by the League of Nations, taken in connection with the Senate's assertion of the exclusive right to interpret its meaning, has caused some of the Latin-American countries to delay joining the League until the Monroe Doctrine is clearly defined. In February, 1920, Salvador brought this subject to the attention of the United States in a formal note in which she argued that, as the Monroe Doctrine was so variously interpreted by prominent thinkers and public men even in the United States, it should be officially defined.[10] In reply Salvador was referred to what President Wilson had said on the subject of the Monroe Doctrine in his address of January 6, 1916, before the Pan American Scientific Congress at Washington.[11] These remarks have already been quoted in Chapter VIII.[12] Salvador was informed that no further definition was deemed necessary. The speech referred to may, therefore, be considered the latest official interpretation of the Monroe Doctrine.

---

[10] The New York *Times*, February 8, 1920.
[11] The New York *Times*, March 2, 1920.
[12] Ante, pp. 306-307.

THE END

INDEX

INDEX

French Panama Canal Company, 187.

Cuba, British or French acquisition opposed by United States, 84-90; annexation schemes, 91-106; " Ten Years' War " in, 107-125; insurrection of 1895, 125-129; intervention of the United States in, 130-133; American occupation of, 136-140; reciprocity with, 140-142; second period of American occupation, 142, 143; enters war against Germany, 312, 313.

Cushing, Caleb, mission to Spain, 119-124.

Dallas-Clarendon treaty, amended by Senate and rejected by Great Britain, 161, 162.

Danish West Indies, annexation proposed by Seward, 264; purchased by United States, 289, 290.

Davis, Cushman K., commissioner to negotiate peace with Spain, 135.

Dawson, T. C., minister to Dominican Republic, negotiates treaty establishing financial supervision, 277-279.

Day, W. R., commissioner to negotiate peace with Spain, 135.

Dayton, W. L., minister to France, 214, 217, 219, 221.

DeLesseps, Ferdinand, begins construction of Panama canal, 146; effect on canal policy of United States, 167-169.

DeLhuys, Drouyn, French minister of state, 217, 221, 225, 231.

Dewey, George, at Manila Bay, 134; prepared to arrest German action against Venezuela, 253, 254.

Diaz, Porfirio, president of Mexico, joint mediator with President Roosevelt in Central American affairs, 280-282.

Dominican Republic, under financial supervision of United States, 276-280.

Drago, L. M., Argentine minister, on war between Germany and United States, 314, 315.

Drago Doctrine, 257-260.

DuBois, J. T., minister to Colombia, efforts to settle differences arising out of Panama Revolution, 270-274.

Evarts, W. M., report on obligations of United States with respect to Isthmus of Panama, 169.

Ferdinand VII, of Spain, dethroned by Napoleon, 27; restoration of, 29; attempts to recover American colonies, 40.

Filibusters, Cuban, 92-96.

Financial supervision, over Dominican Republic, 276-280; over Nicaragua, 283; over Haiti, 289.

Fish, Hamilton, secretary of state, Cuban policy of, 108-124; on British infringement of Clayton-Bulwer treaty, 167; acts as mediator in war between Spain and republics on West coast of South America, 298, 299.

Florida treaty, 52, 85, 261.

INDEX

King, Rufus, correspondence with Miranda, 17-20.

Knox, P. C., investigates title of Panama Canal Company, 185; tries to settle differences with Colombia resulting from Panama Revolution, 270-274; Central American policy, 282-285.

Lansing, Robert, secretary of state, negotiates treaty for purchase of Danish West Indies, 290; suggests adoption of Declaration of Rights and Duties of Nations, 305.

Latin America, and the Great War, 312-318.

Laybach, conference of powers at, 59.

League of Nations, and Monroe Doctrine, 333, 334.

Lee, Fitzhugh, consul-general at Havana, 129.

Lincoln, Abraham, views on Panama canal, 151.

Liverpool, Lord, on conference at Aix-la-Chapelle, 58; on French intervention in Spain, 63.

Lodge, H. C., on alleged secret alliance with England, 266; reservation of Monroe Doctrine, 333.

Lôme, Enrique Dupuy de, incident and recall, 129, 130.

Loomis, F. B., acting secretary of state, 188.

Lopez, Narciso, Cuban patriot, 92-96.

Louis Napoleon. See Bonaparte.

Louis Philippe, suggested as possible ruler for Spanish America, 26; and annexation of Texas, 262, 263.

Louisiana, ceded to United States, 261.

McKinley, William, Cuban policy of, 128-132; demands cession of Philippine Islands, 135.

McLane, R. M., minister to Mexico, 195.

Mackintosh, Sir James, on Monroe's message of December 2, 1823, 78.

Madero, Francisco, murder of, 307.

Madison, James, receives Miranda informally, 20; favors joint action with England against intervention of powers in Spanish America, 70; views on Cuba, 84.

Magoon, C. E., provisional governor of Cuba, 142.

Magruder, J. B., accepts office under Maximilian in Mexico, 224.

Maine, U. S. battleship, sent to Havana, 129; blown up, 130.

Marcy, William L., secretary of state, Cuban policy of, 99-105.

Maritime Canal Company, secures concessions from Nicaragua, 183.

Mason, John Y., connection with Ostend Manifesto, 104.

Maury, M. F., accepts office under Maximilian in Mexico, 224.

Maximilian, Archduke Ferdinand, suggested for Mexican throne, 208-211; offered the position of Emperor of Mexico, 215; not recognized by

341

INDEX

Quitman, John A., relations with Lopez, 93-94.

Recognition, withheld from Huerta, 308. See Belligerent Rights.

Reed, Walter, yellow-fever investigations, 137.

Reid, Whitelaw, commissioner to negotiate peace with Spain, 135.

Roosevelt, Theodore, and Cuban reciprocity, 140-142; signs canal bill, 185; denounces Colombia's rejection of Hay-Herran convention, 186; recognizes Republic of Panama, 189; on acquisition of Canal Zone, 190; creates strained relations with Colombia, 192; on Monroe Doctrine, 251; interview with Holleben on German intervention in Venezuela, 252-254; refuses to arbitrate Panama question, 268; denounces Bryan treaty with Colombia as blackmail, 275; establishes financial supervision over Dominican Republic, 276-280; Central American policy, 280, 281; attempts to purchase Danish West Indies, 290; interpretation of Monroe Doctrine, 326, 327.

Root, Elihu, author of Platt Amendment, 139; attempts to settle differences with Colombia, 268-270; visits South America, 303; on Monroe Doctrine, 330, 331.

Rush, Richard, minister to England, conferences with Canning on schemes of Holy Alliance, 65-67, 72, 73.

Russia, claims to northwestern coast of America, 75.

Sagasta, P. M., Spanish minister, Cuban policy of, 128.

Salisbury, Lord, reply to Olney's dispatch on Venezuelan boundary dispute, 242; agrees to arbitration of the boundary dispute, 248.

Salvador, protests against protectorate over Nicaragua, 285-287; requests official definition of Monroe Doctrine, 334.

Sampson, W. T., blockades Cuba, 134.

San Ildefonso, secret treaty of, 261.

San Martin, José de, takes part in Argentine revolution, 30-32; liberates Chile, 32, 33; liberates Peru, 33-37; relations with Bolivar, 43, 44; death, 45.

Santo Domingo, annexation proposed by Seward, 264, by Grant, 265. See Dominican Republic.

Schenck, Robert C., minister to England, 120.

Schofield, J. M., informal mission to France, 227.

Seward, W. H., views on Panama canal, 151; favors expansion, 165; raises question as to binding force of Clayton-Bulwer treaty, 166; proposes to assume payment of interest on foreign debt of Mexico, 200; declines to unite with European powers

INDEX

345

THE COUNTRY LIFE PRESS
GARDEN CITY, N. Y.

ع

SOUTH AMERICA